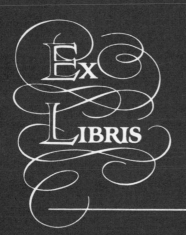

Let Go and Let God

By ALBERT E. CLIFFE

God Can Heal You Now

By EMILY GARDINER NEAL

Carmel, New York 10512

LET GO AND LET GOD

DEDICATED

To the Rev. Norman E. Peterson, B.A., L.Th.,
rector of the Church of St. Columba, Montreal,
through whose
kindness and inspiration these Lessons in Living
were first presented to the public.

Guideposts edition published by arrangement with
Prentice-Hall, Inc.

Contents

Introduction

THE BIBLE says, "In the world ye shall have tribulation." How much we have seen of this in the past few decades, with wars, more wars, and the possibility of still another war to come. These and all our tribulations have come upon us simply because we have not lived up to the laws of God.

We have had the Christian Faith for two thousand years, and yet today we see the whole Christian world divided into sects, warring with and criticizing each other. We have refused the basic teaching of Jesus Christ that we love one another, we have refused to learn how to get along with each other, and hence we see nations unable to live together in any way at all.

The Bible has taught us, however, in a wonderful way, the answer to all the problems that life can throw at each of us from day to day. In other words, you, my reader, can possess within you a feeling that makes you the master of life, that will enable you to walk successfully through all the vicissitudes of life with peace of mind, with hope, and constant courage to face whatever trials may come your way.

By means of faith in a living Christ, a resurrected Christ, you can gain such security that nothing can ever defeat you, no sickness can ever overwhelm you, and by the practice of this faith you can learn to gain victory over life and death.

As a bee needs a hive, a bird needs its nest, and a ship a harbor in time of storm, so do we every day of our lives need a refuge in time of stress and trouble. This refuge is faith. Your religion, your trying to live according to the laws shown us by Jesus Christ, will give you that radiant, vibrant, living refuge.

The true purpose of religion in our lives is to give us the means with which to replace fear, our worst enemy; we need today not merely a formal dogmatic religion, but a religion that does things rather than merely thinks them. This kind of religion is just as real at 7 a.m. on Thursday as it is at 11 a.m. on Sunday.

Every man and woman in these troublous times needs something to hang onto every hour of the day—so that he or she can know how to handle every difficulty which can ever face them. Faith in a living Christ within us teaches us how to *let go and let God.*

This book has been written by a professional biochemist, turned from his work in industry to become a lay reader of the Church of England in Canada and the Protestant Episcopal Church in the United States, who by means of simple faith has found God, and who has surrendered everything to God. From the pages of this book you will glean the basic ideas of how to get along with people in every walk of life, and how to overcome your trials, your fears, your past and your future.

Life becomes a daily thrilling experience when the love of God radiates from our hearts, for then the Christ within us radiates in our words, our appearance, our hands, and we see Christ in everyone we meet.

When we *let go and let God* we have the key to glorious living, and what is far more important—the key to an eternity with God.

Albert E. Cliffe

Let Go and Let God

WHEN YOU have been through a period of worry and tension, it is usually the practice of your doctor to have you take a vacation in some quiet restful spot where you can relax completely, forget your past worries and gain strength.

Very few people today know how to relax, they live in a world of rushing hither and yon. Each day is filled with work, engagements and no time for relaxation. Even when people take time off to go to a movie they usually want an exciting one, thus gaining more excitement for their already overworked nervous systems.

The average man at business is a good example of high tension living. If successful, he tries daily to better his past successes. The excitement of greater successes keeps him in constant tension, and fatigue remains unnoticed until he is in a complete state of mental exhaustion. The busy doctor, teacher, stenographer are good examples of high tension living. These people find that after they retire to bed their active minds will not let them rest, but they go on planning further ideas for the following days.

The rearing of children and providing meals for the family each night takes its toll from the nerves of the dependable mother. She becomes irritable, she cannot get rest even when she retires to bed, and sooner or later she has to seek medical advice to quiet her nerves.

We have nowadays all kinds of machinery in the home to save work, to save drudgery, but they have not in any way relieved the sense of nervous strain of the householder; in other words, we are all trying to burn the candle at both ends. *We do not know how to let go our anxieties.*

1

In this present century man has forgotten how to live, how to enjoy the simple things of life: the sunshine, the garden, quiet walks along country lanes. All of us every day look over our budgets, our costs in living, our economies, but few count the costs of life in terms of nervous expenditures.

Take the average man and woman of our present civilization, as soon as trouble comes, as soon as some little thing goes wrong—what do they do? They reach for a cigarette, a sure sign of nervous trouble, for they have become used to the solace of this potent drug. Many times we find people who suffer terrific pains in certain organs of their bodies, and when the doctor examines them he finds not a single thing organically wrong with them. Nerves, nervous tensions can bring tremendous amounts of real pain to every one of us. After years of struggling with life, we have never learned how to *let go our tensions and fears.*

Many children become nervous types because their parents give them too much attention, too much personal worry about non-essentials, too much being cared for and being watched over. The causes of overactive nervous systems are many, so the doctors tell us, but among these causes we must claim that the worst causes of all are our constant rush and the complexity of the way we think and live.

In spite of the worries of everyday life, we must always keep before our minds the utter need for us to relax, to get rest and healthy sleep. Complete relaxation is the sure remedy for this thing called nervousness. Worry about the little and big things of life, worry about things which you fear may happen to you in the future, all tend to bring about tension. Worry becomes a real habit and if constantly practiced can bring about physical death after much suffering. What can you do about it? Learn to relax, learn to face the tribulations of life without fear, stop crossing bridges ahead of time, for worry is the interest you pay on trouble before it comes.

Show me a worrying person and I will show you a person who does not know how to relax.

Christianity shows us the answer to nervous troubles and tensions. A single constant affirmation that the everlasting arms of God are holding you up, repeated hour by hour until you become convinced that God is now your guide, will often bring you out of worries and fears, yet how many Christians will really *let go* their fears *and let God* handle them?

Suppose that you have a broken watch and you take it to a watchmaker, asking him if he can repair it. He takes out his glass and looks at the works and says that he most assuredly can repair it. Suppose then that you say to him, "Thank you," place it back in your purse or pocket and leave the store. Will you get that watch repaired? Most certainly not, for you have to leave the watch with the watchmaker.

It is just the same with your religious life. You have to get into the habit of leaving your troubles with God. The only complete and sure cure for your bad nerves, as you call them, is to relax in the hands of God and know that He is now looking after your troubles, that He is now guiding you into the quiet waters of inner peace.

If you have a poor tire on your car, what do you do? You can drive more carefully than ever, avoid the bad roads, the side and gravel roads, keeping to the main highways. So it is with your body. If your organs have withstood very badly indeed the wear and tear of life, then you must learn to take care of them until you gain that complete healing which can only come from a real, earnest practice of your religion. To him that believeth, all things are possible, says the Bible; but how many Christians really try to believe this statement?

The most wonderful thing that ever happened to me was this: many years ago *I let go* my past *and let God* take over my life. When I completely surrendered my life to Him, I lost my temper, my fears, my years of deadly illness and sicknesses. It meant facing life every hour with the truth that was in me to replace the negative thinking of a lifetime.

It meant an hourly contact with God, in the street car, the bus, my own car, my laboratory—no matter where I went I had an appointment with Him. What came of it? Peace of mind, health and spiritual prosperity.

After reading this chapter to-day, are you willing to put God first in your life? Are you willing to *let go, and let God* be your mentor from this day on?

Then if you are, you, too, can have no fears, no tensions, no nervousness, no worries. When you take His yoke upon you, your life is a converted one. No longer do the sins of the devil haunt you, no longer can the so-called powers of evil assail you, but you learn to live happily, healthfully, confidently, because having *let go,* you *let God* and abundant living come into your life.

Believing in Life

I BELIEVE with all my heart and soul that God our Father wants us, His children, to live happy, healthful lives, and I believe that my religion, the Christian Faith, is the best answer for us, for a more abundant life. Jesus taught us that he came to bring this more abundant life, not in terms of millions of dollars, not in forms of wealth, but in that peace of mind which is the secret of successful living.

We live burdened with the cares of life, and even our so-called pleasures take their toll out of our nervous systems

—which amounts to a tremendous tax on our daily strength. We expend our mental energies so much that it is no wonder so many thousands of people are tired, discouraged, and sick to the point of death.

If you drive, you know that your battery must not be overtaxed; it needs recharging often if the strain of its daily work is too great. So our human batteries are filled with power for us to use, but only as long as we obey the rules and never waste our energies. Each of us is made up of mind, body and soul; each vital to the other, each essential to the harmonious running of the whole.

Peace of mind is the greatest asset we can have for happy, healthy living. This is an inner victory which only comes from knowing God intimately. Then the material things of life do not bother us any longer—we live in a spiritual world, and spiritual values are the only real values in life.

We each have this power within us and when we learn by faith to control this power, then we know how to use it, how to liberate it for our daily needs.

A lady came to me recently with a serious problem and said to me, "How I would like to get away from it all, how I would like to end my life." I showed her another case I had come across the same day, far worse than hers; far more dreadful things to face than she had ever had to face. I showed her how this lady had got out of her fearful condition. She at once saw my point, was sorry for her selfishness and accepted Christ from then on. She began to recover at once, her pains left. Her fears had gone with that inner faith that God was now working for her betterment. She had always put the emphasis in her life on the negative side of things, and when she got the positive uppermost, then she gained the victory.

The answer to all our problems of living is how we face them, not where we were born, not that we have had a poor environment, not that we had no chance of an education. The answer is always within ourselves. Fighting, struggling against life will never win us a victory. You have to make your own inner consciousness a citadel of peace, knowing that Christ lives there. You become a member of the D.W.C.—Don't Worry Club—leaving your worries to Him.

We all need a safety valve every day of our lives, and we find it in our religion. Christ is the safety valve for your emotions, your wrong thinking. You cannot have a nervous condition when you open this safety valve.

When your body shows illness and fatigue, it is time you looked into the matter. You must find out what has been wrong with your way of living, what sins are dominating you, what hates and criticisms are controlling your mind. You must sit down and see how to gain mastery over these things. You must admit them, and learn to meditate with God, who will give you a glorious victory over everything that has upset you in your past life.

When you show love to your fellowmen, even to those who have hurt you, when you give service and money to your fellowmen, to your church, then you are in a positive state of mind. If you are, however, dominated by the opposites, hate, discord, resentment, criticism, then these forces, being negative, will tear you down and bring you suffering, poverty, and complete failure in life. Negative states of thinking bring nervousness and nervous breakdowns, which no mere electric shock treatment at any hospital will ever cure. The little annoyances of your life are what bring about your greatest troubles. Little things you say "get on your nerves"—this shows you are a negative thinker, you have no faith in God, even though you do go to church and recite a dozen creeds.

Negative thinking will always lead to failure and nervous prostration; but positive faith—positive thinking—

will lead you towards happy, healthy and abundant living.

The positive way of life is the Jesus Christ way—it is always the right way. Look at the face of a Salvation Army lass, radiant with inner peace, joyful, no color on those cheeks from a drug store. She has been to God's beauty parlor; she has gotten that permanent which is a permanent for eternity. She knows Jesus from a daily contact with Him, by a surrender to Him. She believes in life—yes indeed, life everlasting.

Religion is and must ever be the basis of life, the key to the armory of your soul. Its mission is to provide a channel whereby God's spiritual powers may come into your life and mine, to stop us from resisting those things which irritate us daily. To give us trust in our fellowman, to take away all our tensions and to work so that our bodies are not only healed of sickness, but are speeded up. How can you get this peace? Through confidence in the promises of Jesus Christ. Develop this confidence daily as you would learn how to play a piano. Constant hourly practice is essential. *Thou wilt keep him in perfect peace whose mind is stayed on Thee.*

This then is why I believe in life. I know in Whom I have believed, I came to Him, I saw Him, I conquered all things that had prevented my knowing Him before.

I believe most assuredly that Jesus came to bring us a life more abundant; I believe that trying to live is life; by following His precepts every hour of my life, I too shall know the joys of peaceful living, knowing that all my needs will be provided for until the day when He comes to take me to His eternal home.

What are the precepts *you* must follow to know the more abundant life? The next ten chapters will explain to you the faults of your thinking—the way to change your life from negative to positive. I like to call these my *ten steps in victorious living.*

In them you can find the key to what has been wrong with your personality. By improving your personality—by learning what God's laws are for you—you can learn to live so that you will have the health and happiness you need.

THE FIRST STEP IS

Getting Along with People

> "Thou wilt keep him in perfect peace, whose
> mind is stayed on Thee."—*Isaiah 26:3.*

THE MOST important basis for successful living is the art of knowing how to get along with people, how to adjust ourselves from day to day to the different temperaments we meet in our relatives and our friends, how to see the good in them and in their actions and how to ignore the evil they sometimes do to us.

The Bible distinctly tells us that God will keep any man or woman inwardly at peace and in goodwill when that person fixes his mind, his thoughts and his actions, not on material things, not on resentment, criticism and antagonism, but on God.

Therefore, to get along with people, we first of all have to learn how to control our thoughts. There was never a time in the world's history when men needed to know how to get along with people, more than at the present time. Many years ago, men who could not adjust themselves to life could go away into far countries and live alone, finding a home for themselves in the wilderness, in the forest or on a lonely island. In this way they did not have to associate with people, and their negative personalities began eventually adjusting to nature. Today, as one writer has said, "there are no islands any more."

Every man and every woman wants happiness and harmony in life, but if we are constantly upset by the doings of our relatives and associates, we cannot have this harmony. Therefore we must learn how to win the friendship and respect of others, and we must learn how to gain their co-operation every day of our lives. We may be geniuses in some particular way, but unless we have discovered the secret of getting along with people, we will never enjoy successful living.

To be a happy person does not depend upon who we are, it does not depend upon education, it is not just a question of brains; basically it is how we react to people and to conditions every day. We often judge people by the car they drive or the clothing they wear; but remember that we may see a man outside a theater dressed like an admiral who probably never saw the sea and does not even know how to row a boat.

Anyone at any time can interest people, can influence them and lead them the way he wants them to go. If you are one of those people who say they do not care what others think about them, then I venture to make this statement: you are putting on a pose; inwardly you *do* care, because we all like to be able to win friends and influence people.

When we were born, God gave us all the tools we need for successful living, but first of all we have to know how to use them in order to get what we want from life. There are three factors involved: first, yourself; second, other people; and third, methods to follow.

First of all, do you know yourself? Do you recognize and admit your weaknesses? Have you tried to overcome them? Do you suffer from an inferiority complex? Are you timid, lazy, selfish, hot-tempered, cynical, critical, mean, jealous, sarcastic or conceited? These are the little sins that go into the making of your character. We find that so many people think because they do not break any of the Ten Commandments, then there are no other sins to worry about. But there are thousands of little errors in our thinking and in our actions which definitely mold our character negatively. These are sins because in practicing them we are putting them before God and this is breaking the first commandment which says, "Thou shalt have no other gods before Me."

A young lady came to work for me in my laboratory. She was a graduate chemist, had taken a household science course at a university, and previous to that she had taken a complete stenographic course. She was extremely shy. She had tried several religious faiths, but basically she never knew what she wanted to be and she certainly did not know herself.

In a park in Toronto, one noon hour, she came across a tract on "How to Know Yourself." She read it all on that park bench; she found herself because the tract opened her eyes to her weakness, and at the same time she found God. She changed her life; from that moment she decided to give herself to mission work in which she became very happy, successful and well able to get along with people.

If only we would learn every day of our lives to overcome those things in our character which are negative, to *let go and let God* take them over, we would all know what it was to experience harmonious living.

What do you believe about yourself? Have you always been a yes man in your place of employment? To be successful you have to learn to have a mind of your own, to have the courage of your own convictions—for this gives you stability of character. I come across many people in my work who are afraid of facing life because they are filled with the idea that they are failures.

There are thousands of people in offices, factories and stores who have no idea of where they are going from here, who are dissatisfied with their jobs and unable to get along with people. The man or woman whom you do not like in your place of employment has many good points. In disliking them, you can only see their bad points, the evil in them. But before you start criticizing other people you should see that there are no bad points in you.

Have you ever realized that God allows us to live a lifetime on this earth, and in that time He never once criticizes or condemns us? He gave us brains, a free will, talents, and a book of rules to follow, the Bible. If with all this material we cannot find ourselves, then the fault does not lie in our environment, the fault does not lie in God, the fault lies within ourselves.

I met a man some time ago, married and father of three children. This man was everlastingly seeking something he could not find. He devoted five nights a week to his church and his lodge, which placed a tremendous load upon his wife. This in turn brought about her breakdown, followed by doctor's bills and other expenses. One morning he opened the Bible at the text at the head of this chapter. He thought about those words all day. That night he surrendered himself completely to God, he *let go and let God.* He realized that the load he had given his wife to bear for some years was unjust. He now spends his nights at home helping with the housework and the raising of his children. He learned how to get along with his family for the first time, and he gained that inner peace which radiated in a healthy wife, a happy home, increased ideas in his business life, and successful living.

As we go through life every day, we meet many types of people, good people, bad people; some we like at once and some we dislike the instant we meet them. This is the sort of thing that other people find in you. So if you want to gain favor with other people you must first of all build a personality of your own and then you must have a sympathetic tolerance of the other person's point of view.

There is no doubt but that by adjusting ourselves to others, by being considerate of the things in their characters which annoy us, that we build our own character. Dolly Madison, wife of President James Madison, was asked one day how she gained such power over people. She replied, "I have no power over anyone. I merely made up my mind to love everyone, to see their good points, and in return these people see the good points in me and learn to love me."

Therefore, if you are the critical, fault-finding type, if you are super-sensitive to the things you have to face each day, I can assure you this will bring you no friendships whatsoever. These are faults in your character which you must learn to control and overcome.

I often think that the successful salesman or saleswoman has something called *You*point—he or she understands immediately *your* viewpoint and handles you accordingly. One of the first rules we have to learn in order to get along with people is to talk to others about themselves and their habits, their sports and the things they like to do, instead of always talking about our own selves. In this way we learn how to practice cheerfulness, tact, sympathy and gratitude.

St. Paul said, "I can do all things through Christ which strengtheneth me." Do you believe this statement? If so, then why don't you apply it? Life to us all is simply a series of adventures, a series of every-day lessons in living. We must learn day by day how to develop this thing called character, how to overcome the things we seem to have inherited from our forefathers. We do this through our minds, by changing the patterns of our thinking, by becoming positive instead of negative thinkers.

If you will start off the day, as you leave your home in the morning, believing that through Christ and His power within you, you can do all the things you have to face that particular day, you will gain a wonderful conviction of the power which resides within you.

In our daily life we come across many people who show jealousy towards us. Please remember that no one in this world is ever jealous of a fool and that no one can hurt you unless you let them, by fearing them. If you are the type of person who is kind to some people, but an entirely different person to others, then you are two-faced and unstable in many ways. By the law of return you will receive in later years this same treatment from others that you have given people in the earlier part of your life.

It is a strange thing about religion that many people appear to love spending Sunday with God, but oh how they balk at having Him as an everyday guest in their homes or places of employment. Next to God the most important person for you to know is self, your own self. Don't you know that, as a Christian, life was meant for you by God to be a happy experience, certainly not a miserable one. Successful living does not mean accumulating material things, it means inner peace of mind; it means that gift of being able to adjust oneself to everyone else; it also means that all your needs for daily living will be taken care of by God.

Some years ago I had a stenographer who had occupied seven jobs in four years. She was very good-looking but I discovered she was a flirt; she was very vain, snobbish and sarcastic. She definitely had the idea that she could get any man she wanted. She was not interested in her work or her remarkable talents. She was really a selfish and very emotional type. I quickly learned her weak points, at the same time showing her the capacity she had for her particular work. I made her dress more plainly for the office. In a very short time she changed her thinking patterns and began to study books which she saw in my office dealing with the power of thought. At a church meeting one night she gave herself to God. Shortly after that she met the right man and is now a very great help to her husband in his duties. But it was not until she found God, that she found herself. Finding yourself invariably means finding God.

Are you afraid of being called religious? You don't have to show your religion to people by the carrying of a Bible, by dressing in dark clothes, by always having a long face— but you do show your religious convictions by the way you react to people. Many people think that when they accept religion they are going to have to give up many of the things in life which gave them pleasure. Let me assure you that when you find Christ you don't have to give up anything good, because the wrong things in life automatically give you up and you are led into a wonderful enjoyment, the joy of living.

You show your religious convictions by the things you do and say each day, by how you live. You never show them by argument, because every man and every woman has the inborn right to worship God in his own way. Many so-called Christians are miserable, fearful, sick; they just do not know how to apply the teachings of Jesus. Oh yes, they can quote the Bible from cover to cover; they rejoice in telling you how many years they have been saved. But in so many cases these same people know only the letter of the law; they have never learned how to apply the simple teachings of the Master to everyday living, so they do not get along with themselves and invariably get along with no one else. We must learn every day how to study people, how to learn their likes and dislikes and how to cater to them.

In my work in industry I never hesitated to give a pat on the back to the man or woman who did a good job each day, because they always reacted marvelously to my compliments. So many employers are afraid to do this because they fear that if they do, these people will immediately demand an increase in salary, but I have never found this to be the case. When your newsboy, in all kinds of weather, delivers your newspaper with promptness; when your baker and milkman face the storms of winter to supply your needs; when your postman has to face every kind of discomfort to bring your mail; do you think of rewarding these people with a word, a smile or maybe a little gift or tip of some kind? Every time someone does something for you, no matter how small it may be, see that you in return give something to them or to someone else, for this is what makes the world go round. The secret of harmonious living is all in knowing how.

The Bible teaches us that everyone on this earth, Catholic or Protestant, Jew or Gentile, men of every creed and every color, are sons of God. In the Christian Faith we are told that we are heirs to all that God has made; that within us is the Kingdom of Heaven. Have you found this Kingdom? If you have, then you know what it is to have harmony, health and happiness in life. You have gained the art of knowing how to overcome your sins, your sicknesses and your fears.

One gets a marvelous feeling of power when he practices the magic of believing in Jesus Christ, because he then knows that he is heir to joy, eternal joy. We live this life to prepare us for that wonderful life to come. Eternity does not start for you and me when we go through that physical stage called death. It started for us the day we were born, and whatever we make of our lives every day is what we shall reap in the ages which are to come.

Life is a constant overcoming, for the Bible says that in this world we shall have tribulations, but think what thrill and joy there is in overcoming every day some problem which faces you and has defeated you in the past. And with your consciousness of the Christ within, you can overcome all things.

What particular sin is in your physical make-up? What particular weakness? Try to find out after reading this chapter. Know that you can get rid of those negative conditions the minute you try to find the Christ by simply believing that what Jesus said was true. Through faith in Him and what He did for you some two thousand years ago, you can become a new person. Study the Bible every day, believe your Bible every day and let no one at any time destroy your faith in it. To be able to master a piano, to be able to play a good game of golf or tennis requires daily practice, and so does your religion—*everyday practice*. Jesus gave us two commandments to follow: put God first in your life, and your fellowman before yourself.

John the Baptist, we are told, baptized with water but Jesus baptized with the Holy Spirit. Yet He did not give to us this baptism until He had been crucified. The Holy Spirit received by the hundred and twenty people at Pentecost is ready for you, but cannot be received by you until you are ready to receive it. If you will not consent to give up those things in your make-up which are wrong, then you are not ready to receive the gift. If your prayers remain unanswered, you have your foot on the hose, for you have not yet completely surrendered to Him the wrongs and sins of your life. Jesus Christ redeems us today and He will make the best even out of your worst "past."

He more than forgives you. He will turn your troubles and your liabilities into assets. He will make your self-made hells into Heaven. No matter how you have suffered from sickness, no matter how much you have messed up your life, you can this very moment turn over this mess in absolute faith. It has been said, "He unmesses the messer and makes an asset of the mess." Jesus took an uneducated fisherman and, after living with him daily for three years, this poor fisherman became the writer of a Gospel which revolutionized the world. The Christ can take almost nothing and make it almost everything. It is the Christ who brings to us today a full and perfect salvation, and full and perfect healing from sin and from sickness.

Test Him and see if you can prove Him even as you read this book. Remember that the longer you stay away from your adventure of finding the Christ, the longer you will live in sickness and poverty and need. I can assure you that the Christ lives in each man and each woman, and we can find Him if we will only believe.

To get along with people, to have the art of knowing how, we must first find God. In finding ourselves we find Him. This will bring us the true and lasting happiness which was the gift of Jesus Christ to men.

THE SECOND STEP IS

Freeing Yourself from Fear

"Love your enemies . . . do good to them
that hate you."—*St. Matthew 5:44.*

To GET along in life we must know something about human nature. It is the cause of all things which will come to each of us, and the reason we will react to them as we do. If someone makes us angry, if someone does a wrong deed against us, if someone does a good deed towards us or makes us a gift of some kind, the manner in which we react to all these things is always determined by our own particular nature.

For instance, the slow phlegmatic person always takes things calmly and is not very easily ruffled, while the sensitive person is a nervous type and gets ruffled very quickly and goes off on tangents.

Now the best way to make a friend of anyone is to appeal to some characteristic he possesses. Try to learn how to understand the various characteristics of your friends and associates. Find out what things they like and what things they dislike and watch day by day how they react to the circumstances of life.

What is your reaction when a street-car driver slams the door in your face just as you get there? Do you call him all kinds of names, do you say and think how unkind he was? Do you write to the company about his wrong treatment of you? This is entirely wrong, and if you want people to like you, you must first of all learn to like people, no matter what they may do to you. Learn how to overlook the things you dislike in them, see their good points and magnify those points.

There is no doubt that the secret of good living is basically how to know and understand yourself. The events of every day in the business world are often of a disturbing nature, but if you allow these things to depress you, then you have not learned how to understand human nature. It is a fact that if you do not get along with people, you either do not like people or you are definitely afraid of them.

Many years ago I worked under a manager who was very hard to understand. All the employees in every department were very much afraid of him. Then one day I discovered that his main hobby was the study of Egyptology, and I approached him, being interested in the same subject, to ask him if he would lend me two of the books in his library. He was very surprised to find out that I was interested in this subject and that I had once written a thesis upon it. From that day on I had no fear of him and we became great friends. I discovered a characteristic common to both of us, and through an understanding of human nature I solved this problem.

In another company which employed me, the president, who was very wealthy, had a mania for neatness and a terrific hatred of wastage. One day while going to his office with the manager under whom I worked, the president noticed a pin on the floor and told the manager to pick up that pin, as he might need it some day. It was very humiliating, of course, to the manager, to have been so spoken to in front of me, his junior. Some time later it was my job to see the president in connection with some concessions we wanted from him relative to a sales convention, and as I sat down in his office, I picked a pin from the floor and placed it on the pin tray on his desk. He immediately reacted by saying, "Well, I am glad to know that my chief chemist does not waste pins any more than I do." I gained every point which I wanted from that time on. Needless to say, there was no pin on the floor, for I had carried that pin in my hand before approaching him. I knew his characteristics and through that little experiment I was able to overcome the arguments which otherwise he would have presented to me; in other words, he learned to like me because he discovered something in me of which he approved.

The young child has only three emotions when he is born into this world, fear, rage and love, but as he goes through life he gets many more emotional complexes, some of which he learns how to control and some of which unfortunately, control him.

We gain many fears which have no existence in reality at all. Maybe when you look from a bridge to a river below you are overcome with nausea. When you come suddenly face to face with a situation you did not expect, when a serious sickness of some kind overtakes you, fear is the thing that dominates your mind. You must learn to face the thing you fear or you will be a defeated person.

It was my job on one occasion to call on the brothers in one of the monasteries in the Province of Quebec, and as I parked my car I saw a huge mastiff with a heavy fifty-foot chain tied to his neck. There was a big sign in French saying, "Beware of the Dog!" He was very savage indeed, but having no fear of animals, I walked up to him, speaking to him gently in French. Gradually his ears dropped and he lay on the ground and I got close to him. He suddenly jumped up, put his big paws on my shoulders and started to lick my face. At this moment one of the monks came up from the barn. He was terrified because he thought the dog was about to eat me. But I had conquered the dog by showing no fear, only love. Before keeping my appointment, I drove down to the village and brought him some bones. On every monthly visit to the monastery that dog knew the sound of my engine, and as my car drove into the yard his ears would be pricked up, his tail wagging, and he would bark joyfully because he knew he had a friend in that car.

How do you react when you hear some mean remark made by someone about you? When someone borrows your things without permission? When someone enters your desk in your absence? How do you react when your boss tells you to do a job because someone else shirked it? It is knowing the answer to these problems in a positive way, knowing human nature, that makes you know how to get along in life.

This emotion called love teaches you many things, for you have to practice love every hour of the day when living with people. Love in your nature will make people want to agree with you. It will make you want to associate with people who think as you do, who have the same religious views as you have. Love will make you want to do things for others.

Fear is one of the strongest emotions with which to influence people. Take the old-fashioned evangelist with his threats of a fiery hell in the afterlife. Take the patent medicine manufacturer who states that if you do not use his product you will suffer from various hideous diseases. Unfortunately much of the advertising in our magazines today has a fear background. The vitamin advertisements we have seen for years were designed in many cases to appeal to our fears.

You must try to learn day by day how to understand human emotions, and learn to identify people by their reaction to these emotions; but first of all learn how you yourself react to them. Once you solve these investigations, you will understand human nature perfectly.

Samson was the strongest man in the Bible, and able to accomplish wonderful deeds, until a certain day. That day was the day he didn't keep his mouth shut and gave away the secret of his strength. This applies to you. If you want to live successfully you have to learn to keep your mouth shut. God gave you two ears and one mouth, so that you could listen to twice as much as you say.

By quoting someone incorrectly, by passing on a confidence, by misunderstanding a remark, you can cause oceans of trouble for yourself. You must learn when to speak and when to keep your mouth shut. Human nature is the thing that makes some men hewers of wood and other men drawers of dividends. We all have the same kind of brain. We all have the divine right of free will. We all have the power of thought, but it is according to our human nature that we attain successful living.

How many Christians today try to see the Christ in the people they have to get along with? Are you full of criticism for people who belong to churches other than the one you attend? One lady I met told me that she often spent three hours a day in prayer with God, but she never got the answer to her prayers. She was a very sick person, and a very self-righteous one, for she said she never broke any of the Ten Commandments. She detested her next-door neighbor because he went to a certain church; in fact, no one was going to Heaven except those who belonged to her little sect. I eventually managed to convince her of the wickedness of her criticism of others. When she asked God's forgiveness for those things and really believed she had received that forgiveness, she gained a healing from her diseases. We must get an inner conviction of the power that is within us.

In the Christian Faith we are told to love our enemies, to pray for them that curse us, and to do good to them that hate us. This means that forgiveness is the basic teaching of the Christian Faith. As Jesus forgave the men who tortured and crucified Him, how much easier it is for you to forgive those who wrong you every day. Without this forgiveness on your part, you will never attain happy living. Jesus knew the secret of how to get along with people, and He taught us how to do it also. He sensed the personality, the inner thoughts of everyone He met, and you can do this too. There is no room in your heart for fear and worry of any kind when you are a Christian, for then you know and apply in your daily living the truth that makes you free. If you do not control your emotions, or if fear of some kind dominates your life, you can without doubt look forward to diseases coming to you later in life.

The one technique to apply is to develop faith through Jesus Christ. To affirm every hour positive thoughts; to know God is ever aware of you, ever beside you.

A short time ago, while driving in a taxi, an imminent collision with another car became apparent, due to the other driver coming out of a side street at a terrific speed. I had no fear, I relaxed completely; not for the crash which was to come but for the crash which was not to come. I knew that God was in our car and as we pulled up a little further along the street after a close call, the taxi driver, with perspiration running down his face, said, "God was in my car tonight." This gave me a chance to explain to him how he had proved God by the experience and how he could prove Him every day of his life; God was at the wheel with him wherever he was driving.

Has going to church ever taught you anything about how to get along with people or how to understand human nature? Going to any church should be a refresher course in faith. It should be a re-conditioning center where your mind gets an overhauling once a week to enable you to gain greater faith, to learn lessons in how to overcome the problems which are about to face you.

A lady some time ago told her minister that she was no longer going to attend his church; she preferred to attend my Bible class for the simple reason there was no collection taken, and it did not cost her anything. Are you that kind of Christian? Are you the kind who spends dollars during the week for entertainment but does not want to give anything to God, or to the church on Sunday? What have you ever sacrificed to God? According to the law of giving and receiving, you will get nothing back if you give nothing of yourself in service or money, or both. The more you sacrifice in this way, the greater will be your reward. According to the Hindu teaching, this law is called Karma, and Karma means come-back; in other words, what you sow you reap, and that of course applies to giving. Ask yourself what you have sacrificed for God that you might have the things you need in life. I can assure you from practical experience that I did not know successful living until I learned to be a successful giver.

The New Testament to me is a book on how to gain power, how to know people, how to enjoy radiant living and how to insure myself for all Eternity, in which I am now living and in which I will still continue to live for ages after my soul leaves this physical body. From it I learned to accept the Christian Faith, the teaching of the Master in all its fullness as given by my Bible. I had to learn to master my weaknesses and my errors of thinking. When I learned to do this, I discovered the secret of human relations.

In my laboratory every day it was my job to prove certain formulae. In my religious life, I prove God often, many times a day. My religion is faith in Jesus Christ and His atonement for my past sins and sicknesses. That faith applied hour by hour with constant practice gives me freedom from sickness, teaches me how to understand human nature, gives me all the things I need in life.

I know as a scientist that the very air we breathe is full of terrific atomic energy. So I believe that God's energy is around me, at all times available to me, whenever I choose to take the good which God offers to me so freely.

Chemistry is based upon laws, laws which I can prove every day. Those laws never change. For instance, I take two parts of hydrogen and one part oxygen and I get water. No matter how many times I mix these gases in this proportion, I get the same results. Now, your religious life teaches you the same kind of laws which work for you. Once you come to believe in Christ, that through Him you can do all things, you contact that invisible power which is always flowing within you and, as that power flows through you, it brings this thing to you called life.

This faith, this contacting of God's laws is what makes sick people well, and the more you believe, the more your faith develops, the more you will come into this thing called *attunement*—attunement with God. To tune in on a radio you tune in to a broadcasting station, and the vibration tuned in to puts your instrument in harmony. Your religion as a Christian is to tune in to the source of life, which will give you a perfect broadcast, the Christ within.

Your full realization of this will teach you how to understand His nature, and from that moment will come a complete understanding of human nature.

Let go, my friend, of your fears, your tensions, your worries and your anxieties, *and let God.*

THE THIRD STEP IS

Practicing Kindness

"Be ye kind one to another, tenderhearted,
forgiving one another."—*Ephesians 4:32.*

THERE is no doubt but that this text teaches us the beautiful teaching of the Christian religion, which is love, kindness to one another, always forgiving one another. How often do you find these qualities in the church you attend, in Christian churches? This to me is the great weakness of Christian people today, for we find within church organizations so much resentment and criticism and condemnation, which, of course, is opposite to the love which Jesus Christ demonstrated so magnificently.

Human beings are very complex creatures. We are all alike at bottom, but within our minds we are vastly different, in our sentiments, our interests, our abilities and activities. We are very much like a wheel, for at the hub we all have the same basic common sentiments, but at the rim we are all different from each other and seem far apart. We all start off at the hub in our childhood with two simple fears, of noise and falling, but as life progresses and our experiences vary from day to day we acquire characteristics, fears and habits different from those of anyone else. Take two boys attending high school, probably born in the same social class, living close to each other, their family and other ties very much alike. Once they get through school or college with their different talents, they meet different types of people and have different experiences from day to day. These two boys grow up into young men and into mature age with entirely different likes, dislikes and temperaments.

We can classify people into certain set patterns but we have to look into the question of personalities in order to solve the problem of getting along with them. Take the case of a wife who is the dominating, aggressive type. She is usually a good talker, a gossip. But on the other hand, often her husband is a clinging vine, very retiring and completely dominated in his home life. Many active, progressive men have wives who are quiet and reserved and who very seldom take any part whatsoever in public life.

The best way to understand the differences between men is to divide them into two categories, introvert and extrovert. The former is a person who is usually shy and retiring, who likes to spend his spare time alone in study, with some favorite hobby, or just reflecting. The extrovert, we find, has many social, public and other interests. Generally speaking, musicians are introverts while successful salesmen are typical extroverts The introvert is usually hypersensitive, easily embarrassed, writes more fluently than he speaks, does not make friends easily, worries a lot. He often spends a great deal of his time day-dreaming. He generally resents being ordered to do anything, but is very easily spurred on to do things by praise. If he plays any game at all he is invariably a poor loser. Now the extrovert is the exact opposite. If you are learning how to get along with people, try to sense these qualities in the people you meet, then you will know exactly how to handle them, what to do and what not to do. If a man or woman is hypersensitive and easily hurt then you must be extremely careful what you say to them. You get along with the extrovert by getting him to talk about himself, about his sports and his outside interests. Be a good listener.

When you are handling an extrovert, let him talk. He will talk a blue streak about his conquests, his business, his ideas, the sports in which he is interested. He is the type who acts quickly on impulse, and very seldom worries about what happened yesterday or what is going to happen tomorrow.

Every person has some of both qualities, but those which predominate put him into one or the other class. I employed a research chemist for some years who was a typical introvert. He had a very great complex of superiority because he had a doctor's degree, and he was also extremely argumentative. He could not get along with men at the laboratory. I finally gave him a laboratory to himself. This worked very well for a while, but eventually he looked to other fields for employment, and in fifteen years he held fifteen jobs simply because he did not learn how to adjust himself to people.

On another occasion I knew a girl stenographer who was an introvert, extremely shy, did not like meeting people, and seemed to get tongue-tied when suddenly thrust into company. She had lived for years in a room at the Y.W.C.A. She did not attend church meetings or socials of any kind, and did not meet people. In the office she did not get along with the other girls because she was hypersensitive. This was followed by a nervous breakdown. Her psychiatrist did his best to teach her how to know herself. She came to see me privately one day after her illness, telling me she was a very defeated person. I tried to show her the weaknesses in her character and got her a job in a summer hotel, where part of the day she had to meet the incoming people. She had to mix with different people after hours, and she got a new slant on living. She changed her appearance, got to be very attractive, and today she is the permanent hostess in that hotel, having married the hotel manager. However, this change did not come about until she learned how to overcome her introvert nature.

With these basic keys in your possession, you can unlock anyone's characteristics and know how to adjust yourself to those people. We all have some of both these qualities; if we were one hundred percent introvert or extrovert, we would probably be insane.

Suppose you come across a man who does not seem to like to make friends, changes his mind a great deal and is very often stubborn in his ideas. This being the case, never do anything to bring out his stubbornness, and certainly never mention the fact to him that he is unstable or that he never knows his own desires. Find out his other characteristics and keep his good qualities in mind.

I knew a man who was employed for nearly twenty years by one company. He was an introvert and there was no future for him in that company. By bringing this tendency to his attention and by teaching him how to overcome it with constant study and practice, he was able to change his personality and is now the personnel manager in the same company.

To understand people we have first of all to be kind to them, to respect their ideas, their religious viewpoints, their sensitivities and their qualities.

Many years ago the head of a large institution and farm called me to see their calves, forty of whom were seriously ill with pneumonia resulting from a fire. The veterinary had ordered them shot, but they were very expensive and bred very carefully, which meant a great deal to that institution. We prayed about it right in the barn beside the calves, and thanked God for having begun their healing Immediately an idea for a medication to use came to me; I followed it up in practice, and everyone of those calves was saved.

That one kindness, that one demonstration of faith in God, resulted in the company for which I worked getting orders totaling thousands of dollars, from that particular institution.

Kindness must come before all things in our daily lives. The text from your Bible which heads this chapter tells you to be kind to one another and to forgive one another. How often do we find tremendous hatreds and bigotry between our different church denominations, yes, and even between churches of the same sect. We see this exemplified day after day. This, of course, is not the fault of the churches, it is the fault of those who profess and call themselves Christians and yet are so filled with their own self-righteousness that they forget all about being kind to one another. There is a tendency to dualism in every man and woman, a tendency to good and to evil. Each of us has a little of Heaven and a little of earth in his make-up. The reason we live on this earth is to prove that Heaven is within us throughout our daily lives, so that we shall also have Heaven in the life we are to live when we leave our physical bodies.

No one ever just *finds* life worth living, because every single one of us has to *work* to make it worth living. The real proof of a Christian is his kindness to his neighbor, his relatives and his friends, under every sort of condition. This kindness works wonders over yourself, and it works wonders over everyone else; in fact, there isn't anything in life that will work so many miracles as love and kindness.

What is your relationship to your Creator, God? He is never what we picture Him as being. It is not what we think about God that counts, but what He thinks about us. How have you proved in your life your divine relationship to Him? His was the mind, the Divine Mind that created the earth, the universe, and you. You are made in His own image; your soul is the only real part of you, eternal, everlasting and indestructible, and your own mind is that part of you through which God works and by means of which you contact divine power.

Forget the old ideas you were taught ages ago of a God of wrath, a God who sent you sickness to punish you, and demanded an eye for an eye and a tooth for a tooth. Jesus told us His Father was a God of love. He is all love, and when you show love to any person, or to an animal, you are expressing God. Our main reason for being on this earth is to express God. Everyone of us is a means by which God does His wonderful work among men. Therefore, when you are dominated by criticism or resentment or temper, you cannot express God, and you are breaking His laws; and when you break any law you have to pay the price for the breaking of that law.

Into our cities are brought power lines of very high voltage. At the outskirts of the cities there are gigantic transformers where the high voltage is stepped down to a voltage low enough for use in our homes. This is an exact example of what the Christian religion means. Jesus is the transformer of God. He is the only "somebody" no one of us has yet been able to match, this man Jesus Christ, the teacher. We must first of all believe that He came and inhabited human flesh. The Christ came down from the Father and was made man. He taught us a way of living so that we could live more abundantly, and we must try to follow that pattern not just on Sunday but every hour of our lives.

Jesus said that no man could get to the Father except by Him. When I came to a realization of what Christ could mean to me, I became a conqueror, for I got a living, vital sense of His presence which took away from me all fear of men, of evil, of disease. If, however, I made a serious mistake, if I fall into error, then I have to take the punishment that goes with the breaking of that law, and I have to realize that I have not walked with Him as I should.

You will become a revitalized person when you come to accept Jesus Christ. In our churches we usually see a cross made of brass or wood. It is not there for the purpose of adoration or worship; it is only a sign or symbol. It is usually an empty cross, a token to me of a Man who died upon it two thousand years ago for my sicknesses and my sins, but who became a resurrected Person. His Spirit lives within you and within me, and it is up to us to believe this. If you will do this religiously every hour of the day and practice this faith in His power within you, then you too will have a resurrection from every error, from every wrong that can come into your life.

The Christian way of life is not just sanctity; it is sanity, for you cash in on the promises of God when you learn to walk in His way of life. Your devotion to Him transcends all other things in life. You gain a healing from sin and from sickness, and develop a happy, radiant, successful personality, confident that all the details of your life, all your needs on this earth are now being taken care of by God.

I had to prove the theories of my science every day in the laboratory. In my religious work I prove God every day by prayer. You can do this too. Realize every moment that God is now waiting to operate through you, and that your mind can now open to this super-power to solve your every doubt or difficulty. All you have to do is to tune in your mind to His wave-length and all other wave-lengths will be blotted out.

How do you tune in on God's wave-length? By faith, faith that God lives, faith that God is good, and faith that all the hosts of Heaven and earth must move to an increasing purpose when attuned to His power.

You make every day a testing time for your happiness.

You wake up and live in the reality that with Christ at the helm you can have life, and can have it more abundantly.

When this change comes into your life you will no longer see the evil in other people. You will see the Christ in them because kindness and love become your dominating impulses. In chemistry I learned that coal under heat and pressure becomes diamonds. The black sticky-looking tar from coal gives us aniline dyes, beautiful colors, all the colors of the rainbow. The slag refuse from this produces wonderful crystals. Mud is made into the jewels of costume jewelry.

So it is that the stresses and tribulations, the trials of your life, can produce many wonderful things for you. The hard knocks that you may have to take when you have the abundant faith of the Christ within you, will change your coal into diamonds, your sorrows and sickness into beauty. The mud of your defeats you will transform into jewels of kindness and love, because through your faith, the super-atomic power of God is at your disposal. Make this affirmation: *"I am,* therefore *I will, I do, I have."* Say to yourself, "I will now arise and go to my Father. Nothing can stop my progress from this day on because I believe that God is ever with me. Through this Spirit of Jesus Christ within me I am never alone and I have nothing to fear."

Let go your problem, let go your anxieties, *and let God* fill you with kindness and love.

Getting on the Right Track

"And if thy right hand offend thee, cut it off. . . ."—*St. Matthew 5:30.*

POSSIBLY the above text has puzzled you, because it would be a very serious thing to take it literally and to cut off one of your hands. However, the meaning of it is quite hidden and quite metaphysical. It means that if you have any characteristics in your nature preventing your spiritual growth, your success in life, or which hurt other people, then you must cut them out, you must learn how to control them and replace them with love. Love is the predominating thing and is the whole basis of Christian religion.

The Bible tells us that if a man says he loves God, and yet at the same time hates his brother, he is a liar. So to understand people we must first of all start off by learning to understand ourselves, and particularly our characteristics. There is hardly a day in our lives, hardly an hour in which we do not think critical thoughts and say critical words of other people, but before we criticize anyone in any way we should first of all see that our own lives are free from error. We are so prone to see the evil in another person, but seldom do we see the wrongs in our own thoughts, our own actions and our own ways of living.

In our present day and age, more articles, more books, more "bunk," have been written about character analysis than about anything else, and for years we have known of people who make a profession of reading character by the leaves of tea located in your teacup. But it is true that if we really want to get along with people, we must practice the skill of reading their characteristics. However, it must never be simply guess-work.

Thousands of people follow astrology, phrenology, palmistry, and all these have been put to the acid test by scientific men and have been found wanting. How do you size up people? Do you think that tall men are more attractive, more dependable than short men? Have you found, or do you believe that fat men are more likable than thin men? Do you think that tall men are invariably better leaders in every profession? Have you got a conviction that the bumps on your head describe your good and bad characteristics?

The constant habits of a lifetime, the same reactions to the same conditions definitely affect your face, your body and your nervous system. The best clue to a person's character is to watch how he reacts to certain happenings in his life. Watch what he does when he is surprised, shocked, disappointed, pleased or condemned, and make a mental note of it. The constant practice of watching your friends in this way will tell you their inner thoughts.

You know very well that, when fear strikes you, you grow pale and possibly tremble. If you are sad, tears will come to your eyes. If you are happy, joy will increase your heartbeat and give you a better color. The changes you see on the faces of people are always reproduced in their inner organs. This is why the constant practice of thoughts of fear or failure will bring about physical and mental upsets. Shock very often produces the disease known as diabetes; resentment carried on over a period of years often produces forms of arthritis; while worry produces many ills such as stomach ulcers and heart diseases.

Every man and every woman should start practicing early in life the art of controlling the feelings and emotions, for emotions produce certain characteristics in the face. If you laugh a great deal, you get happy little lines at the corners of your eyes and your mouth. If you worry a lot, you get wrinkles across your brow and long deep lines down your face. If you hold feelings of inferiority, you generally shrink away from people and gradually develop rounded or stooped shoulders.

In living this life and noting thousands of people during the years of your life, you will find that by the time many people make the most out of their life, most of that life is gone. In going through life you must remember that the man to watch is the man behind the man in front of you.

When the executive of a company is interviewing a prospective employee, possibly for a sales division, he may suddenly say, "Well, what do you think you can do for us?" Very often the man becomes disconcerted, he is taken off his guard, and by the man's reaction to that question a great deal can be told of his characteristics. The executive sizes up a man very quickly by constant application of this type of psychology. He does not want a "yes" man, nor does he want a man full of his own importance.

In a school which I know of in Canada, when the boys line up each morning they are checked over by one of the masters for cleanliness, for neatness, and to see that every boy has a handkerchief in the top lefthand pocket of his coat, and one in his trousers' pocket, to see that his shoes are shined, his teeth cleaned, and his hair brushed. Boys who go to such a school very quickly get out of slovenly habits, and when those boys grow up to be men, that habit of neatness has grown so much that they cannot leave the house without going over those details which mean so much in their appearance.

Neatness in appearance always shows an orderly mind and orderly thinking. The woman who does not replace a button on her coat or who is careless about the sewing of the hem on her skirt which has come loose, the girl who does not care about the way in which her hair is dressed or whether a button is missing from her blouse, is never successful in the business world, or the social world either. Those characteristics show her mentality very plainly: sloppy, untidy, disorderly thinking. Such a person is generally undependable.

When you come across a man in your office or factory, perhaps a foreman or a boss of some kind, who has a dominating personality, you will find almost invariably that this is due to an inferiority complex. It is a part of your lessons in living to learn to study the emotions of those with whom you associate every day of your life.

Some time ago I spoke to a man taking candid photographs of people on the main street of our city, and I found out that he was most successful because he had studied people; he had read character in them. He said to me, "After you shoot pictures of the first million, you know whose photograph to take." The people wearing smart clothes invariably bought the photographs. He never took a picture of an old man or woman, never wasted his film on a man with an old hat. He could tell from the way people wore their clothes who would be willing to pay twenty-five cents for a photograph. This man, by practical experience on the streets of a big city, was a good student of psychology, and therefore most successful in his line of work.

In this question of reading character, try to find out what pleases the men or women whom you want to understand, also what angers them, what amuses them, what frightens them and what hurts them. Many people carry poker faces all day long, but you will get beyond the poker face by studying in a very simple way their reactions to the problems they have to face day by day.

The story is told of a colored man who said to his minister that he had got religion. The minister said to him, "So you are going to lay aside sin!"

"Yes, sir," said the colored man, "I has done it already."

"Well," said the minister, "are you going to pay your debts?"

"Oh," said the colored man, "you ain't talking religion now, you is talking business."

How many of us think this way? When your business is touched in some way or other, when your business is affected by religion, do you forget all about the latter?

Religion is something we do not just practice once a week, it is something we must live in our thoughts, in our actions, every hour of the day. Not by telling people how good we are and how sinful other people are, but by the way we react in love and kindness to our fellowmen, by the way we learn to study people, saving them embarrassment, trouble and fear in any way possible.

People who call themselves Christians should be the finest folk in the world to get along with, but are they? I am afraid that thousands of Christians, members of churches and regular in their attendance, are very hard people to get along with simply because they have not learned how to find themselves.

Money, fame, position and wealth are the material things that have no reality; in fact, they do not last and are very easily lost. They seldom bring peace of mind, for many millionaires do not know harmony, peace of mind, or the happiness which every Christian should experience. To get a direct answer to prayer is the finest lesson in how to live because it teaches you how to get peace of mind, and shows you the joy of living. By adventuring daily with God, you can learn how to make a success of your life.

To know Jesus Christ, to realize that the Christ Spirit lives within you and within every person you meet, will give you a revitalized life due to the magic of believing. Your life is made by what you think every hour of the day, and just where you are in life today is due entirely to your past thinking. You are what you think.

If fear dominates your life, you reap that fear in sickness and poverty, but when you substitute faith for fear you gain dominion over all negative things, you gain success.

When you learn to believe in God in a very simple child-like way, you get the answers to your prayers; criticism and resentment never find a place in your thoughts, and you gradually come to see Christ in everyone with whom you associate. You start to radiate that personality which was in Jesus Christ, and your positive thoughts day after day, when properly applied, are always healing thoughts.

To me, any church should be a reconditioning center where you can go to get your mind overhauled. All of us need a great deal of mental conditioning. When we get our minds renewed we live in a positive way, and life is then a very different experience indeed. Religious faith puts terrific fight into a man so that he develops resistance to defeat, to failure and to sickness. The obstacles you meet from day to day, the tribulations you have to face, all become stepping stones to happiness. Believe that God is now answering your prayers, believe that you are now receiving and, according to Jesus Christ, all things shall be added unto you. Faith without works is dead. We must act on the inspiration we receive as the direct result of positive prayer. We all need inspiration, and we get new ideas from God every hour of our day when we put our trust in Him—but we have to follow that inspiration up with perspiration—we have to work to prove our faith. Remember that the bee that hangs around the hive never gets any honey.

It is always well to remember that faith is far stronger than fear and that God is far more powerful than any supposed devil or power of evil.

A food chemist will tell you, by an analysis of a cake, the percentage of each ingredient that went into the making of that cake, and from that analysis he can duplicate the formula. Such a thing is very easy to prove in a chemical laboratory. Have you realized that it is easy for you when you start adventuring with God, to prove that He is God?

It is always easy to read a man's character when he has had a decisive experience with God, because he radiates something that the godless man has not got. The more you realize the faith, the power of God within you, the more easily you gain mastery over all the problems of your life.

I met a man some time ago, extremely successful in business, but completely defeated in private life. He had no faith in God, no religion; he had a very unhappy home, and his wife was at loggerheads with him. He did not drink, he had no wicked sex life, he just couldn't get along with his wife. He came to see me on the eve of a divorce action. He saw and accepted my teachings about God, and gained an answer to his prayers. He made a demonstration, he proved God. A few days later he told his wife of the change that had come into his life, but she had already seen it. She came to see me the following day, for through the change that had come to her husband she had gained a happy home, and he had gained success in his private life as well as his business life.

Possibly you think that because of your evil life God has deserted you, but God has never been absent from your life since you were born, not for one hour! He has been there with you, waiting for you to follow His rules, waiting for you to find Him, waiting for you to live up to the code of Jesus Christ. The prodigal son took his substance, and spent it on riotous living and the joys of a material life. He tried everything once. Possibly you have done the same and have imagined yourself to be away from good, away from God. But, like the prodigal son, you can come back to that Father who is all love, who is waiting to receive you this moment. He is always willing to forgive, to receive you back into His fold, into His family and to give you health, happiness and peace of mind.

Christianity is not just a way of living, it is not simply a membership in a church, it is life itself, it is vitality, it is vibrant energy. Christianity correctly practiced is a healing, throbbing, vibrant, creative energy. It is a deep therapy which can drive to the very roots of society by breaking down sins and infected centers. It will rebuild your life, mentally, physically and spiritually. It will give you the overcoming of all things. The Bible says, "In Him was Life." The life that was in Jesus Christ is also in you. In Him is creative energy, and this is the tremendous dynamic energy of life itself.

If you will start, with the reading of this chapter, on a new page of your life, if you will accept the cross of Jesus Christ as your symbol of redemption, you can be resurrected today from all the failures that have been yours. You can begin right now to take from your character the things that have made you a failure in life. You can start to practice immediately to read the character of everyone else. You can make a rediscovery of Christ.

Will you not then *let go* your past *and let God* put you on the right track. If you will do this in all sincerity right at this moment, you will feel the thrill of Jesus Christ as He touches your heart, and all things will be added unto you now and through all eternity.

THE FIFTH STEP IS

Establishing Right Relationships

"And whosoever liveth and believeth in me shall never die."—*St. John 11:26.*

To BELIEVE with all your heart and soul in Jesus Christ means that you will always get along with people. If you thoroughly believe in and live the Christ-life, you will never know the slow death that comes from the lack of right relationship with God and people.

As we journey through life we must learn how to get into right relationships with other people. We must stop seeing their defects, we must forget and forgive the wrongs they do to us, we must show love and kindness and be really sincere to everyone we meet.

In order to get into a right relationship with anyone, your first idea must be to find out their special interests, their views on religion, their pastimes, and learn to talk to them particularly about the things they like. Be sure to keep yourself free at all times from criticism or condemnation, especially of any other religious sect, remembering that all good roads lead to God, and that every person on this earth has a right to worship God in the way that suits him best. Never start to discuss political or religious views with those you want to please. It is always more effective to deal with what a person does outside his working hours than whatever his vocation may be.

A good salesman tries to see his products through the eyes of his customer. He tries to think how he would react if he were the buyer instead of the seller. This is a lesson for us, for we must always try to see ourselves as others see us rather than as we see ourselves.

I have found out from experience that it is also a good idea to get the other person interested in you for some reason or other. A young lady of my acquaintance was seemingly detested by the head of her department. But one day this young lady found out that the manager was a collector of hammered brassware. The lady in question had some very fine pieces brought by her parents from India, and she took these down for her manager to see. That was the beginning of a new-found friendship. They established right relations with each other due to one common factor. I know of another case where a collection of stamps was used by a man at loggerheads with his chief, to establish common ground between them.

Are you the type of person who does a great deal of talking? Maybe you have plenty to say about nothing when you do say it. A good listener is always popular.

The most valued possession of every man and woman is sincerity. When you start to cultivate a friendship, do not use pretense, but keep confidences in the strictest manner. In establishing right relations it is always well to remember that patience, moral integrity and humility are factors that you need very much indeed. You will probably have to learn how to swallow your pride as well as control your emotions in order to win friendships, but it is easy to do when you learn to know yourself. If you are a highly critical person, then you will find that everyone else criticizes you. If you are hypersensitive, then the sooner you stop hitting at others, the quicker you will overcome your sensitivity.

"Whosoever believeth in me shall never die" means that if you will accept Jesus Christ as your guide, your redeemer, your friend, then you have a sound basis for successful living with people of every creed and color, for in this way you have established right relations with God.

When you have a daily, yes, an hourly appointment with God, you will become so confident of His presence and guidance that you will withstand all the trials of life; you will overcome your hereditary characteristics; you will overcome sickness and you will lose your fear of death. There is no death—it is merely a passing over, a release from this physical life into a wonderful spiritual life for all eternity. When you come to believe that the Spirit of Christ lives within you, His intelligence becomes your intelligence, a source of ideas, inspiration and guidance. You lose every fear you ever had when God controls your mind, and you believe with all your heart and soul that He is mindful of your every move and is standing by to fulfill every righteous desire of your heart.

The Bible says that we must be reborn, we must be born again mentally and spiritually before we come to this wonderful understanding of God. Our thought patterns must be reborn, completely changed, and we must recognize the errors and fears of our daily lives, and make amends, and learn how to overcome these conditions which have been getting the better of us for so long. This is when we begin to find the Kingdom of God within us. Every day will become a spiritual adventure with God, enabling us to rise above every difficulty and temptation.

A Canadian Merchant Marine captain had lived a very materialistic life, but on three occasions when his ship was sinking he was saved by his prayers. Yet he still doubted God. He had laughed at any evangelistic messages he heard until he came one evening to a lecture which was meant for him. He accepted in simple faith that day the fact of what God could mean in his life. He asked His forgiveness for his sins, and he became a completely changed person. He was born again. He did not have to give up his drinking habits and other evil passions. They gave him up. He lives today a new life, for he knows that God is with him on the bridge of his ship, and his newfound faith has brought many another person to find that same Christ.

Jesus said on one occasion, "Be of good cheer," to a person whom he had healed. This means cheer up, no longer will you have a life of sickness or dismal living. By accepting Jesus Christ in all His fullness, the tendency to have a long, sad, sanctimonious face disappears. The smile of Christ radiates from your face and you are automatically cheered up even when the greatest of difficulties come across your path.

A woman came to see me some time ago filled with fears

of all kinds. She had lived a lifetime of pleasure, had been a leader of society, but after thirty years it brought her the disease known as claustrophobia. I told her during her first visit the simple story of Jesus, how willing He was to forgive and forget; that in fact He was now washing her past away and she was beginning a new day if she would only surrender to Him. She broke down with violent emotion, and at the end of my prayer for her, her tensions were gone. She was released immediately from all her fears. From that day on she practiced the magic of believing; she believed that her sins and the errors of a lifetime were washed away on Calvary two thousand years ago, and she has become a radiant personality spending most of her time as a social worker among the needy.

You are not facing life alone, you are facing a future, an eternity with God. I do not know nor do I ask *what* the future holds for me, but I do know *who* holds my future. I know with an absolute faith that God will never let anything come my way that He and I cannot handle together. You first have to surrender, then you have to supply the willingness and the tools, and God supplies the power. When God actually becomes a reality in your life, anxiety goes, but when anxiety dominates your mind, then God goes.

The head of a girls' college, after a nervous breakdown, came for an interview with me. She was filled with deep fears of a past experience and she had built a wall of negativeness between her staff, her pupils and herself. All her life she had been a strict martinet for discipline, and she always demanded too much of others and herself. There was no room for the emotion called love in her life. She was a completely repressed and defeated woman. Her psychiatrist had been unable to help her and it was very hard for her in her first lesson to believe that God would remake her, that she could be reborn after years of living without any faith in God.

However, she accepted my teaching of childlike faith. She threw open the windows of her soul to Christ and an amazing change took place in her personality. The causes of her school irritations dissolved. She lost many of her inhibitions because now she looked for the good, for the Christ in her staff and in her pupils. She radiated in her voice and presence this conviction, and as the months went by she was able to establish perfect relations with all those with whom she came in contact.

What Christ did for this woman He can do for you. Are you filled with nameless fears? Are you filled with doubts and worries? Then let them go and let God take over your life. If you will let Him, He will remake your entire life and you will reap the harvest which Jesus promised, a life more abundant. The greatest thrill comes, not through sensation, but with the knowledge that a complete surrender has been made of that life to Christ. When you feel the touch of His hand, the thrill of new life will glow through you, and sickness and need will never dominate your life again. When Christ rules your life completely, all negative things fade away and you gain the health of mind and body that God expects you to have.

If we would only spend half the time in prayer that we spend in learning material ways to bring success, we would gain a thousand times the results we otherwise obtain. All my life I considered that I had established the right relations between myself and God through my church. I lived very strictly according to the letter of the law. I acknowledged my sins, but within myself I did not have a personal relationship with God, and therefore I did not know how to establish right relations with my neighbors. Then I came in simple faith to the foot of the Cross; I came to love Him with all my heart, my body and my soul. With my rebirth came my healing and, instead of fearing a God of wrath, I came to accept divine love from a Saviour who died that I might live.

The joy of triumphant living is mine today, but only so long as I live according to the teachings of the Master. Day after day we have to make conquests over temptation, day after day we must gain in a spiritual way, but at the end of each day comes the knowledge of having again *let go and let God:* thus do we reap the thrill of another day's adventure in right relations with God and men.

THE SIXTH STEP IS

Building a Name for Yourself

"If any man be in Christ, he is a new creature."—*II Corinthians 5:17.*

EVERY WORD we say, every act we perform helps to make or mar the impressions the world has about our doings. Courage and self-confidence make good reputations; fear, failure and distrust unmake them.

Many people who read this book are not getting one-half the success out of life they should, for they have not yet learned to use the tremendous power locked up within themselves.

There are some distinct principles for building a reputation. First of all make up your mind what kind of a reputation you would like to have. Then try to show to everyone you meet the characteristics that will gain that end. Be consistent every hour of the day with everyone, and under no conditions belittle yourself, for you are a son of God.

People will talk about you every day. They will remark that you are timid, boastful, kind, selfish, intelligent, stupid, cheerful or sad. They will say that you are worth knowing or that you are a person to be avoided. Remember that a good reputation makes the process of getting along with others easier, and besides gains for you real rewards in the afterlife.

Shakespeare said, "The evil that men do lives after them, the good is oft interred with their bones." The good you do every day is, oh, so soon forgotten when a mistake you make becomes public. It can be held against you throughout your life. Very often the people who boast most about their Christianity are the most unwilling to forgive.

Try to get a clear picture in your mind as to the kind of man or woman you want to be: then think and act according to that mental picture. Live up to your best ideals every hour of the day. You cannot just sit still and gain a good reputation, for you must do something to build that reputation.

A good choir leader has a reputation for getting the best out of his choir; a chef in a restaurant, if successful, gains a reputation for bringing crowds into that eating place.

The story is told of a lady watching a fisherman landing a fish. "O, the poor little fish!" she cried.

"Yes," said the fisherman, "but if he had only kept his mouth shut he would not be on the end of my line."

Is this your weakness, my reader? Has your reputation been marred for life because you never know when to "keep your mouth shut"? I knew the manager of a large company who, one evening, drinking with a competitor, boasted about the sales and production of his company. That one mistake cost his firm a fortune. He didn't know how to control his tongue. Many a secretary loses her job because she talks to others about the contents of letters she has written. Knowing when to speak and when not to speak is a wonderful characteristic, and plays an important part in the reputation you are now building. Many virtues are necessary every day of our lives. We must be kind and helpful, we must be tactful if we want people to like us. Knowing when to say the right thing is a wonderful asset; but a caustic, sarcastic tongue will never reap a good reputation. Meanness means unhappiness for the one who applies it.

The housewife who keeps her home in perfect order at all times stands in good repute with her friends. The person who watches the clock in an office or factory, who just does the things he is supposed to do and no more, never gets along in life. He builds the wrong reputation, he never receives advancement.

I know a saleswoman in the dry goods department of a large store. She studied at night all she could about the manufacture and printing of linens and cottons, and became so interested that she spent one whole vacation at her own expense visiting certain mills which made the goods her company sold. She gradually became very well versed in her products. She built a reputation for wonderful and interesting service to the customers who came into that department, and became the manager of the company after a few years.

Another woman I know worked in the silverware department of a downtown store. She took a correspondence course on silverware which included the setting and arranging of tables. This resulted in her being made adviser for special luncheons and various other functions. She did not have a high school education, yet today she is in charge of a huge store's department for advice on parties and catering. She built a reputation.

Every person who reads this book has talents and abilities waiting to be used, just as these people I have cited. Your mind from day to day will be filled with ideas, but it's up to you to use them according to your faith. Generally speaking, people want to find out how much they can rely upon you, your knowledge, your wisdom; so it is wise to know your real abilities and prove you know what you are talking about. If you have no confidence in yourself, how can you expect your friends or your employer to have any confidence in you? Remember that we have no reputation at all when we are born, it is something that grows with our living. Every hour of every day in every way we are building the reputation we will have later in life.

One of the greatest weaknesses among people is inconsistency. We find people who are kind today and unkind tomorrow; who offer help to some people and turn their backs on others. We should always act in a friendly way to everyone we meet in order to prove the dependability of our character. Remember that a reputation for telling the truth is one of the finest strongholds in life, for unless we stop our first attempt at lying to get us out of trouble, by a succession of events this can lead to our destruction.

The Bible says that if a man be in Christ Jesus he is a new creature. This means that if we live the Christian religion, if we live in Christ, He lives in us. Our minds are filled with His spirit, and we talk to Him, we pray to Him until the presence of God becomes a reality to us. Old things become new. With Christ at the helm, your past reputation can be overcome and you yourself be a new creature.

Many Christians think they live up to the rules of the Ten Commandments, but how often are they filled with self-righteousness. They think that because they do not steal or lie or commit adultery that they have complied with the whole law. Yet how often do they suffer illness and disease, how often suffer poverty, because they never dream that Jesus Christ died for their sicknesses as well as their sins. This type of person often has a reputation for meanness, for lack of charity towards his neighbor, especially towards those who attend churches of a creed different from his own.

My "Lessons in Living" work has taught me that the world today is crying out for God. He has never forsaken us, but in these pagan days humanity has forsaken Him. The answer to this cry lies not in the willingness of God, but in our willingness to accept, through this thing called faith, a belief that Jesus Christ has sent His spirit to every man and woman. It is for us to recognize it and make it the greatest reality of our lives.

Today the power of God within every person is like a sleeping giant which has to be awakened by faith so that it may spring into action. How would you like to start right now to use the law of life? Would you like to prove God right at this moment as you read this book? Would you like to prove that tremendous power, His life, His love available to you at this moment, no matter how great your depression or sickness?

Then believe that you are one with God whenever you wish to be. God is a living, dynamic, vibrant force, a living reality just as available to you as electric power when you touch a switch.

Jesus Christ built for Himself the finest reputation ever held by any person who has inhabited this earth. If you will accept Him right now with faith, you can start building this moment the same reputation that was His.

When a man comes to me who is defeated in life, on the verge of bankruptcy and suicide, it is my job to teach him in simple words how to re-pattern his life, how to change his fears into faith, and how to put God first in his life, so that all things will be added unto him. No matter what your ability, the world will defeat and break you if you do not gain the consciousness of Christ and remember that when you accept Him you have then not only your own ability and power but that mystic force as well which is backed with indescribable resources.

As we go through life we may get the advice of lawyers,

specialists and various experts, but if we would only re-member that the one supreme authority is God, what new creatures we would become! He is the only real expert who can turn your sadness and failure into joyful, happy living. Would you not like to close this book with the assurance that no sickness will ever come to you, that your job will now work out successfully, that no one can hurt you, that no situation in your life can ever again be hopeless?

Then make up your mind to come to the Saviour, to find the Christ within you, to really let go and let God take over from this moment on. He will be the friend of a life-time; He will never turn you down. He will start building for you now a new reputation, and He will give you proof hourly that life is not for dying, life is for living.

Do not just read these words and let them go by without trying to discover this power which I have found. Get the conviction that the Christ Spirit is within you now, that His power is your power, that His love will be directed through you to others, and you will begin to gain a reputation that will take you through eternity. *Let go* your bad reputation *and let God* build you a new one.

THE SEVENTH STEP IS

Adjusting Your Life

"He that doeth good is of God. . . ."—*III John 11.*

IN OUR last chapter we spoke about the traits of character people like to see in us. But how are they going to recognize them, how can we bring our good traits to the attention of the other fellow? This is an easy matter, for it is far harder to hide your real nature than to reveal it.

People judge you by what they see and hear, and their ideas are formed by many things: your expression, appearance, actions, interests and motives. From these various ideas they form a conclusion as to whether they like you or not, as to whether you are going to be hard to get along with or not.

Try to look at all times as if you had confidence in yourself and your own appearance. Your height or weight does not matter, for you can get along with people whether you are thin or fat, short or tall.

The story is told of a very tall girl who lived in New York City. She found her tallness a bar to getting ahead in life. She found it difficult to get boy friends, and she became very sensitive to her condition. Then she began designing her own clothes: hats, suits and dresses. She made them herself. People began to look at her because, though tall, she dressed in such a way as to minimize that impression. They had something to look at now. She conceived the idea of starting a dress shop for tall women, giving such women ideas on how to dress in order to reduce emphasis on their height. Today she is the head of a million-dollar corporation, developed through overcoming a handicap of extreme height. She adjusted herself to the other person regardless of her handicap.

The clothes you wear are very important, for no one can help noticing how you dress, whether you are a man or a woman. They show whether you are neat or untidy; whether you have good taste or lack it; whether you are conservative or radical. Clothing very definitely has an effect on the people you meet, so it is well never to go to extremes.

I came across a woman with a very untidy appearance: no care about her hair, safety pins instead of buttons on her coat, holes in her stockings. All of this showed untidy thinking, and when I took her to task about the matter she said that God looks at the inside, not the outside. That, of course, was the wrong way to look at it because, if she had known God, she would automatically have adjusted herself to Him, and neatness in appearance would have followed.

The expression of your face at all hours of the day is of the greatest importance; it is a true indication of what you are thinking. People with a sour expression usually have a sour and selfish disposition. People who wear a scowl give the idea that they do not like people, and a well-wrinkled forehead often shows lack of confidence, and an excess of worry. Look at your face every day in a mirror. If you are a Christian, your habitual expression must be a smile. Think joyful thoughts, because joyful thoughts give joyful lines to your face. Learn how to be alert every moment of the day, and your face will automatically have that alert expression. Feel confident about your place in life, and your face will show confidence. Every emotion you give rise to in your mind reflects itself upon your face, and the thoughts you think constantly radiate in your facial expressions. If you are a worrier, you invariably show it. If you are an optimist, you show it also, for the play of emotions is always reflected by the play of your features. You can't assume a course of action whereby your face is to show the same features to everyone you meet, for you have to adjust yourself to the particular men or women you are meeting under particular circumstances. One person might be impressed by a business-like appearance, another by your gentle tolerance, and another by your sense of humor.

You have to practice adjusting yourself to the different natures of the people you are trying to get along with. A young lady with several boy friends never tries the same tactics every time; a man never uses the same tactics with every man in his office. Remember that people will try to sound out your real motives in what you say or do, for the thought behind your actions and the key to your being consistent and having people see in your appearance the right motives is to always *have* the right motives towards everyone. We like people who are helpful, we like people who appear to like us. Everyone likes everyone else he meets to appreciate him; so, to adjust yourself to people, you have to learn to like people, to make yourself like them. This means forgetting the bad points and seeing only the good points in them.

Two men met on a train in the United States and one said to the other, "What is your occupation?"

The other replied, "I am a missionary from India, where I have converted five thousand people to Christ."

"Well," said the first man, "I lived in India for years, and never saw a Christian."

"Then what did you do in India?" said the missionary.

The man replied, "I was a government official and I used to hunt tigers. In my life I have killed scores of them."

"I never saw a tiger in the thirty years I spent in India," said the missionary.

One man was looking for tigers, and found them; the other man was looking for people he could help, and found his goal. Neither saw what the other was looking for.

It is the same with you and me; we find what we look for in people. We seem to look for the evil, to try to find a hole in the other person's armor, seeking to discredit him, refusing to see the good in others.

If we are tolerant of other people's errors and mistakes, we can expect them to be tolerant of our own mistakes, for everyone has some good qualities in him, and we must see those qualities and magnify them. The person who tries to pull down another's character is usually a Jekyll and Hyde himself, a type with many weak spots.

Every person we meet likes to feel his own importance. One of the main things to do, then, is to give him a chance to talk about himself. People like to grant favors, and it is often a good point to ask a favor of someone you want to get to like you. Most people have hobbies of some kind. Find out what they are and discuss them sensibly. People like to be asked for advice. This is often a good way to start a real friendship, for people like to share confidences.

I knew a man who could not get along at all with another man in his office who was a Welshman. One day he said to him, "It is very strange, but do you realize you belong to a race that has never been conquered?" This hit very hard at the heart of the Welshman, and was the beginning of a real friendship between them.

The key to adjusting yourself to any person is to act as if you liked them. Get the Boy Scout motto deep in your mind and do a good turn to someone every day, for the constant practice of this is basic Christian teaching.

"He that doeth good is of God." Do you realize that you were placed on this earth by God so that He could express Himself to men through you? For God can do nothing except through us; we are the keys on His piano. God is all good; every good deed we do, every good thought is a means for God to express through us, and this brings us to the point of seeing the Christ in everyone we meet.

We are told that Jesus Christ was a carpenter's son, yet His mission on earth was to construct a spiritual temple in the hearts of men, to teach men the spiritual laws He knew.

We are all apprentices in His workshop. Every day we work to unfold soul qualities like those expressed by the Master to make us loving, kind, forgiving, and perfect. Love is the most powerful and attractive force in the universe, and the more love you show your fellow man the more good things will be drawn into your life.

We have to know what God is before we can love Him,

but it seems strange that many so-called Christians will not believe how wonderful God and His power can be to them. First of all we must believe that Christ dwells within us; this simple belief puts us in tune with a power that will develop creative abilities in our minds.

Successful living depends upon how well you can adjust yourself to other people. The Christian Faith as taught and practiced by Jesus is the only answer.

We have today many Christian sects, the members of which often show hatred to each other, refusing to love each other, and filled with condemnation for others who practice a different Christian creed. This is all because they will not try to follow the plan of the Master, Jesus. Do you realize that Jesus spent His life going about doing good in order to express the will of His Father? Have you ever realized what tremendous love would develop in you if you made it your sole purpose to serve the good which is God by serving your neighbor? What have you done for someone during the past week, for instance? The greatest joy in life is the joy of giving. The greatest happiness in life is found by expressing love wherever you can.

If we would realize the law of love, there would be no bad relations, no bad marriages, no need to fear the rapidly rising divorce rates. The way to love is to give service wherever you can. If you have never learned to give in money or in service to God, then you have not yet learned to love God. In not trying to serve Him every day of your life, you are disobeying His rules for living, you are working against His Kingdom.

The Bible says, "Do good to them that hate you." Why? Because when you persistently do good to the people who wrong you, you eventually make those people like you.

It is well to remember that the only treasures, the only permanent treasures, we can lay up are those in the heavens of the mind; the only gold that can be trusted, that can be continually depended upon, is the gold of spirit. We are told that Jesus never owned anything; yet how rich He was in the treasure of spirit, the thing we need so much in this materialistic world.

Some religious leaders have said it is a Christian duty to be poor, but to me this is not the teaching of the Master, for He definitely said He would give you all things you might need in life if you would put love for Him and your fellowman before everything else.

You are not a Christian simply because you follow some creed or ritual. You become a Christian only when your heart becomes centered in Christ. You may belong to a church, you may have found Christ in that church; but you may also have lost Him in the same place because you have not lived up to His teachings. Do you show love and friendship to all the members of your church, or are you filled with criticism towards some members of the congregation? Once you believe deep down in your heart, once you get into a personal relationship with God, you become centered on the Christ within and receive in return an abundance of health, happiness and harmony.

You never have to beg or coax God in order to bring His good into your life. God is like the sun; He shines on everything. It is up to you to get out of the shadows, to grow out of the basement in which your mind has lived so long. Open the windows of your soul and lift up your faith with conviction, and your life will be whatever you wish it to be.

As you close this chapter, consider your own life. Think of the people whom you have not been able to get along with; then make up your mind to *let go* the evil you saw in those people *and let God* bring you a new vision in regard to them. Change your thinking habits and let God adjust your life.

THE EIGHTH STEP IS

Using the Force of Ideas

"For whosoever hath, to him shall be given,
and he shall have more abundance."—*St.
Matthew 13:12.*

It is a well-known fact that the average man and woman
find it easier to do things according to their emotions than
by applying their reason. In our daily contacts, therefore,
we should try to keep away from arguments of any kind.
Arguments create bad feeling and often result in a sense of
humiliation.

In my life I have known many managers who seem to
take delight in making their employees feel small in front
of other people. These men are the most detested men in
any organization.

You may, as a result of an argument, convince someone
against his will that you are right but, invariably, in so
doing you lose a friend. The best way not to get along with
people is to try constantly to prove that your knowledge
is superior and that you are invariably right.

Human beings love to discover things for themselves,
they like to form their own judgments. They usually resent being told what conclusions they must reach. In order
to get someone you know to do something for you, plant an
idea or suggestion; then train their imagination and their
emotions the way you want them to go. In making a suggestion of any kind, turn a person's attention to that particular thing. The power of suggestion is stock in trade in
any profession. The magician on the stage uses the power
of suggestion to the nth degree in trying to make you

believe the very opposite of what he is doing.

This is a story of a certain prize fight between a big man and a small man. One of the men near the ring said, "It looks like Sullivan and Corbett all over again." The little man, hearing this conversation and registering the thought in his mind, got the idea that again the little man would be beaten. This suggestion took him completely off his guard, thereby defeating him.

How often during the day do you face the negative thought that it is impossible for you to do the thing you want to do, and so are beaten from the start?

There are many people who are contrary by nature, and it is simpler to suggest to them the opposite course of action than the one you want them to follow, in which case you will nearly always win out. The medical man often uses strategy of this kind. In my own spiritual counseling I have interviewed many people who came to see me apparently on the verge of suicide. They got a definite sadistic pleasure from hurting relatives and friends and by threatening to do away with themselves, but when their bluff was called they certainly did not do any such thing.

There is the story of a daughter who had been absolutely forbidden by her mother to keep company with a certain young man. The father, however, took the opposite tack, and told the mother to invite the young man to the house. After the visit, he praised his daughter's friend, saying what a nice chap he was. The mother was very upset and told her husband that this was a very dangerous practice, to which the father replied, "Yes, but not so dangerous as placing obstacles in her way." The mother's treatment of complete detestation for this young man would possibly have caused the girl to run away and elope with him, for she was a very determined girl; but the father, having encouraged the young man to come into the home, turned the tide, and the infatuation did not last a month, for the daughter had realized by this time that he was not at all suitable for her as a husband.

We must never laugh at the fears of other people, because often they are very real to them, and we should not attempt to remove their fears by means of argument. It is a good policy to listen to their long tales of woe, then gradually submit adroit suggestions which help lead them away from their stupid obsessions.

Suggestion is the most potent of forces used by publishers, politicians, and even evangelists. Take, for example, a new book—let some book critic give a particular work a splendid write-up and you will find thousands of people flocking to buy it. The same thing applies to a movie or a stage presentation: the greater the crowds, the more people there will be to follow those crowds. We see mass suggestion at work every day of our lives.

If a man goes to the office in the morning looking pale and out of sorts, he will probably go home before noon quite ill if enough people tell him how sick he is looking. This is really the power of suggestion. The women of our day commonly use cosmetics. This gives the suggestion of good health, and very often enables the user to feel better by means of the power of suggestion than she would otherwise have felt.

When you see a man polishing a lady's automobile, it is almost certain that this couple is engaged. When you see a woman polishing a man's car, you may be sure they are married. These are suggestions purely by appearance.

Your subconscious mind produces in your daily life evidence of the thoughts you send back to it. The constant repetition of fear, anxiety and worry thoughts will bring upon you the same thing multiplied many times over, but the constant practice of positive thinking, making affirmations hour by hour that God is now healing your fears and worries, will bring magnificent results.

How many times have you heard the phrase, "believe you can do it and you will do it"? Belief enables you to do things that were otherwise impossible, for the act of believing is the starting force which leads to accomplishment. The more you believe, the more power within comes to your aid. The practice of suggestion is used by all coaches of football, baseball, and other sports. The more the coach gives his team the conviction that they will win, the more sure is the victory for that team.

If you were faced with a sudden fright, such as meeting a ghost on a dark night, you would run with unbounded energy, for there are great reserves of strength in your subconscious mind which give superhuman strength to meet all the fears you will ever have to face.

The Mohammedan has a religion which compels him to pray five times a day; regardless of what his work may be, at prayer time he stops everything, kneels on the ground and says his prayer ritual. This gives him a great conviction that God is with him. In Haiti there is a cult of Voodoo, which is entirely a religion of mass suggestion. Dictators such as Hitler, Mussolini, Peron and Stalin owed, or owe a good deal of their success to the mass suggestion of pictures placed in every corner of their countries. Many years ago, in Canada, we would see a sign on every farm fence and barn, from coast to coast, advertising a certain baking powder. This was really mass suggestion to make people think that the only baking powder was the one mentioned in this advertisement: it was a profitable suggestion. I can assure you there is magic in the art of believing and the power of suggestion.

The story in the Bible of Jacob, and how he became so wealthy, reveals his mastery of the art of suggestion. Moses, too, was a past master at this art. If you remember, David, the small shepherd boy, killed a giant with his sling shot. Why? Because he knew he could do it.

Today on every hand we read in newspapers and magazines that the world is in for a terrific depression, that it is growing from bad to worse. When these suggestions circulate, money runs to cover, and the depression we talked about and pictured in our minds becomes manifest only because of our fears, only because men and women take part in this wrong suggestiveness.

We see also many articles written in the daily newspapers that war with Russia is inevitable. The more we talk about it being inevitable, the more we get a real fear complex and the faster we produce this war which does not need to occur at all.

There will never be another depression or war if the people of every civilization will realize that it is their own fear thoughts, suggestion en masse, which create the ideas of these so-called hard times and international conflicts, and which sooner or later bring them into being.

Success in any walk of life is caused more by mental attitudes than by anything else; so is failure. The Roman Catholic Church places great faith in the ceremonies of the Mass. During that service certain things take place, all of which are suggestions that exert a tremendous influence over those who believe in them.

Good luck charms, sacred medals, talismans and amulets have no power of themselves. It is the magic of believing on the part of the recipient or user that makes them really effective. Alexander the Great and Napoleon were both convinced that they were superhuman individuals, and they became so because they absolutely believed this. *You can do this too.*

St. Peter, we are told, at the suggestion of the Master began to walk upon the water; as long as he believed, as long as he did not see the wetness of that water, he was able to overcome a physical law.

"For whosoever hath, to him shall be given, and he shall

have more abundance." This means that to him that hath faith, shall be given the truth that will make him free of every negative thing. It means that more health, more happiness, more harmony in living will be added unto him. It does not mean wealth in dollars and cents.

It does mean that if you will accept the suggestion that Jesus Christ was God and that His spirit lives within you, then by practicing His teachings, you will never doubt any more that you can overcome in the world everything negative that you can possibly have to face.

Faith depends entirely upon suggestion: the more you believe that God is now healing you of sin, sickness and poverty, the oftener you use this affirmation; the more you will become convinced of its truth and the faster you will gain the perfect answer to your prayers.

You may say, "How can I believe that I am getting better when I am still very sick?" It is never you who are sick. The soul is never ill, but the physical body in which your soul lives has from some cause or other demonstrated the sickness. When your mind becomes the dominating factor in your life, when you believe that God is now healing you and repairing the house in which you live, then the necessary change will take place.

In my counseling work I met a woman who had suffered from terrific nervous headaches for many years; she could not get relief. There were many negative things in her life, fits of temperament and resentment which she had to learn to overcome. When she came to Christ really convinced that He was now healing her, she lost the desire to do these erroneous things; she saw the Christ in her enemies, and suddenly her nervous headaches were over.

A man once visited my clinic completely discouraged and defeated because he was heavily in debt and had at the same time to find another home, which seemed impossible. He applied this magic of believing. He made affirmations every hour, thanking God for having begun to find the home he needed, but at the same time making sure that hate no longer dominated his life. In one week, the home he needed was found, and in moving from the house in which he had lived for many years he found a trunk in the basement which contained what he thought were many old worthless gold stocks. He took them down to a broker and found that they now had considerable value. He sold them and paid off his debts. The lesson to be learned from this story is that he had riches all the time in his own possession. You have those same riches available to you, for within your own consciousness right now is your future happiness, your future health and your future success.

First believe; then make use of the power of suggestion that Jesus Christ, who is now your captain and your pilot, has begun to give you strength, to give you ideas, and to give you happiness. Make this your belief, your affirmation, every hour of every day.

An artist came to see me who had had several nervous breakdowns and who was filled with fears. She had tried many different religious faiths but never gained the answer to her prayers. She attended a lecture on the magic of believing and, on asking God's forgiveness for her lack of faith in the past, she decided to rely upon the Christ within herself, and began to thank Him every hour for having begun to solve her problem.

The following morning she got out of bed with a new idea in her mind and, within four days, she had painted her first picture in many years; for her religious fears and troubles had left her. This picture showed real life, far better than her former works, and came from her new consciousness of God, from within! This was the beginning of a successful career.

Remember to look upon God as a friend. Remember

also that all your life must be lived according to laws He has made. Believe that He is willing to give you now His Kingdom. Trust that He will solve every problem you have to face at this moment, if you will practice the magic of believing.

The way to get along in the world lies in the thought, the suggestion, that once you accept Christ by simply letting Him be the dominating factor in your life, and take Him at His word, believing that He is now showing you the way to a life free from error and a life more abundant, then the self-imposed prison you have lived in for so long will disappear.

Learn how to *let go* the negative suggestions of the human side of your nature, and learn how to *let God* bring happiness to you. You have the ability for successful living. You have the tools. The power you use is faith and the tools are your thoughts and ideas. Learn today how to use them, not for yourself but for God. Thus you will become a radiant, happy Christian, living in Christ and He in you, for you will have gained every righteous desire of your heart.

THE NINTH STEP IS

Discovering Your Underlying Motives

"God so loved the world that he gave his only begotten Son."—*St. John 3:16.*

PEOPLE give many reasons why they do things, but many of them are only secondary, because so often they will not give the real motives for their actions. Sometimes it is a case of shyness; sometimes they are afraid to hurt your feelings; and sometimes they don't want you to know certain facts about their lives.

It is your duty, if you are learning to get along with anyone, to find out to which emotional class he belongs; then by appealing to that dominating emotion you will win your point.

Possibly you want an increase in salary, and the boss says you are worth it but he can't afford it. How can you find out the real reason?

Suppose you are at the head of a Sunday School and the attendance is dropping off. Maybe the students are not interested. How can you solve this problem and get at the real motive?

Suppose you owned a restaurant and wished to increase your clientele, what motive can you appeal to other than reasonable prices, good food, and a clean restaurant?

To understand why people do what they do, you must be able to discover the motives which underlie their acts. You will often find that the real motive is something far removed from the act itself.

You will notice that leading men in your city often head drives for charities. They are chosen to a certain extent because of their place in the community, but chiefly because they are men who love publicity, who will do wonders and give plenty when they see their names in the headlines.

I remember a lady some time ago, whose little boy complained of a headache and could not go to school, but at eleven o'clock he got out of bed and dressed and was very anxious to get his lunch. His headache had gone. His mother discovered afterwards that he was to have had a school examination that morning which he was afraid to face. This was the real motive for his so-called headache.

Perhaps your corner drug store will offer you a more expensive product than the one you want to purchase, stating that it is much superior to the one you had in mind. But is it? In many cases the druggist gets a better profit on that article. You must always try to get at the real motive.

Many people write me from time to time in glowing terms about my work and want an interview to see me as soon as possible, but when I get down to brass tacks and discover the real motive, they usually want a position in my particular field, and at several hundred dollars a month more than they could earn anywhere else. Be very careful of the gushing person who tells you how wonderful you are and how much he appreciates you, because often this is distinct proof of his insincerity.

Sometimes people are actuated by motives of which they seem to be unaware. A lady who came for an interview one day told me that her marriage was a failure because she had discovered she did not love her husband. On discussing the pros and cons of her life in the past, I found that she did love him but that he had a superior education and wanted to mix with people of the same cultural background, among whom his wife felt inferior. Gradually through the years she felt out of place and developed an inferiority complex. Once this matter was straightened out between husband and wife, the whole situation cleared up beautifully, and they have lived happily ever since.

In solving your problems with other people, do not take only the obvious facts into consideration, for apparent reasons can be very misleading. Try to find out the hidden motives.

We often find in church organizations and clubs that friction is common among members because of different temperaments. When we hear of these frictions the real motives are not always given by either side, and we must try to find out what it could have been, and study the emotions and the conditions involved.

A man who was a very good worker with me in religious

work suddenly stopped attending my meetings. When I asked him why, he said that he hadn't been going out at all in the afternoons, so I began to look for the hidden motive. Knowing his temperament, I discovered that I had given some task to another man to do, which he felt should have been given to him. He had allowed resentment to build up in his mind, and this caused him to stop attending my meetings. Once he found out that I had discovered his hidden motive, we got the matter straightened out and he again became a very useful man in God's work.

Possibly the plumber who comes to repair your furnace or your water coil will give you a sales talk on the use of a gas or electric heater. The real motive may be that he gets a better profit from such a sale than he would for the repair work or for replacing the old coils.

To succeed in any phase of human activity we must first of all be able to work in harmony with others, to win their friendship, their respect and their cooperation. People of every nation, every creed and every color can get along together when they have the right motives. "For God so loved the world, that he gave his only begotten Son, that whosoever believeth in him should not perish, but have everlasting life." The real motive behind the coming of Jesus Christ was not to give us a formal church in which to worship, not simply to give us a creed or a lot of dogmas or a theology, but to show us a way of living, a way to happiness, and the only way to life everlasting. Every one of us has been given special talents and abilities. We must develop mentally and spiritually every day of our lives. Jesus came as a human being to live as we do, to face the same temptations we have to face, to have the same physical make-up and the same emotions we have. He had to face the same diseases of the flesh we have, but He conquered all these. He not only conquered disease but he conquered death so that you and I could gain the Kingdom of Heaven. He sacrificed everything for you—what are you willing to sacrifice for Him?

Jesus often said that it was the Father within Him who did the work, and He told us that this power is now within us. Marvelous, unlimited spiritual power which we can contact by means of faith, and which will bring to every person in every nation peace of mind, health, joy, harmony, and everything needed for successful living. The things which have made your life unhappy in the past can be completely eliminated by conscious use of this power.

How can we contact it? By faith, by the magic of believing, by constant, hourly contact with God in prayer. Jesus taught us His relationship to the Father, and He showed us how we are all related to the Father in the same way.

We are made up of two parts, the physical part which always wants to say, "I can't," and the spiritual part which says, "I can do all things through Jesus Christ." We must learn to love God, to love Jesus Christ with a love greater than any other love and, in order to prove that love, we must follow His teachings and His life as closely as we can. Many Christians follow the teachings of Jesus Christ with the idea that God in any form is outside of men; they feel we can all call upon Him but He very seldom answers us.

To live a Christ-life is to follow Jesus' instructions, to find God's presence dwelling within us, to be filled with life, love and power—all of which are ready and willing to flow forth abundantly the moment we are willing to give up the errors in our lives and to take Him as our partner for the rest of our days.

Some time ago a man came to me in the depths of despair, entirely unable to face life. Full of fears of he knew not what, full of doubt, a complete introvert, he felt the time had come for him to end his life. He had no knowledge of God, but he learned from attending two of our lectures something of faith. He came for an interview and he was taught how to pray. He asked God for forgiveness for his past, but what counted most was that from that moment he came to Christ. He had begun to find the Christ within him. Alcohol, and the other things which had dominated his life completely, left him. He had no desire for them whatsoever.

I advised him to pray every hour, wherever he might be, thanking God for the guidance he was now being given. At my suggestion, he also took a sales psychology course to help him to gain confidence in himself. He is now a happy, successful salesman. And he regularly keeps his hourly appointment with God, because he knows that when he began to seek for the Kingdom of God within him, he found power, he got at the real motive for living. He has *let go* his past *and let God*.

The real motive for our life on this earth is for us to express God through His Son, Jesus Christ, every day we live. God will never force us to do anything against our wills. If we want Him to do anything for us we must let Him. Jesus said that signs and wonders would follow a belief in Him, but never will God work any miracles for us until we first of all submit to His will. This is the basic, the integral part of the bargain of living.

Do you want happiness, peace of mind? Then to gain these things you must first of all be willing to sacrifice your sinful desires, your wrong emotions, your sins. Once God takes His rightful place in your heart, these things fade away; they give you up and you gain that inner peace which makes life worthwhile. It is not just a case of following Christ, of following God, it is a case of letting Christ, the perfect Son of God, be manifested in you, in all your doings.

There are many Christians who expect at some time to be saved from sickness and trouble, but the true Christian is one who knows that he is now saved from those things by the indwelling Christ, and in faith constantly affirms this truth until it is manifest in his life.

What fears have you who read this book today? Are you afraid of your future, your health, your finances, your job? Then, in silence, when you have finished this chapter, close your eyes, hand over all these fears to God in absolute faith, and pray, believing that you are now receiving that for which you ask. Thank God for having begun to bring health and happiness into your life. This is positive prayer. It completes the circuit between you and the power called God, and the answer to such a prayer will astonish you.

Simply believing that Jesus died on a cross for you is by no means sufficient. There must be much more than this. There has to be a real change in you, a real call of some kind, a real merging of your soul with God. The healing Spirit of Christ is here today, available to every one of us, to meet all our needs, to revitalize our lives, and to regain for us the Kingdom of which Jesus spoke so often.

Won't you come to the conviction right now that you want to accept Him in simple faith? The real motive in life is for us to find the Christ in ourselves and in everyone we meet. When you make a sincere effort to find Him you will be gently led from the canyons of despair into the fertile valleys through which run the waters of everlasting life. You who seek truth, health, peace of mind—these things come only from the fountainhead—they come only from God. They come only when you learn to lean on Him in absolute faith.

Won't you get at the real motive right now as to why you are on this earth? God has a prospect in view for you, and maybe this book will bring a consciousness to you at this moment of how changed your life can be.

Won't you try at this moment to let go everything in your life that has brought you failure and fear? Won't you really give God a chance, and let Him, let God take over the control of your life?

To *let go and let God* means a complete overcoming of the unsound motives in your life and the glorious realization of eternal happiness with Him forever and ever.

THE TENTH STEP IS

Overcoming Any Feeling of Inferiority

"If God be for us, who can be against us?"—*Romans 8:31.*

STRANGERS we meet from day to day are apt to take us at face value. If we have a feeling of inferiority towards them or towards life in general, it will very quickly show up. We must therefore do something about it. The Bible tells us why we should never feel inferior to anyone.

In trying to improve our position in life, in trying to adjust ourselves to others, we should tear ourselves apart mentally and find out if there are any such traits of inferiority in our characters.

The cross-eyed man almost always develops an inferiority complex because of his handicap. People who are shy or timid, people who are weak by nature, people who have a secret sin upon their consciences, invariably dislike meeting people because of a sense of inferiority.

Possibly you have developed a dislike of meeting new people. Possibly you may find it difficult to remember people's names. Hence you withdraw from the public as much as possible. You may not have had a high school or university education, and therefore cannot discuss with some people some things with which they, because of their superior education, are familiar. So you avoid such discussion.

Now whether the difficulty is real or whether it is imaginary, the results are the same. You become whatever you think. If God is with you, how can you possibly feel inferior to anyone? You have equal access to all the good that comes from God. You can demonstrate your faith in His ability to give it to you by living His life. So change your thought patterns right now. Make up your mind to beat this feeling by faith in God, and you will.

He can who thinks he can!

As we read through the pages of history we find that Julius Caesar, Napoleon and Edison, all had developed a feeling of inferiority, yet they were great men in many ways; so do not be ashamed of your inferiority complex. Do as they did, and lick it!

In our modern age we have a type of doctor known as the psychiatrist. When a patient goes to him filled with fears, anxieties and worries, he analyzes all his past life, all his past ways of thinking, and from that deduces the reasons for his present fears. He tries to outline the things he should do in order to overcome those fears.

Many years ago, I had a secretary who was filled with a sense of inferiority. The first day she arrived she told me that she couldn't possibly do my filing, and she was very much afraid of the dictation she would take from me because it would be full of technical words.

The story of this girl's life was a very interesting one. She was the only child of two invalid parents, and all her spare time had been devoted to them because they had no other care. Her previous position had been a very depressing one with unpleasant people. Conditions at home, where there was no outlet for entertainment which most girls have, had added to her misery and caused her to become obsessed with the idea of being inferior.

However, while she was in my office she heard no negative remarks, she was given nothing but positive thoughts every day. She was taught gradually not to be afraid of technical phrases or words. She found the work extremely interesting.

Gradually she refused to accept feelings of inferiority, and month by month one could see a wonderful improvement in her personality. In five years, or thereabouts, this girl was the finest secretary I had ever known, and she left me to take a position as private secretary to a big executive.

Now, the people who succeed in life are those who, when they get into wrong ways of thinking, when they seem to face mountains of difficulty, refuse to accept these things. They refuse to believe that conditions, or people, or events can ever down their ambition or their spirit. They refuse to believe that any condition in life can interfere with their success. They know that nothing in life can hurt them unless they let it.

If you have had thoughts of failure, defeat and inferiority, get this idea now. Simply believe that the Bible means what it says; for when you begin to live right, when you begin to live within the laws of God, you will find that your negative tendencies are gradually overcome, because of the power within you, in which you are now trusting. This power, of course, is God.

With most people it is not the fact that they have had a failure or had a defeat which has beaten them; but it has been a holding of negative thoughts, the anticipation of failure in their own mind. They convince themselves that they are inferior to certain of their friends, their fellows or their neighbours and the longer they hold this thought the more inferior they become to everything and everybody.

One very wet and cold Monday morning in the month of March, I got into a taxi. The driver was a veteran who immediately began to rant in no uncertain terms about the vile weather. As I sat beside him on a long trip, I discovered that he was single with a good war record and that he had had two years' university training in engineering before the war, but on his return he felt that he could not complete his education, therefore he bought a taxicab and his sense of inferiority had grown to the point of obsession with him. I also discovered that he had many characteristics which go to make a good salesman, so I told him that with his background and education he should try to locate a job in engineering sales. He said this was exactly the thing he would like to do, but how could he do it?

I then quoted this text to him, "If God be for us, who can be against us?" He said he went occasionally to church with his mother but God did not mean very much to him. However, in that taxicab he came to a conviction, and before I left him I prayed with him, thanking God for having begun to find him the right job. I gave him my card and told him to come to see me when that job arrived, as I knew it would.

Ten days later he came into my office, quite a different person and radiant with happiness. It seems that the Saturday before he picked up a man to drive him to the airport. The man noticed how optimistic was this driver, who, though it was a dull morning, said it was a beautiful day. Before they got to the airport the passenger, who was a sales manager of an engineering firm, had asked the young man to come and see him when he returned. The driver did this, and was immediately placed on the staff as engineering salesman. He was just the man the sales manager had been looking for. And now after almost two years in that work he is most successful. He gained a complete overcoming of his inferiorities, was living successfully, but not until he *let go* his fears and his doubts *and let God*.

We must remember that thoughts of victory, thoughts of overcoming even small things, are the seeds from which victory springs, and you, while reading this chapter, can sow the seeds right at this moment that will give you victory over the things that have defeated you to date.

Several thousand years ago a noted philosopher known as Pythagoras said, "Man, know thyself." This simply means know your power. When you realize your own power of thought and what you can do with those thoughts to contact divine power, you can overcome every obstacle and every tribulation that may happen to you in life.

Do you realize that there is enough atomic energy in the body of every man and woman to completely destroy the whole of New York City? As this is a scientific fact, how can you have a sense of inferiority towards anything, when this power is within yourself? Similarly, there is enough power in you to withstand every sickness you ever have to face. You will overcome all your troubles by trusting this power to work for you.

You will become what you imagine yourself to be. If you believe there is no future for you, if you believe that through certain conditions you have no chance to get anywhere, then that is actually what you will prove.

People who get ahead in life, who defeat these inferiorities, are those who refuse to accept them. These people refuse to believe in defeat, for, as I said before, it is the thought of defeat which produces defeat.

When we believe in a divine power within us, when we practice thinking thoughts of absolute faith, we realize then the meaning of spiritual victory, and learn from day to day how to deny the power of evil in our lives.

Train your mind every hour of every day to think victory and, by the magic of believing, victory will be yours every day of your life.

An inferiority complex is a disbelief in your own self,

your own powers of mind. This to me is a sin, for every human being has been made in the image of God and is perfect, whole and complete. We all come across people in our lives who suffer from pride and conceit. Strangely enough, this is usually an indication of an inferiority complex, and they are using this method to hide a feeling of inadequacy. You will notice how some small, short men like to be in the forefront a great deal. They like to strut around in front of people, and when talking to you or others seem always very sure of their abilities; yet how often are they not filled within themselves with fears and doubts, depending upon this bold front to hide their inner complexes.

A certain woman complained to a newspaper in her town because her picture had not appeared in the society column. As a baby this woman had always cried for her rattle and her toys, and someone had always handed them to her. All through her life there was someone ready to do things for her; she expected to be "babied," and so developed a strong sense of inadequacy. This developed into a complete manifestation of inferiority later in life, and made her resent being left out of anything.

There is a story of two frogs. They fell into a pail of thick cream. One frog was filled with fears and inferiority, so he didn't swim around very much before he began to be choked by the cream, and drowned. Not so the other frog. He knew he was going to get out of that pail somehow, and he said to himself as he looked over his shoulder at the drowning frog, "That isn't going to happen to me!" So he placed his front feet against the pail and started to paddle for all he was worth with his back feet. In no time he had a pat of butter. As soon as he felt that solid island beneath his feet, he hopped out.

This little story illustrates in simple words the problems we all face in daily living. We go ahead with good intentions to tackle something new, but when an obstacle confronts us that we have not faced before, we often feel inferior to it, and our new proposition becomes a failure. We have to have stamina like the frog, we have to do as he did and know there must be some way of getting out of a pail of trouble.

But we have more power available to us than has the frog, for we have God power—the greatest power in the universe ready for us to use whenever we change ourselves, whenever we become converted from error into a life of radiant living.

Know yourself—change yourself.

We can all do this if we will believe that "if God be for us, who can be against us?" If you will simply believe this passage from the Bible and practice it every day, you will gradually develop tremendous faith in God, and you will find that this faith releases forces which come at once to your aid. Religious faith puts power into every man and woman to gain complete resistance to, and demonstrate a complete overcoming of, defeat.

Start now, believing that if you really trust God, if you really try to live according to His laws, you are building on a solid foundation. Every day you thus train your mind never to accept defeat, never to accept inferiority.

Has your Christianity been practical? Does your faith in religion act as a working instrument to solve the problems of your life.

I can assure you that when you constantly live in tune with God your inferiorities change into power and the impossible things of your life then become the possibles.

During my counseling work I interviewed a young lady who had made a serious mistake and got into a great deal of trouble. The more she worried about the child she had given birth to, the more she worried about her sin, until finally she came to the point of suicide; for though she had asked God's forgiveness, she had not learned how to forgive herself. This one mistake in her life brought about a feeling in her of inferiority and fear towards everyone. She eventually came to the realization that God had forgiven all, that He had forgiven her momentary error; and she lost her inferiority complex, and became a happy, well-adjusted person.

However, it was not until she let go her fears of what friends might think about her, it was not until she let God take over her life, that she gained this overcoming.

We are living in an age when we find on every hand apparent signs of a complete decline in orthodox religion. The world seems to have cancer of the soul and, if your religion is simply a formal one, mere attendance at church on Sunday, then it is time you did something about it. It is time you began to believe in this power called God and that He is for you in everything that is good. This being the case, how then can anything in opposition to God ever exist?

God is a very loving Father, always willing to give us the Kingdom if we will learn to know Him, if we will learn to love Him, if we will learn to believe in Him.

A lady came to me one day who had lived a very sinful, very selfish and very sophisticated life in society. Though she had plenty of money, she was most unhappy, for she had been chasing butterflies all her life which she had never been able to catch. She came to ask me to teach her how to pray, for she could not believe that God, whom she had entirely forgotten, would ever forgive her selfish life.

I told her that this was an assured fact, and we prayed believing that we were now receiving. I taught her the meaning of Calvary, and how through that Calvary some two thousand years ago the errors of her life were now blotted out. She learned how to practice in a very simple way, praying every hour of the day for one minute, in thanksgiving to God for having completely wiped out her sins. Thus she gained that thing called peace of mind. It is a pleasure to talk to her today because she carries the light of faith in her eyes, and every day of her life she experiences the joy of helping someone in need.

You have no doubt noticed that on pictures of Saints there is a halo which surrounds every holy person. Do you ever realize that every one of us is surrounded by an aura of light? This light which comes from us, which radiates from every part of our body, comes from our thoughts, and this is the part of us which attracts or repels other people. This is how you sense whether you like or whether you dislike new people whom you meet from day to day.

Remember that the whole world is run on the law of cause and effect. Every effect in your life is produced by a cause, and these causes usually are actions which come from your predominating thought processes. How careful then we should be with our thought patterns every hour of the day; because for every thought we hold predominantly in mind, we shall see the effects outpictured in life, according to this unfailing law. If we continually think thoughts of fear and inferiority, then those things will be produced throughout our lives as natural consequences or effects.

Possibly, though you are a Christian, you do not wish to give up certain wrong things in your mind: the way you handle your emotions or the way you handle your temper. If so, then by the law of cause and effect you will never know spiritual success. Happiness of a permanent variety will never be yours in this life or in the life eternal.

However, if you will from this moment begin believing in God as a tremendous source of divine energy, if you will believe that He is intensely interested in your life, and if you will believe that His laws must be adhered to, you will begin to think of God first, and yourself last. Then this Christ power within you will demonstrate every day the complete overcoming of everything that has defeated you in life. When you first come to that conviction, you are what the Bible calls "reborn," you are born again and your eternal salvation starts from that moment, for that is the moment when you start to really live.

There is an old hymn which says, "Come to the Saviour, make no delay"; and if you are willing to believe those words, they will bring you to the fount of joy which will enable you to convert your inferiorities into success, your sickness into health, your poverty of mind into abundant living, your fears, your doubts and your sorrows into a wonderful awareness of joyful living.

Every one of us as he goes through life must die daily in a mental sense, for his negative or evil thoughts must each day die. New ideas, new thoughts, positive instead of negative, new faith must be born in us from day to day. It matters not what fears have beset you in the past, what inferiorities are now holding you back. It matters not what you have reaped in life hitherto, if you are willing today to make a new seeding time and believe that tomorrow holds promise of a harvest that will bring you life more abundantly.

It is the easiest thing in the world to learn how to *let go* your sense of inferiority *and let God;* for if God is for you, what and who can be against you?

Your Code for Life

"Be ye transformed by the renewing of your mind."—*Romans 12:2.*

IN EVERY chapter of this book I have tried to show you how powerful is the action of thought, and I can assure you that thoughts are things. In the last ten chapters, in particular, I have tried to give you specific steps in victorious living that will make those thoughts the right things.

Your whole life, your health and happiness and your success in life are entirely determined by your thoughts; whether you think constructively or destructively, positively or negatively, you build up your thoughts and carry them through to action every day. These actions produce results which mean victory for you and a complete overcoming of everything negative, or they can mean complete defeat and years of ill health.

The power of right thinking is the power of faith, for it is only through faith in God, absolute steadfast faith, that we fulfill the requirements of the code for happy living.

The basic teaching of my "Lessons in Living" Bible class is that we are to see the Christ (the good) in everyone, in place of the evil. A real, lasting faith in all good things, a faith in spiritual powers, works out successfully for those who constantly and consistently hold that faith.

A lady once said to me, "I wish I had the amount of faith you possess." Every person on this earth has potentially the same amount of faith as I have; those who meet failure and defeat are those who allow their faith to be dominated and ruled by fears.

Suppose you accidentally cut your finger, you immediately place a bandage on the wound and forget about it;

82

then a day or so later you take off the bandage and look at your healed finger. You had no doubt, you knew it would heal, so it did. But it is really God's power within you that performs that healing. Now, if through a demonstration of absolute faith like this a cut finger can be quickly healed, why not use the same absolute faith to overcome any sickness, any disease which might befall you? This same faith that healed your finger is the same faith that will solve your every problem, because it is faith in the God within you.

What kind of a person do you want to be? Have you really tried in the past to overcome your fears and your failures, to develop the personality you like so much in others? We are told by a great school of learning that out of all the people who attain successful living, only fifteen per cent have college educations; in other words, eighty-five per cent of those who develop into successful persons with attractive personalities, do so without the benefits of a university training.

Possibly as a child you were taught in your religious faith that this world was a very dreadful place in which to live. It may have been painted to you as a vale of sin, sorrow, sickness and misery; and, if you have accepted this type of religion and constantly think negatively about the world, you will produce exactly that kind of a world you have built up in these wrong mental pictures, and you will completely fail in meeting your life's problems. If, however, you acknowledge Jesus Christ as your guide, if you accept His teaching as the code upon which to base your life, then you will find this world a very wonderful place to live in and you will realize the joy of living.

Doubts, fears and sicknesses will come your way from time to time but these things will no longer trouble you for, by means of your devotion to Jesus Christ and by living His way of life, every tribulation, every sickness overcome, must prove a stepping stone to your success.

Remember well that Jesus Christ said, "I am come that they might have life, and that they might have it more abundantly." If, therefore, you have not been enjoying more abundant living, the fault is your own.

Should you ever take a trip to the Rocky Mountains, you will discover a most amazing plant, bright green in color, known as saxifrage. This plant grows on the flat faces of steep rocky slopes. You will wonder at this miracle of nature, how any plant can withstand winds and storms when it has no soil in which to anchor its roots. This plant makes its own soil for its roots; its seeds contain a strong acid which rots the rock, and by so doing it develops its own soil.

Now this is a secret for you to take note of because you can become an "overcomer" if you are willing to create from your thoughts and your everyday deeds the soil that will give you courage, faith, ideas and initiative to overcome everything which life can throw at you.

You can create miracles in your life by achieving things which others with less creative minds, and less determination and faith, say cannot be done.

Saxifrage keeps bright green at all times upon a bare rock. You too can keep your life green and thriving if you will keep your thoughts and your spirit undaunted. Never fear man or devil, for within yourself you can create the substance by which you live and rise, by which you achieve your dreams. Saxifrage adjusts itself to certain conditions, and very rigid conditions at that, but have you ever realized that all life is an adjustment? The secret of getting along with other people is in being able to adjust yourself and your temperament to the conditions under which you live and work.

Every day you must be willing to learn lessons from your

weaknesses and your failures. Every one of us has God-given power within to overcome life's obstacles, but it depends entirely on the code he has chosen.

I read some time ago a statement regarding practical faith in practice which said, "To be a good Christian, we must get religion like a Methodist, experience it like a Baptist, stick to it like a Lutheran, pray it like a Presbyterian, glorify it like a Jew, be proud of it like an Episcopalian, practice it like a Christian Scientist, propagate it like a Roman Catholic, work for it like a Salvation Army lassie, enjoy it like a Holy Roller."

What is your code for living? If you belong to any particular Christian denomination do you automatically criticize other branches of the Christian church? Do you believe that only your sect has the secret of happy living? In this difficult age in which we live it is essential that we should have an undivided Christian faith. We must overcome the hundreds of divisions; we must see and know and experience Christ as He meant us to. Theology alone does not give you the essential code by which to live, but the simple teaching of the Master applied is the only way to happiness in this world and in the next.

His code is the only code to follow, and once you come to a complete conviction of what God can mean to you, once you realize that His power is available to you at all times, then that is your day of salvation, that is the day when you change your thinking pattern and make up your mind to live a new life.

I knew a chemist many years ago who had a very phlegmatic personality. He was satisfied with the small things of life but he never made headway in the company that employed him and never offered any new ideas that might be of use in his employer's business, but was content to go on in the same old routine manner.

He went to church regularly, but God did not mean much to him, until he came across a certain book that awakened in his mind the tremendous latent powers within himself. This gave him courage, and month by month as he practiced his new-found faith, God, who had now become a reality to him, brought new ideas to his mind. He gained a new and positive personality, was able to adjust himself to his employers and his fellow employees, and in a few years rose to the top of his organization.

All his life he thought he had believed in God and had fulfilled the laws of his church, but he had never made his faith in God real until he was faced with defeat. By *letting go and letting God* he demonstrated an overcoming of what had been in his life one long series of defeats, sickness and failure.

The greatest things in life are faith and character, for these give you mastery over all things on earth. As you develop them you learn to know no fears, you begin to find that no power on earth can hurt you unless you let it. Faith and character comprise the armor you need to withstand evil temptations and wrong emotions. The person who develops a character marked by integrity, honesty and truth is the one who wins the greatest rewards in life.

Success must never be judged as the attaining of fame and fortune, for these things cannot go with you into that life everlasting to which we all must go when we have completed our training period on earth. The material things in life are very unreal for they have no permanence. The only real and lasting things throughout eternity are the spiritual values, and these, of course, come from your thoughts, your mind.

The Bible passage at the head of this chapter states that we are transformed by the renewing of our minds. This simply means the changing of your mind from a belief in fear and failure to a belief in faith and happiness, from sickness to health, from poverty to abundance, from negative to positive. You can transform your whole life by the renewing of your own mind, by the gaining of a real spiritual experience.

It is often the case that many a so-called Christian will go through life without much thought of God until he gets into serious trouble and, when there is no one to turn to for help, he invariably turns to God. We often hear the word conversion used in connection with religious meetings. To me, this word simply means the changing of your mind, the recognition that you have lived without God for so long and have reaped the natural harvest which follows such a life, and suddenly you have a religious experience which gives you a proof of God, and in this way you make a demonstration. Whenever you see the word "demonstration" in any of my writings, you will know that it means an answer to prayer when one has prayed, believing. It is a proof that God lives, and that He is always willing to answer when we live up to His laws.

What kind of life have you lived? Are you loaded down, as you read this chapter, with problems you cannot solve? Have you lived a life of empty pleasure and sin? Have you tried to find happiness in alcohol or other materialistic pleasures of this world? Then learn to realize that none of these are real, none of them have lasting values, and none of them will bring you successful living. You must begin to practice faith in God, whom you cannot see, hear or touch, and I can assure you that this magic of believing in Him is the magic that will change your entire life.

Jesus Christ came to show us a way of life, and though He lived on this earth some two thousand years ago, He, by His life, solved our problems of today. His death took away our errors and our sins and our sicknesses, too; but when His physical body left this earth He gave us a Holy Spirit, who now lives within every one of us. And it is up to us to find the Kingdom of God within us.

When Jesus was asked where Heaven was, He did not say it was a place of pearly gates and golden streets to which we go in an afterlife. He said the Kingdom of Heaven is within us, but if we have been experiencing sickness and failure hitherto, we certainly have not found that Kingdom. "Seek ye first the kingdom of God and his righteousness and all these things shall be added unto you."

The Christian Faith is so simple in its basic teachings that when you accept that faith as your code for living, and genuinely try to live up to it hour by hour and day by day, you will see all things added unto you.

When you look upon the form of a cross, do you ever think of it as the arms of the Master outstretched to you, saying twenty-four hours a day, "Come unto Me all you who are in sorrow, all you who are heavy laden with worries and fears, and I will give you rest"? This means here and now, not just eternal rest after death. Are you willing to believe that Jesus Christ is now awaiting your call, at this moment; that He wants you to follow His code, that He wants to prove to you that He lives, that He wants to give you the joy of living?

There is a statement in the Bible which says, "He was in the world and the world knew Him not," and oh, how true this statement is today—for we find even in many churches a complete lack of the living Christ. To be sure, we have plenty of theology, we see plenty of the ritual and formal type of religion. We hear about learned divines constantly arguing over set forms of church teaching and dogma but all this sort of thing of itself will never give us a way of life. It is essential that we come to Christ ourselves, believing that He will heal our sorrows and He will forgive our backsliding.

What kind of a religion have you? Is your religion a Sunday one? Do you think you alone have found the road to Heaven? If you are a member of a church, then practice the faith of that church; find the kingdom of God there and prove God through your faith every day of your life. Mere attendance at church once a week will never, in itself, give you a realization of the Christ within you.

I interviewed a lady who had suffered nervous strain for years, and she told me she was sick and tired of praying to God. She had always prayed, if it were His will, would He please cure her, but she had never gained an answer. Subconsciously she had accepted the fact that it was not His will to cure her. So, month by month she went along still suffering this pain. However, when she was taught to pray with the conviction that it is always God's will to heal, she made a great effort to really believe that she was now receiving, and from that day she lost her nervous pain. It was no miracle, it was simply a case of what the New Testament calls knowing the truth; for, when we know the truth, it makes us free from all evils.

How anyone can believe that God, who is all love and who knows nothing else but love, sends poverty, sickness or trouble to anyone, is hard to understand. These things happen to us all from day to day, but they are never sent by a loving Father, though He allows them to exist so as to refine our characters. But He has given us a means, through the teaching of His Son, of overcoming these things.

We should realize that all the health we wish to have, all the financial needs for successful living are ours for the asking. This is what is meant by the Kingdom. "Ask and ye shall receive." You never have a care about sickness, never a fear about your position, never a doubt about being able to pay your debts, when Jesus Christ comes into your heart by means of faith and becomes a reality to you. Then you learn to love God with all your heart and with all your strength. You learn to hand over your problems and the things in life which puzzle you to Him, and thus you enter into the joy of life.

Jesus sometimes told the people He healed, to cheer up and do things! And He says to you every day, "Cheer up, children of God, live according to my pattern." Renew your mind in the pattern of God and all things shall be added unto you. The name of Jesus, what magic there is in that Holy Name! There is no other name whereby we can be saved from sin and sickness and fear. Jesus said that the things He did we can do also, and even more wonderful things shall we do in His name. Therefore, why not accept His code, and really begin to live.

You can tune in this moment on God. You can really believe and with that beginning will come the finding of the Kingdom of Heaven within.

What have you ever given to God, in service and in money? You can get nothing in this world for nothing. Before we ask God for anything, we should be prepared to make a sacrifice in service or money to Him or to our fellow men.

You cannot draw water from a pump until you first pour water into that pump, after which you get an abundant supply. You have to give to the pump first and this is the Christian code of life. You must always be ready and willing to give to God throughout your life, for, by an automatic law, whatever you give will be returned to you many times over.

The only code to live by is the code of the Saviour. It is your code and my code. Try to learn a lesson from this chapter and you will embark upon the most thrilling experience of your life; you will have begun to find the Kingdom, to create a new life for yourself. By consciously using this code of the Christ you will be what you want to be; you will learn to let go the past and to let go all anxiety.

The power you need is within yourself right now. It is

not necessary to look elsewhere for the key; you, and you alone, have the key to successful living within you.

Your Guide to Happiness

"He that will love life, and see good days
. . . let him eschew evil and do good."—
I Peter 3:10-11.

How many people who call themselves Christian really love life? How many really love living? For centuries the Christian church seems to have taught that we live in a very sinful, very depressing, very wicked world; that there is no happiness on earth for a follower of Jesus Christ, and that the only happiness for those who follow the Master comes in an afterlife.

When these thoughts were predominant in the church, it is no wonder that we had a long Victorian era, when it was considered a sin to even smile in church or to wear bright clothes. The teachings of those days produced exactly the conditions which dominated the thoughts of the people who lived in that age.

If we hold such negative thoughts until they dominate our minds, if we look for sin and sickness in everyone, we will certainly find it.

Every day can be a blue day to you, every night just another night of misery; you produce in your daily life these very things by constantly impressing wrong ideas upon your mind. Every person living on this earth is as he is because of the pattern of his past thinking, and if your life has been unhappy up to now, then it is time for you to change your ideas and begin to practice a Christianity that will radiate happy living into your experiences.

Many of you enjoyed, no doubt, during the last summer a wonderful vacation, going to new places, seeing new areas of nature, meeting different people all living very different lives from your own. You came back with a thoroughly different picture of life from that which you had before. You came home refreshed, after being absent for some time from your daily toil, your daily worries, the people who annoyed you. Oh, how much you enjoyed the change. You lived happily during your vacation.

Was it a miserable world to you then? Did you not enjoy every minute of it? Did you not love the beauties of the sea, the forest, the countryside, the lake shore? Was it a hell on earth to you or was it a picture of God's perfection? You had a complete change of scene and peace of mind. In those few weeks you changed the pattern of your thinking, and what did you find? In the beauties of nature you found God and you found a heaven on earth. You loved life while on your vacation, didn't you? Then why is it not possible to enjoy this happy living three hundred and sixty-five days a year?

The Bible says, "He that will love life and see good days," and this tells you very definitely that the Master, Jesus Christ, knows all about life, knows all about the good in life, all about good living, and He wants you as a child of His Father, to share that good life, to be happy with Him right now.

Can you imagine the Master, Jesus, as a sad-faced, weary, miserable-looking person, a man without personality, a negative individual thinking only of the miseries of life? Would such a man have brought Lazarus back from his eternal home to continue on such an earth if it were a place of misery? It isn't common sense.

Every day in our newspapers we read about atomic weapons, atomic wars that will wipe out our present civilization, but God gives us the insight into these atomic weapons, the power of the atom, not for war but for peace. Man, however, with his selfishness and sinful nature and complete unawareness of God is able to use them for his own selfish aims, but that is not the will of God.

The people we find who are the most worried by these articles on atomic warfare are those who have never found God. The only answer to this Armageddon which we face is that the standards of our race and our age must be changed; our beliefs about God must be changed; nations must get back to God. Yes, I venture to say that the so-called churches of God must get back to the simple teachings of the Master.

No meetings of the United Nations can ever be the means of changing this world into a world of peace; first we must change the lives of individuals. We must begin to think rightly, to live rightly, according to the laws of God, and peace will follow.

Everyone, regardless of his age, can completely change himself, and this change will help to change those with whom he associates. Our happiness and the happiness of our relatives and neighbors depends upon every one of us. Once we find the Christ within, we radiate that light to others, and can change our home life, our occupational life, our community life and, eventually, the life of the nations.

A mother told me of how she had come to a complete restoration of her faith and religious convictions through spiritual reading. Oh yes, she had been a regular church-goer, but at home she lived in constant fear of sickness for herself and her children. She had adopted a very nagging habit toward everyone, for she suffered constantly from nervous prostration, and at night was too tired to go out with her husband. What a difference in her life and her home since she began to practice the teachings set forth by our Lord. The children can now have their friends visit them in their home; the mother does not mind the upset they make. She has given up the constant irritations that occurred every day in her life. She had thought that her duty to God was simply to go to church every week. Now she finds the Master with her in the kitchen, at the wash-tub, or wherever she may be occupied. Of course, all this needed perseverance and constant practice, but she has now found the guide to happiness.

You too can find this nearness of the power within your-self. You must come to the realization that it is a very happy and practical thing to be a Christian and to radiate happiness and health every day of your life.

Many years ago I met an old lady of eighty-six who lived in a small thatched-roof cottage in Ireland, and every day of her life had to descend a five-hundred-foot cliff by a narrow path. She raked the seaweed after the tide went out, dried it, then burned it and carried the ashes to the top of the cliff. These were sold to a factory which gave her about twenty-five cents a week; she paid eight cents a week for her house and, radiantly, she told me how happy she was and how good God had been to her. One of the sons raised in this tiny cottage won the Victoria Cross in the First World War.

What about you? Could you be happy for blessings un-told under such conditions? You can make your life a happy one if first of all you will forget and forgive the past, if you will learn to live one day at a time, believing that a radiant future is yours.

Fears and diseases will follow you no more when you learn from the depths of your heart how to let go the evils of your life and let God take care of you.

There is a simple technique for living the Christian life. First of all you must believe in and accept the teachings of the Master. You must read about Him every day in the

Gospels. You must make an appointment with Him every day to talk to Him. Through this simple faith you will demonstrate a life of overflowing abundance and overwhelming happiness. You will learn how to put yourself last in your life, and your fellowmen before yourself. You will then have a most powerful mental attitude towards life. This is faith, and the Bible is full of stories of what faith has done for others and what faith in a living vibrant Christ will do for you. Nothing in this world will be impossible to you.

What about the promise, "What things soever ye desire, when ye pray, believe that ye receive them, and ye shall have them"? What a marvelous promise this is, and how true you can prove it to be.

Stanley Jones says that it is much more fun being a Christian than going to the devil; one feeds a life, the other satisfies an impulse. One ends in a mess, the other in the joy of living.

Many things will happen to you when you take Jesus Christ as your guide to happiness. Many little coincidences will take place in your daily life which you had previously looked upon as good luck. But they are all part of that divine plan, for the world is created by a God who runs it on laws, and when you live up to those laws, then you *let go and let God*. The joy of living becomes a daily coincidence with you.

A business man came to see me some time ago who had failed in business. While he seemed to have good ideas, he did not have enough working capital. After discussing his life with me, we discovered he was filled with criticism and resentment of former employers and his life was dominated by these resentments. He had to ask forgiveness of his employers. He had to ask forgiveness of God. He had to seek peace and follow it; he had to surrender his life to Christ. Then he gained his answer. Several offers of capital came to him from sources he had never known before, and the more he practiced living one day at a time, the more he forgot that wicked past, and the more successful he became.

Do you believe that God wants you to live a miserable life? Do you believe that He wants you to have worries, anxieties and sicknesses? That is not the teaching of the New Testament. The way I interpret it, He wants you to be happy and to radiate that happiness.

Many people want to be happy but do not know how. They take their happiness from the material things of life; but do you often see happy faces leaving a movie or cocktail bar? Not really happy faces.

Then we have that type of Christian so proud to tell you how long he has been saved, who thinks it a crime to smile in church. I often wonder why so many Christians frown so much in their daily lives and in their jobs. They don't realize that it takes twenty-seven face muscles to form a frown, and only eight to make a smile. This kind of Christian naturally overworks his face.

The teachings of Jesus make us happy, radiant, joyful, successful. Jesus makes you glad; He makes you sing. Do you learn how to prove Christ in your church? Does going to church make Christ a reality to you? The finest cathedral in the world is only a pile of stone if we do not learn how to find the Christ there, if we do not learn lessons in living in that cathedral which will be a guide to happiness for you and me.

Your guide to happiness is the Christ—His way of life.

Do you want it? There is a price to be paid. You must surrender your whole self to God through Jesus Christ. Pray for it, act on it, believe it, and you will begin at once to feel His power in you. Plant this idea firmly in your mind, affirm it every day, strive for it. Try to make yourself worthy of being a temple for His Spirit.

Bury your sins without doubt or fear, and your fondest dreams for happiness will come true. There is not a soul upon earth who cannot make his or her life a marvelous thing, a tremendous experience.

Let go those things in life which have kept you from happiness, *and let God.*

There Is Magic in Believing

"If thou canst believe, all things are possible to him that believeth."—*St. Mark 9:23.*

As you go through life you will find that people in general are more interested in themselves, their own health, their own success, than in anything else.

The Bible says that any Christian can achieve any good thing if he is willing to believe strongly enough in it. This is a force, a factor which few Christians seem to realize and, not realizing it, they do not use it to achieve happiness and success.

There are many leaders in the world who have reached the top of the ladder because they have found this source within them and, having discovered it, use it from day to day. The science of right thinking is as old as man, for the Bible says, "As a man thinketh, so is he." If you have not been able to succeed in life in some particular way, then that tells me at once you are lacking in belief, you have not yet realized the power of the Man inside you, the Christ within. If you are willing to believe in this power which you cannot see, feel or touch, and practice that faith every hour of the day, then all things will become possible to you.

In our everyday lives we see so many people interested only in those things which must be left behind when the soul passes on to eternity. It is most regrettable that in churches of every denomination we find people who are not interested in the study of spiritual matters, particularly as they apply to daily living.

There is genuine magic in believing for every one of us. If you constantly think about past failures, if you allow past sins to bother you, if you hold resentment against someone who has wronged you, then you have no faith, then you become a failure.

Some years ago a lady in this city who had studied the magic of believing for several years was left a widow. After the funeral expenses were paid, she had a credit balance of twenty-nine dollars in the bank. In these intervening years she has become a very successful business woman and now owns outright her own hotel, worth over a hundred thousand dollars. She proved her magical faith.

Many of us are filled with the idea that, because we read our Bibles each day and say routine prayers and attend church once a week, that we are the only real Christians. This sort of worship is often based on a faith that goes no further than the lips, whereas real service to Almighty God has to come from a conviction, right from the heart.

A woman came to see me several months ago suffering from a nervous rash which a dermatologist had been unable to heal. On discussing her problems we discovered what was wrong with her thinking. She gave up that wrong to Christ, and her rash disappeared in twenty-four hours. It has never returned. Her constant fear was of something that had happened years ago; this fear caused the rash. The moment she gained faith in God, through the magic of believing, her "incurable" condition disappeared.

In hospitals today, every recovery from a serious operation depends on this faith, and the person who will not release his or her fears after an operation will make no recovery at all.

Are you afraid of certain things happening to you? Are you afraid that some disease is in store for you, or that later in life you will be left without means to support yourself? Then these things will happen just as you plan them in your own mind, because you are using wrongly your power of believing, you are placing your faith in wrong thoughts, in evil thoughts, instead of the good which God expects of you. We produce in our lives whatever we think, whatever we fear. A beautiful building, beautiful clothes, any work of art, a radio, a steamship, an airplane —all had their origins in thought, in the minds of men. No empire, no fortune was ever built without thought. Yet have you ever realized that your thinking patterns today can make you successful or bring you complete failure?

In many universities today the power of thought transference is being studied. It has been definitely proved that thoughts are things. Every thought you think goes out from your mind on an electrical impulse, on an ultra short wave, and it is possible to train people to be receptive to thoughts.

What are you willing to sacrifice from your present ways of living in order to make your dreams come true? Are you the type of person who feels that if he sits in a draft he will get a cold? Do you think if you go out on a wet day without your rubbers you will get the flu? You surely will, because of your wrong mental pictures, using the magic of believing for the wrong things. You need never have a cold at any time. Why should a little bug that you can't even see under a microscope be capable of dominating your blood stream, your body? Why should you be afraid of some dust from a flower which results in giving you two months of hay fever each year?

The moment you make up your mind to overcome your fears, the moment you really practice the magic of believing in this power within you, you will never demonstrate or produce any of these ills in your physical body again.

We hear a great deal about the science of hypnotism, and it is very easy for a psychiatrist to demonstrate to you or to anyone how your subconscious mind believes everything it is told. I have on many occasions seen a psychiatrist hypnotize a person, attach to his hand a postage stamp, and then tell the person this was a super mustard plaster that would blister his hand in three minutes. After exactly three minutes had elapsed the victim would scream with pain, and in each case a blister covering the same area as the postage stamp was produced.

We should all learn how to make positive statements, positive affirmations, every day in our lives. As we leave our homes in the morning we should say to ourselves, "Underneath me are Thine everlasting arms." And with that conviction will come complete freedom from fear of anything evil that might assail you. Such positive assertions, faithfully repeated, will build up in you the power of believing that God is now protecting you, that God is now doing wonders for you to bring you into happy living.

On the other hand, of course, repeatedly denying God's ever-present help, will gradually wear down your resistance to evil things, because you have built up the evil in your mind instead of your God power. For instance, tomatoes were once believed to be poison, and many people actually died through eating tomatoes, because they put their magic of believing to work in the wrong direction.

I often wonder why so many Christians look on the dark side of life, fearing the future, fearing death, and fearing life itself. This world was made by God for our happiness, for our happy living, and it is only man's negative thoughts, man's selfishness which have produced the very things he fears. No follower of Christ need ever suffer sickness or poverty, need ever be without any good thing which he needs, and all that is required is to follow the principles of the Master and practice the magic of believing in God, every hour of every day.

Have you ever realized that when you hear an unsavory story about some public figure and, whether or not you know it to be true, you accept it and so condemn that person, you are forgetting all the good things he has done. This does not hurt the man in question but, through wrong use of your belief, through wrong mental pictures, you will produce failure and sickness in your own life.

As a chemist I have faith in science, and I can prove it every day. The salt we use so commonly is made up of two deadly poisons; combined in a certain manner they produce a commodity which is absolutely essential for every one of us. This is the magic of believing the laws of chemistry.

Christian faith is the greatest spur to success. Take the case of the Maid of Orleans. She had a dream early in life which made her believe she would be the leader of her country. She gave her life to prove an ideal. Her firm belief in God's will for her enabled the armies of France to rid that country of its enemies, and today this simple maid is revered as a Saint.

When a boy is very young he lives in a world of imagination. He plays cowboys and Indians and, as he plays, really believes that he is a cowboy or an Indian. A little girl as she plays with her dolls lives in a real fairyland, really believes during her hours of play that she is a mother— and look at the happiness our children get from practicing such beliefs. Jesus said that we could not enter the Kingdom of Heaven unless we had the faith of a little child. Only by the magic of believing in Him will we find the Kingdom of Heaven within ourselves.

Have you ever thought that you probably produced your present insecure position in life through believing in the wrong things? Maybe you loved to let your temper go, maybe you have on many occasions lost control of your emotions. Maybe you thought it the right idea to be modern and to ridicule the old-fashioned ways of your parents. These are all wrong mental attitudes, and will produce in years to come the equivalents of your wrong mental pictures, in suffering and defeat.

The basis of all healing is faith. In order to recover from sickness a person must have faith in his doctor, his surgeon, his nurse, and the medicines which are given him, for without this faith the patient would never recover. How many times have you not seen a patient go down hill rapidly when his doctor told him there was no hope of his recovery?

Once I was asked by a medical doctor to visit his wife, who had suffered two strokes, was partially paralyzed, and whose blood pressure was so high that she was in imminent danger of a third stroke. This woman listened to what I had to say about God's healing power, and so complete became her conviction and faith that in two days she got out of bed, took a bath and did her own hair.

When all human means had failed, the power of the magic of believing in Jesus Christ destroyed her fears and brought healing to her physical body.

When you learn to swim, to ski, or to ride a bicycle, you are using this thing called faith, believing you can do these things. It is just as easy to fasten your imagination and belief upon God, who is willing to work wonders for you if you will let Him.

Think of God as a wonderful Father, and picture yourself every day as a happy, healthful person; then make it come true by the constant hourly practice of tuning in on God through faith, handing over your problems to Him and you will reap that abundant life which Jesus came to bring.

I am no theologian and I have no desire to study orthodox theology in any university. I simply believe that God is my Father and that I am His son and that my mind is a part of His divine mind—and by this magic of believing I can be in tune with that tremendous mind of His at any time I choose and, by so doing and by so believing, I can gain the answer to any problem which I have to face.

I believe with all my heart that Jesus Christ is divine and that He came to show me a new way of living, a new way of loving. When I came to Him, giving Him my heart; when I placed Him first in my life; when I told Him it wasn't what I wanted to do but what He wanted me to do; then this communion with God brought me release from all my past errors.

This communion with God many times a day is simply communion or fellowship with the principle of life. This is what gives us ideas and brings peace and harmony in our lives.

In the New Testament, St. Paul says that those who took the sacrament of the Lord's supper unworthily, without thinking about it, suffered from diseases and poverty, and died. But if we are willing to come with a pure heart, with simple faith, then, through the elements of bread and wine, we receive, in a spiritual way, power to overcome all things. We make a communion of fellowship with God and with our loved ones, and we take His power, which comes to us by faith, to enable us to withstand the perils of life.

What you get out of religion is entirely up to you. You can make your faith a super atomic dynamo or you can make it a routine affair without progress. You can be healed right now and your healing can start at any time regardless of how serious your condition may appear to you, if you will let go your fears and give God His rightful place in your life.

How can you afford to refuse this man, Jesus Christ, when you see every day in your life what faith in Him can produce? This Christ became a reality to me many years ago; and the freedom from pain, from sickness and from fear which I have had in these intervening years is what I am trying to offer you through the medium of these words today. What He has done for me, what He has given me, He is willing to give you, if you will try to practice the magic of faith, the magic of believing.

Yesterday Ended Last Night

"Seek ye first the kingdom of God, and his righteousness."—*St. Matthew 6:33.*

WHAT do you desire most from life? If it is good then the Bible says that you can have it. It says that if you seek first the Kingdom of God, all things shall be added unto you: peace of mind, freedom from worry, the best of health, all your material needs including food and clothing.

Many people feel they cannot have successful living without trying to live the life of a saint, without being saints themselves. The Bible does not say that you have to be perfect as Jesus Christ, but it does say that you must seek His Kingdom first of all. Try to find God by devoted living.

I do not believe for one moment that saintliness is the answer to this question. It is righteousness. The ancient Greek meaning of righteousness is the dictatorship of the kingdom within. In other words, let your life be dominated by God, let go of evil emotions. Let go of wicked tempers and evil things. Believe that His creative Spirit within you is now working for you, and His Spirit within your mind will work out and solve your problems in life. *Let go and let God.*

Only by daily contact with God, thanking Him ahead of time for the things He is going to make possible in your life, will you gain abundant living. Jesus Christ used and taught this method. It's up to you to follow His teaching.

If we look in the Old Testament, we find that David thanked God and praised God with his Psalms, particularly when he was in trouble. Daniel thanked and praised God when he was in the den of lions. St. Paul, we are told, sang hymns and praised God when he was in prison and, as a result, God opened the doors of that prison and let him out.

Wherever we look today, we see people living in prisons of their own thinking. Many people go on suffering day after day through constantly thinking of their past evil living. Many of them are held fast by that devil called alcohol, which they still continue to drink knowing full well that each additional drink brings them into a greater prison than ever before. These people have never learned how to turn their thoughts to God, which is the only way to gain release from this downward pull. They do not believe that their bodies are temples of His Holy Spirit.

How many people are held day by day in the prison of a bad temper? It is all very well, when your evil tongue has spent itself and you are exhausted, to say the devil tempted you. No devil, no satan, tempted you at all. You are passing the buck to some being you have never seen, instead of taking the blame upon yourself for allowing your temper to hold you in bondage.

How many people today are living in sorrow and sickness because of their resentments towards people and conditions that brought misery to them in past years. They will not let go the memory of a past that is dead.

So many Christians let little things, the non-essentials in life, disturb their peace of mind. For instance, one lady who attended my lectures in Toronto refused to sit in the church. She preferred the Sunday School, because she said she did not like to see me dressed up in my vestments. She will wonder why her prayers are not answered, yet she will no doubt stubbornly refuse to remove this "grit" which is blocking her channels and wearing down her bearings.

Maybe you have failed, in your journey through life, to find life really worth living. Maybe you have married the wrong man or woman. Maybe you have gotten into debt and feel that your life is an utter failure.

No man on earth has ever failed in life so long as he retained his faith in God, so long as, day by day, he sought the Kingdom of Heaven.

Throughout the years I have been engaged in spiritual work, I have found that most people need a lesson in living in such a way as to forget the past. It is not easy to forget the memory of someone who has deliberately hurt us, who has done us a great deal of damage materially. It is never easy to forget, but unless we are willing to forget and forgive as Jesus did, how can we expect God to forgive us our errors of thinking day after day?

I had to begin seeking that Kingdom within myself and, once I found it, by constant faith, by constant hourly practice of turning to Him, I gradually gained a greater consciousness of the powers available to me and to you every single second of every day and night.

I had to learn first and foremost that all my yesterdays ended last night. There is no yesterday to remember, there is no future to worry over; it is only *today* that exists, and we all make history for ourselves each day we live. The day we make the decision to put God first in matters great or small, that definitely is our day of salvation.

Then no enemy can invade your heart, no alcohol or emotional reflex can ever dominate your life, when you trust that power of God which is within your soul. Please believe me when I say, right at this moment, that all your yesterdays with their records of failure, resentments and hatreds ended last night.

No longer need you live in fear of that past, no longer need you fear the sicknesses you suffered in that past life, if you will only put the past behind you and live for today. If you refuse to do this, then your life will be a failure, not only as long as you live in the physical world which we know, but in that life which is to come.

Some time ago I met a woman who had an epileptic daughter, one who had suffered from this disease from birth. Previous to the birth of this child, the mother had fallen into a certain type of sin, and, from the birth of this baby, she was filled with tremendous fears, believing that God had sent her an epileptic child as punishment for her sin. Naturally, under these conditions, the child made no headway whatsoever and it was essential in this case, as in many others, to heal the mother first. She had to be taught that she had been forgiven long ago and she had to learn how to forgive herself.

I explained to her that God did not want this sin brought up from day to day in her consciousness when He had already forgiven her many years before.

How the child came to be an epileptic is not for us to know. I explained to the mother that it was sufficient to know that God's grace was enough to heal that child and, if she would come to a complete surrender of her past fears and let go that past and let God take over, then not only would she be healed but the daughter would also recover.

This is exactly what happened. From that day to this, that child has never had an attack of the disease.

A great man said some time ago, "Duty and today are ours. The results of the future belong to God." Have you ever realized that there is not any limit to the question of God's goodness to you as His child? Have you ever realized that you are deliberately limiting God's goodness when you are not willing to forget your past? No matter what you may think about hereditary conditions that have come down to you, no matter what you think about your past existence and its evils, God can and will redeem it and give you perfect understanding of your relationship to Him.

When we start to practice the teachings of the Master, every trouble we have to face, every experience of failure in our past life and present, becomes a stepping stone to successful living with Christ. Every trial is a spur to greater success and a greater future than we have ever known.

Many years ago the cotton industry in the United States was almost blotted out by a bug called the boll weevil. When this happened, did the planters get scared and run away from the country? No, they began to fight with every weapon of science available to them, and they licked it completely. It is now only a memory in that area.

May I ask you, as you read this book, what boll weevil, what bug, what fear is now sapping you? Do you think because your parents died from some organic disease that there is no health in you and that you will inherit that disease? Have you been told already that there is no hope for you as far as your bodily health is concerned? Then, if so, a fear bug has got you within its grasp and, if you continue in this way of thinking, this fear bug will master your life. You should remember that the things that are impossible to man are always possible to your Father, God.

A short time ago I received a letter from a woman in a coastal city, thanking us for the marvelous healing that had taken place in her son, incarcerated for several years in an insane asylum. She had written for my literature and requested my Bible class prayers. She was taught to pray positively, believing that she was now receiving. She was taught not to look back into the past, that God had already forgiven that past in the boy's life and had begun his healing, although he himself knew nothing about what was being done for him.

She was no more a saint than any one of us. She was no closer to God than any one of us, but she let go her fears of insanity, she let go her yesterdays, and in a very short time her boy's mind came back to normal and he returned home happy and sane.

A man attended my Bible class a few Sundays ago and told me that he had come from a distant city six months before for treatment in one of our hospitals; his condition was chronic neuritis of the legs. He could not walk at all and he was being sent home as incurable when, the Sunday before, he heard a sermon given by me on the subject, "Healed by a Touch." This sermon came to him in the hospital by radio and as the sermon ended, he said he put forth his hands from the bed and said, "Jesus Christ, I am touching the hem of your garment. Now my healing has begun." One hour later he discovered that he could bend his knees in bed, he got out of bed and found he could walk. After one week he was able to come to the Bible class before he left for home without the aid of crutches or a cane.

He was a Christian man but had never come into such a consciousness of God until on that Sunday morning in his hospital bed he suddenly let go his fears and God took them away.

When you begin to practice every hour of the day a consciousness of God, you get this thing called righteousness. When you learn to thank God for the lessons of your past life and realize that all your yesterdays ended last night, then the worries of those yesterdays no longer have any hold upon you at all. The same blessed assurance that "Jesus is mine," that Jesus is in you, that you have accepted Him, that you have found Him, that you will live with Him forever and forever, becomes a daily, hourly conviction and you know you will never let Him go.

Our physical bodies can be placed in prison but no one can ever imprison a thought. No one can ever cage up an adventurous spirit, and this is what makes human beings different from animals. This is what the Bible means when it says, "For as many as are led by the *Spirit of God,* they are the sons of God." Would you not like to feel that you were a son of God? that you have for your Father the greatest power in the universe? that you will never again feel alone in this world? When this conviction comes to you, when you realize that Jesus Christ suffered tortures and death for you, your sicknesses and your sins, then you will have an urgent desire to put Him first in your life.

No longer will you say, at any time, that it cannot be done. It can be done if you say it can. Ask forgiveness for your past and pray right at this moment, thanking God for having begun a new life for you today.

The Bible tells us that there is but one power in life. So forget the devil and all his works. Deny his mythical ability to hurt you. Throw him out of your heart and mind. Believe that you can do all things through Jesus Christ who strengtheneth you. You will then learn that life is for living, happy living, radiant living.

All your yesterdays ended last night. Today you start adventuring with God; so plan to begin the finding of that Kingdom of Heaven within you right now. Find His righteousness, and you will learn the secret of how to *let go* the failures and evils of your life *and let God.*

The Ten Commandments—and You

In the course of my work I have found it to be quite common for people to have the idea that they strictly live up to the Ten Commandments so long as they are not conscious of deliberately breaking any one of them.

Such people do not lie or steal or commit adultery, but they seldom realize that there are many, many sins not listed in the actual words of these commandments that are definitely in the same category.

Let us take the first commandment, "Thou shalt have no other gods before me." To the great majority of Christians this means we must not worship any pagan gods like Mohammed, Buddha, Confucius or a thousand other gods. But the metaphysical or spiritual interpretation of this commandment, as it is worded, does not mean just that particular idea.

Of course no Christian would worship a statue, a crucifix, a religious relic, or any of the pagan gods; but when we put pride, resentment, criticism, condemnation or hatred first in our lives, when we constantly think and act upon these thoughts, we are placing these things before God. In this way we deliberately break the first commandment and, in so doing, we have to suffer the punishment that goes with it. God never punishes us; when we do wrong we punish ourselves because in holding wrong thoughts, in performing wrong deeds, we, of our own free will, disobey God's teachings.

Likewise, the man or woman who puts money, social position or other forms of false security before God is breaking this first law every day.

The average Christian would not like to be accused of

bearing false witness, but do not many of us repeat idle gossip without proving the accuracy of our statements? And how many people mar their happiness by coveting other people's possessions, their success in life, their health, their positive attitude towards life, instead of going direct to their own Father in simple faith for these riches of the Kingdom which He is waiting to pour out upon them to fulfill every righteous desire of their hearts.

I cannot conceive of a single person who could truthfully say he never breaks any of the Ten Commandments. In attempting to break them we break ourselves, for God's laws are immutable.

It is well therefore for all of us to discover ourselves, to find out how in a thousand little ways we have tried to break some of God's laws, maybe are trying to break them now. Let us then root them out, do something about overcoming these evil characteristics, and in so doing we will learn how to *let go* and *let God's* laws work for us.

The Law of Cause and Effect

"And the fruit tree yielding fruit after his kind."—*Genesis 1:11.*

ONE of the most important lessons we learn from the Bible is that everything in nature, everything in life, everything in mind, produces after its own kind. Trees, plants, vegetables, the animal kingdom, all produce according to their own classification and the farmer knows only too well that whatever he sows in his fields, that only will he reap; he never expects anything else.

As we look through the Bible, we find the story of Elisha

and the widow who had just a little oil, yet when Elisha blessed it, he brought unlimited wealth to her, not in money, but in oil, after its kind.

When the crowds had no food to eat, Jesus took a few loaves and fishes. He fed thousands with them and there was an overflow of food. He produced bread and fishes, after their kind.

So it is with us, every hour we live: whatever we think, whatever we allow to dominate our minds, so we produce in our physical bodies. If we persist in thinking fear and poverty, then, unfortunately, these things we will reap according to law. By that same law, thoughts of health and abundance will produce after their kind and our lives will show forth these blessings.

Possibly you have met a person who often says, "I can't afford to give. I am too poor to give anything to anyone." This person has built up a very negative idea of substance and through the years of his or her life that person will never have anything to give, because he will never receive.

Our abilities and talents, the skills we possess, are all forms of power and, if we want to increase our stocks of these things, we must put them to work. We must have faith in them by thinking success thoughts, thinking health, thinking happiness, thinking victory.

We are told in the New Testament of a man who gave talents of silver to his servants. One of the men was so afraid of losing this money that he buried it in the ground. For his lack of foresight and lack of faith, he was discharged from his job.

Every man and every woman has talent and ability along certain lines, but oh, so many people have long since buried their talents. We heard a lecture in our parish hall which was an inspiration to all those who heard it. The lecturer had the ability to write, to lecture and to paint, but she only had these abilities because from childhood she had used the talents which God had given to her.

Every man and every woman wants happiness. We all want to have a dollar or two to spare. We all want power of some kind in order to overcome past failures. Therefore, we must first of all put to work every talent we have, great or small, that they may grow day by day as we learn to put more faith in that power within us that guides us and inspires us with new ideas and new confidence in our innate abilities. This is the power of God working through us by way of the Master, Jesus, when through faith we have let go our sense of separation from Him.

Some time ago a woman was left a widow with two children to look after. She had no money that Christmas to buy gifts for her friends and relatives, so she prayed earnestly for it. She prayed believing she was now receiving. One night she had a dream. She saw a Christmas tree filled with envelopes on the branches. As she looked at the envelopes, she saw that on each one was written the name of a friend or a relative. The next day she sat down and wrote nice letters to them, letters of sympathy to sick relatives, words of courage to an uncle faced with difficulties. She wrote ten letters of blessing. All her life she had never believed she could write in this way, yet she did.

One of her friends said afterwards that she had got a wonderful message from her letter and it had brought peace of mind to her. The uncle wrote that his troubles had been solved through her advice. What came to her in return? The greatest blessing of happiness that she had ever known. From then on she started to write, and today is a well-known columnist on an American newspaper.

The minister of a church I went to some years ago felt a great need for funds in his church but the congregation lived in a very poor section of the city. One Sunday he got the idea that he would take up the collection at the beginning of the service and asked all who had received blessings from God recently to give well—to God. He was amazed at the amount of money that was given that day.

In the Jewish faith and the Buddhist religion people are taught that before any member of their religion ever asks for a blessing of any kind from God, he must first of all sacrifice some material benefit for God.

Many people come to see me from day to day privately, asking for advice, for help, but many of them never remember to give anything to God for the benefits they are coming to receive. The world is filled with people who want something for nothing, who never realize that one of the basic laws of life is that we must give before we can get.

The Master said that he that findeth his life shall lose it, but he that loseth his life for His sake shall find it. What does this mean? Simply that he who gives his life in the service of his fellowman shall find it in so doing and shall reap abundant living.

Have you ever realized that what you keep to yourself you lose, and what you give away is yours forever?

During my life I have met many married couples who had made up their minds to keep up their business careers and refused to have a family. I have seen many of these couples grow rich, but almost invariably there was a reckoning, when one or the other, sometimes both of them, would come down with a very serious sickness requiring months of hospitalization. Where did their money go then? What they decided to keep for themselves they had lost.

During our earthly life God has to work through men and women, and He cannot be shut out. He must be expressed some way or other every day of our lives. All of us must come to the realization that we are inseparable from God.

What must we do to win that victory over defeat which is the goal of all humanity? What must we do first of all to gain spiritual supremacy? We must give and give freely of whatever we have in talents, or service, or money.

The farmer in the spring casts the seed into the ground. Then he covers it up with the earth and awaits the harvest. He waits in perfect faith believing that the law will work for him once more; although he has nothing to show you, he knows that it is on its way. And so, in the fertile soil of your mind, this law is just as dependable. Sow your good deeds, then cover them up and in due season your own will come back to you. This is how you lay up treasures in Heaven and they never fail to wing their way to you in time of need.

Have you recently told a story about someone which was not quite true or which was mean or unkind? Then look out, for this same law will bring back to you after its own kind; you will reap sorrow, sickness and trouble. When you do something to help someone else, then that something brings you closer to God, for in this way you allow yourself to be a channel or an outlet for God, and automatically you will reap what you have sown.

I met a young lady who had suffered from many sleepless nights and had no peace of mind. Eventually she developed a nervous breakdown. Years before it appeared, she had deliberately lied to her employer and now she was reaching middle age and was many years older than she had reported to her company. At this stage she felt she was about to be found out. When she spoke to me about it, I said, "Go to your manager direct and confess it. Tell him why you did it and what you have suffered."

She did this, and gained peace of mind and with it freedom from all her nervous trouble. Her manager very kindly and generously forgave her. She had been mentally picturing for months being discharged from her job and being unable to find another one.

Many people think it is quite the right thing from time to time to get away with little lies, but every lie you tell means that later on in some way it will come back to you to cause you embarrassment or dismay.

Make a change in your pattern of thinking today. Take God as an active partner into your business, into your life. You need finances for that business. Say to Him, "Father, thank you for bringing to me what I need for my business." Then try to see how you can give better service to your customers, to your friends and relatives. Try to see how much more you can give financially to charitable organizations or to your church. You are rich according to your own kind of thinking.

We often read in books about the unpardonable sin. I have never had a reasonable interpretation given to me of this statement, but I personally think that if there is an unpardonable sin it is the damming up of God's powers within us by refusing to believe that His power is available to us every moment of our lives.

When you constantly suffer from sickness, you are lacking in faith. When you are surrounded with debts, those debts have come to you by your own wrong thinking, by your lack of understanding, and you are reaping exactly what you have sown; in other words, you have shut God out of your life in one way or another.

At a lecture recently a lady was present who had decided, on leaving, that she would place fifty cents in the love offering box. However, the lecture appealed to her so much she felt that she could not give that amount. She had to sacrifice, so she put a dollar bill in the box which was more than she thought she could afford.

She had a friend who had been trying to find a job, and the next morning an idea came to her at breakfast. She went into her room and prayed about it and acted upon the idea and succeeded in getting the person who needed it an excellent position. This was no coincidence. The sacrifice she made at that lecture opened the way for abundance to her fellowman, and in turn it has brought a more abundant life to this person.

She did not say in her mind, "If I give that dollar to God I want so and so for it." She did not say, "If I can get a position for so and so, I will make a sacrifice." No one can bribe God, at any time, but if you only knew this wonderful law of giving you would certainly operate it successfully every day because in so doing you open the door to divine love wherever you are, whoever you may be. This is God's way of doing things.

If you are in trouble or in sorrow or in sickness, right now as you read this chapter start praying. Don't expect an angel to suddenly appear to you in person, but know and believe with all your heart that God works through ordinary folk like you and me, and that it is through ordinary people that good will come to you.

Have you ever thought of the fact that God is willing to wipe out from your consciousness and your life all the things that have been wrong up to date? That you can come to a conviction right now that God's wealth, God's health and God's success are all yours for the taking? "I am come that they might have life, and that they might have it more abundantly."

The law of cause and effect simply means that whatever we think or do in life will come back to us in due course, returned with interest exactly in kind. We must invariably reap whatever we sow.

There Is No Death

"They shall hunger no more, neither thirst any more . . . and God shall wipe away all tears from their eyes."—Revelations 7:16-17.

THE Bible tells us that in our afterlife the beauties of that world to which we go will be far greater than anything we have ever seen before.

We have no conception whatsoever of the magnitude or the greatness of the beauty that we shall see after we have crossed the valley of the shadow. Every tear will be wiped away from our eyes; no fears, no anxiety, no debts, no worries of any sort at all shall beset us.

Something beautiful seems to come to people when they come to the end of the road. I have seen the happy light in the eyes of those who were passing on, leaving behind the physical body.

As I sat at the bedside of my father who had been unconscious for days, he suddenly looked up and recognized me and the other members of the family. Then he read the text on the wall beside him and he said, "I certainly do know that my Redeemer liveth." He told us that all around his bed were his mother and father, his brothers and sisters who had gone on before and his face lit up with a holy light as he talked to them and he talked to us. Then suddenly he was gone.

Was this imagination? Certainly not! For a few moments he had hovered on the edge of that new life seeing the physical as well as the spiritual. This I have seen on many occasions. It is part of the goodness of God that after a lifetime of tribulation we can take up, if we wish, the joy

119

of living with God forever and forever.

Are you certain of that joy in an afterlife? Could you write a letter to God today and say, ". . . faithfully yours." Will God say to you when your number is up, "faithful servant," or do you care?

The Bible teaches us that life on earth is but preparatory to that life of permanent happiness in Heaven to which all souls can go when the period of training is over. Whether you have been born to poverty or wealth, whether you have lived in the top ranks of society or the ranks of the poor, makes no difference whatsoever. But all of us go to that new life with one possession, our character.

The size of the house you live in, the money you have tried to accumulate, or the fortune you have made are all left behind because these things have no value when you come to the end of the road. You came into this world with nothing, and you leave it with nothing except your character and the lessons you have learned in life.

What handicaps have you overcome? What sins have you fought and won a victory over? Is this world a better place because you have lived in it? Is anyone happier because of your goodness to them? What have you done for Jesus Christ? All these things help to build your character and develop your soul. This is the purpose of your life on earth.

What is this separation called death? It is not death at all; there is no death. It is the gateway to eternal living, when we all get the rewards we have won through our faith, through our religion, through our belief in God, and Christ, His Son.

In the New Testament we read that Jesus said to one, "She is not dead but sleepeth." To another, "Lazarus sleepeth, but I go that I may awake him out of sleep." So Jesus looked upon death as really sleeping, for He taught us very definitely that the body is but the temporary home for the soul and that this thing called death is but graduation to another and far happier life.

Is this happy land to which we go located in some distant planet? Oh, dear, no! That life is right here and now around you every day that you live. It is simply a transference from a physical to a spiritual plane, each completely interwoven with the other. There never has been a beginning for God, and there will never be an ending. The continuity of your life is not interrupted by your death because there is no death to the soul who has found Christ.

The statement is made in the Bible that the soul that sinneth shall die. This means that if we die deliberately in sin, then we shall never see God. Could you dare take a chance of dying like this? Can you risk an eternity away from love, away from God, just because you preferred the thrills of your emotions, the material pleasures that the world provides, of money, of pride, and sins of all kinds. No one can take such a chance as that.

Yet you, and you alone, can say whether or not your soul shall see the beauties of Heaven . . . and God.

I have seen many people obsessed with a terrific fear of dying; and yet when they came to that final day they found it just a peaceful passing along the road. They got a glimpse of that brightness, a glimpse of their loved ones waiting for them to come over. Rest assured that there is someone there to meet you when you leave this plane.

When you came into this world the loving devoted hands of your mother were waiting to receive you; so, when you leave this world, loving hands, angelic beings, will be waiting to welcome you into that beautiful land where sorrow is no more.

We are apt to shed tears and to mourn about our loved ones, but as Christians with a real undaunted faith in Jesus

Christ, we should never shed those tears, for that shows a lack of faith, and by holding fears for our loved ones we hold them back from progressing along the heavenly road.

If you are doing this at the present time, then release your loved ones and let them go. If your son should win a scholarship to a university and take his four years there free of cost to you, how happy you would be. Then look upon death as a scholarship into the highest school of all. So why should we fret and cry about it, why worry about it, why fear it?

Do not fear the coming of this crisis into your life; it is never a dark lonesome road to travel; it is filled with light and joy and happiness, and God wipes all tears from your eyes over there. The Chinese people wear white at their funerals to show their joy at the release of their relatives from a world of trials and sorrows. We should do the same thing for we know that our loved ones have won their great reward. If you have tried to live with Jesus Christ, then you too will win your reward, the greatest that can ever come into your life.

Through the whole of my life I have had many psychic experiences which have afforded me the opportunity to look into that other world beyond the veil. In my religious work, these experiences have grown from month to month, and during healing services I have seen many glorious sights. My psychic researches have taken away from me all fear of death because I know there is no death. It is a gateway to life everlasting.

A clergyman told me this story. While he was visiting a dying member of his flock, the man's dog scratched at the room door to be allowed to enter. The sick man said, "I am like my dog. He does not know what is in this room, for he has never been in it, but he knows I am here and that is good enough for him. He wants to come in. Just so, I do not know what is in the many mansions of Heaven, but I know Jesus Christ is there. That is enough for me; I ask no more of Heaven."

Many of the subjects I have given in my Bible class have been dictated to me by my loved ones long since passed on. This does not mean for one moment that I wish to be labeled as a spiritualist. In my psychic work I have seen the great danger of people who constantly try to look beyond the veil. We must remember that while we are surrounded by powers of good, we are also surrounded by thoughts of evil, and I know from experience that many a medium, in giving the answer to a problem, is simply tuning in on the subconscious mind of the individual. The message does not come from the spirit world.

It is not our purpose to deliberately spend our lives peeping into that other land, for when God wants us to see with our spiritual eyes, He will open those eyes and give us the lesson He wants us to learn.

In all my lessons I have taught that evil can never win a permanent victory over us. The much feared religion of communism may conquer the whole world, but it is basically evil and therefore will be overcome finally, and only good will prevail. The next few years may be very difficult ones for this world. But evil will be finally destroyed and false conceptions of its power along with it.

"I am the resurrection and the life. He that believeth in me . . . shall never die," said the Master. This teaches you that there is no death, for, when your soul awakes in that other world, you will have a more glorious body than you have ever owned. You will go to that plane of thought which you have prepared for yourself, and the more you learn God's laws, the more you progress.

Jesus said, "In my Father's house are many mansions," and I am sure He did not mean houses. He meant many planes of thought; and according to the way we have lived, so we will find ourselves. In that future life you will have a full memory of your past life. The character you have developed here will go with you, and the moment you arrive at that other shore, you will have angels to guide you and teach you how to get a greater consciousness of God. You will grow spiritually over there just as you did here.

The Holy Communion service of our church was developed through the centuries, a passing on of the teaching of Jesus when He gave this fellowship as a symbol on the night before He died. We are taught by that service that we join in a spiritual fellowship with God and all our loved ones who have gone before. I have found that this teaching gives the greatest confidence to those who are willing to accept it, for they can have that fellowship every hour of the day. They can actively associate with others who are living vital lives.

I do not think for one moment that God allows those who have preceded us to just look upon the sicknesses and sorrows which we have to undergo in this world, but I earnestly believe that at certain times in our lives, when good can be accomplished, they are allowed to intervene in human affairs.

The physical body is used as an instrument of the soul just as a fountain pen is used as an instrument by the mind. If you lose your pen you don't cry about it, you find another pen or pencil to write with. The loss of a pen does not silence you forever on what you wanted to write. As you go through life, no one sees your real person, they just see your physical body. As I preach in the pulpit you cannot see me, you only see the house I am occupying, you cannot see my sins, my virtues, my hopes. Yet what am I but the sum total of the component parts of my soul, which is indestructible and eternal?

I do not believe in the materialistic hell painted by the church of long ago. It is not a place of fire and brimstone, filled with little devils and their pitchforks. It is the place of complete separation from good, from God. Can you imagine a worse punishment, when you think of what you might have been, than the pangs of eternal remorse? This is far worse than material fire which, of course, could never harm you in a permanent way, because your spirit cannot burn.

The paradise to which we go at death is a place of rest and growth. Our loved ones in this realm are sent to help us along the path we now must travel, and their instructors are angelic beings. What are angels but thoughts, messengers of God?

The Bible teaches us that judgment comes to all of us after death, but none of us need fear that judgment if we have done our best, if we have tried to live with Christ, overcoming those things which are wrong in our lives. God will not condemn us to an eternity of hell for some misdeeds we had performed in our former life.

I was called to the bedside of a lady who was dying, and she had a great fear of death. Her family did not want to tell her there was no hope, but she had sensed it already; so I showed her the beauties of a Christian life, and she prayed very earnestly with me at her bedside. Immediately she lost her fear of death, and something seemed to tell me to pray fervently then for her recovery. So we prayed believing we were now receiving, and she made a most amazing recovery from the edge of the grave.

Today she is living a happy, healthful life. A better Christian I have never met, and she is now ready whenever the call comes to her. The end of the road does not mean termination to her, for she knows that divine beings are waiting on that other side to receive her.

What about you? Can you face God if He calls you home this very moment? If not, then it is time for you to think what you might have done in your life and what you still can do for God. Learn how to make your faith a realistic one. Make your religion live with you every hour of every day by putting God first in your life and make up your mind to live with Christ. If you do, you will gain an overcoming of everything, including death.

You will thirst no more and God will wipe all tears from your eyes, forever and forever.

There can't be death where God is, and God is everywhere!

What God Means to Me

As a child I had a very great fear of God. To me, He was a vengeful sort of person, always trying to catch me doing some wrong thing and then trying to punish me for so doing. I well remember the second commandment and what it meant to me, "For I the Lord thy God am a jealous God, visiting the iniquity of the fathers upon the children unto the third and fourth generation of them that hate me."

How terrifying was the Victorian picture of a sadistic God, and how wonderfully different is the picture of God given to us by Jesus Christ: a loving, merciful, devoted Father always willing to forgive His wayward children.

Throughout my life as an Episcopalian, I have certainly believed in the Christian aspect of God. I always realized my sinful ways, but I did not realize that His power was my power to use, that Christ lived within me, until after many years of illness, and then having but less than a year to live, I discovered the God within, which has brought me many years of complete freedom from illness and has indeed given me life more abundantly.

Although, according to the teachings of my church, I had given myself to God at my confirmation, I really did not know Him in a true sense, nor did I have any idea that the healing power of Christ was now available to me. I believed that God forgave my sins—oh, yes; but I did not think He forgave and released me from sickness as well, if I would only believe. Many a time I prayed for healing, if it were His will, and when that healing did not come, then I accepted this, believing it was God's will for me to suffer sickness.

The reading of a book called *In Tune with the Infinite* brought me to a new conception of this Divine Being. This new idea I adopted and practiced daily, yes, hourly. Soon after this new life had begun, I came to a very real conversion at the radio in my study, after hearing an evangelist speak the word that was certainly meant for me that eventful day. On my knees I gave myself to God, thanking Him for my conversion and giving Him in all sincerity my heart and my devotion. Practicing my new-found faith hour by hour, daily overcoming temptations and fears, I found that my healing from many years of sinus, hay fever and stomach ulcer troubles had come. I found the Kingdom of Heaven within me and, oh, how my ideas of God changed.

Years of careful study and hourly prayer put me in constant touch with the Infinite, and daily demonstrations of my beliefs came to me. I gained the answer to my prayers and my viewpoint in life was completely changed. I learned and proved that Jesus Christ came to bring us a life more abundant. That I must live from day to day, resting in the consciousness of God's presence within me at all times. I went to the communion table of my church now with a new conviction, a new reality. I discovered it was a power-house for me, and I believed that in taking that sacrament I was indeed receiving strength and power to conquer all ills.

The more I studied the spiritual meaning of the New

Testament, the more I got out of my faith. Then I came to
a belief that God was the one creative power in the whole
universe, at all times available to me for good. My Bible
said that God was spirit and that they who worship Him
must worship Him in spirit and in truth.

God to me is all life, all power, all love. You cannot see
spirit, you cannot see love, you cannot see wisdom, yet
these are all manifested in this Being, our loving Heavenly
Father, called God. Wherever there is life, there also is
God. They are inseparable. Every human being is the
highest manifestation of divine creation, divine energy.
Therefore is it any wonder that God, as told in Genesis,
gave man dominion over all other things upon the earth?

Once I realized this, I suddenly came to the conviction
that I had dominion over all germs. How could a cold
draft give me a cold? How could getting my feet wet produce cold germs in my system? I refused to let such things
have dominion over me. I realized that all food was God's
food, so how could any food of any kind give me indiges-
tion or stomach ulcers? I learned, oh, how truly, after years
of suffering, that stomach ulcers come not from what we
eat but from what is eating us, which means our worries,
anxieties and resentments. Once I gave these up and refused to hold them in my thoughts, then came healing of
body and soul.

God is the name given to that unchangeable principle
which is the source of all life, of all existence. As God He is
impersonal, but as we come to know Him day by day as expressed in each one of us, He really becomes personal to
us, a very personal, very loving Heavenly Father; and
every person of every color and creed becomes a child of
God when he learns to live in Christ and according to His
teachings. Then verily indeed we all become sons of God,
and we seek more and more for the good that is in us and
we find more and more the good, the Christ, that is in

every person whom previously we have disliked and resented.

My new-found faith in such a loving God brought to me daily proofs that He is indeed the giver of all good things, that He and I are always connected, that praying in faith is just like tuning in on a gigantic radio, and through that radio I can draw upon this power within me for all the good I want or need.

For the past few years I have indeed been blessed with a constant stream of answered prayers; all of them givers of joy and happiness. The more my prayers were answered, the more I wanted to spread the glorious message of what I had found myself. No longer would I ask God to heal someone "if it were His will"; it is always God's will to heal. I prayed believing that I was now receiving. I had complete and absolute faith, and have been able to pass on this faith to thousands of persons who have found release from suffering through it.

God means to me today "perfect everything," and the more I devote of my life to Him and His work, the more He shows Himself to me in everything I may do. We read in scientific books that there are thousands of lost arts in the world, completely forgotten, but the greatest of all these is the art of living as shown us by the Master. Yes, we recite creeds, we attend churches; but we have lost in the Christian church of today the art of living with Jesus Christ. Many of us found Jesus, yes, years ago, but oh, how easily have we lost Him in this maze of materialistic existence. Mary found Him in the temple where she had lost Him, and so, too, must we seek Him where we have lost Him, within our own consciousness, within our own selves!

Day by day I see the lives of men and women recreated by this Christ within. Each day I live I wonder at the goodness of the God I have come to love so much, when

I see how easily and surely He forgives sinful living when the heart is opened to Him. This in itself is a miracle, indeed.

A man I heard of recently was in bed with a creeping paralysis for nine years, had lost the use of his legs and feet and toes, and had only partial use of his hands. I talked to him over a phone by his bedside. He did not know God at all; his life had been filled with making money. I taught him how to pray, believing, and we remembered him daily for the next week. When I went to see him the following week, he had the use of his hands, and his legs from the knees down. He came to Christ that day. That is what God means to me—Christ the forgiver, Christ the healer, God, all divine love.

A woman steeped in a lifetime of sinful living, and now at the point of suicide, came to see me asking for help. She had to be taught how real and how good this God I worshiped is. She asked forgiveness for her past life, she came to Christ, and was not only instantly released from her past evil life, but was cured of all her pain and ills. She is now rehabilitated, has an excellent job, and is steadily growing in grace with her new-found Christ within. This is what God means to me.

The art of living with Christ can be yours today if you are willing to pay the real price for it, taking up your cross, following in His footsteps, looking upon life as He looks upon it, and then reaping the reward of your Christian living with life more abundant.

For ages religion has been looked upon as a science rather than an art. We have taught it in precepts, in dogmas and in creeds; not in realities, not in absolute faith. Since the second century man has, through the church, formed varying dogmas, differing from century to century; hating, detesting those who differed, those who refused to accept them. In the Middle Ages the church devised devilish means of tortures to force its ideas upon those who refused to accept them. This was done in the name of a God of Love! Let us all try to find this Christ within so that we may all worship Him in spirit and in truth and that He may so fill our hearts that we all worship together in spite of our so-called differences.

The Kingdom of Heaven which I have found is the kingdom of human relationships, based on Jesus' teachings of two commandments whereby we put God first in our lives and our fellowman before ourselves. Believe in the power of the living Christ within you, let this sink deep into your mind and heart and soul, and you will also learn, as I have, what God can and will mean to you.

God has come to mean to me the source of all my supply, all my strength, all my happiness, all my needs, and my life itself. He has become my daily guide, my loving guard and pilot in everything that I do. I have come to love Jesus with an undying love, and with this increase of my faith has come the living in a spiritual world. My whole life then I devoted to the winning of souls for Jesus Christ. I am not merely interested in the healing of physical ills, but in bringing a new discovery of Christ to every man and woman I find who needs Him as I did. He lived and died for me; therefore I live for Him, and Him alone.

What does God mean to you?

GOD CAN HEAL YOU NOW

DEDICATION

To my husband Alvin Willard Neal
and
for the Glory of God

This Guideposts edition published by special arrangement with Emily Gardiner Neal, c/o Scott Meredith Literary Agency, Inc.

Acknowledgments

SPECIAL thanks go to my husband, Alvin, and our daughter, Diana, whose patience, understanding and interest did much to facilitate my work; and to Ethel T. Banks, for her unfailing help, encouragement, and faith.

I take this opportunity to acknowledge my incalculable and continuing debt to the Rt. Rev. Austin Pardue, D.D., Bishop of the Diocese of Pittsburgh; and the Rt. Rev. Wilburn C. Campbell, D.D., Bishop of West Virginia. The ministries of these great Churchmen have served as never-failing beacons, leading me, as they have led many others, from the rocky shoals of cynicism and disbelief into the safe and quiet harbor of the Holy Spirit.

To all those too numerous to mention individually, who have given me so freely of their time and cooperation in the preparation of this book, I am deeply grateful. Without their assistance it could never have been written; and without their witness, it would never have been written.

—EMILY GARDINER NEAL

Contents

PART II

HEALING MINISTRIES

Bible References

A. The Healing Miracles of Jesus

Two blind men: Matt. 9:27–31
The dumb demoniac: Matt. 9:32–33
Deaf and dumb man: Mark 7:31–37
Blind man at Bethsaida: Mark 8:22–26
Widow of Nain's son: Luke 7:11–17
Ten lepers: Luke 17:11–19
Woman whom Satan had bound: Luke 13:11–17
Man with dropsy: Luke 14:1–6
Ear of Malchus: Luke 22:50–51
The Nobleman's son: John 4:46–54
Impotent man at Bethesda: John 5:1–21
Man born blind: John 9:1–7
Lazarus: John 11:32–44
The Syrophenician's daughter: Mark 7:24–30. Matt. 15:21–28
The centurion's servant: Matt. 8:5–13. Luke 7:1–10
The blind and dumb demoniac: Matt. 12:22. Luke 11:14
The "possessed" man in synagogue: Mark 1:21–28. Luke 4:33–37
Peter's mother-in-law: Matt. 8:14–15. Mark 1:29–31. Luke 4:38–39
Two demoniacs: Matt. 8:28–34. Mark 5:2–20. Luke 8:27–39
The leper: Matt. 8:1–4. Mark 1:40–45. Luke 5:12–14
Daughter of Jairus: Matt. 9:18–26. Mark 5:21–43. Luke 8:40–56
Woman with an issue of blood: Matt. 9:20–22. Mark 5:25–43. Luke 8:43–48
A paralytic: Matt. 9:1–8. Mark 2:1–12. Luke 5:18–26
Man's withered hand: Matt. 12:9–13. Mark 3:1–5. Luke 6:6–10
Lunatic (epileptic) boy: Matt. 17:14–21. Mark 9:14–29. Luke 9:37–43
Blind men: Matt. 20:29–34. Mark 10:46–52. Luke 18:35–43

B. The Multitudes Healed by Jesus

St. Matthew 4:23–24
8:16–17
9:35–36
11:4–5
12:15
14:14, 34–36
15:30–31
19:1–2
21:14

St. Mark 1:32–34, 39
3:7–11
6:5, 53–56

St. Luke 4:40–41
5:15
6:17–19
7:21–22
9:11
13:32

St. John 6:2

Twentieth Century Miracles

MIRACULOUS healings reminiscent of the New Testament are occurring in churches of every denomination all over the United States. They are the result of a revival of one of the Church's oldest and most dynamic ministries—the healing of sick bodies as well as sick souls. This ministry of the early Church, though never wholly lost, has been mislaid for many centuries. It is being rediscovered today with thrilling results.

A woman suffering from brain cancer, diagnosed by an internationally known clinic, was given about one year to live. She attended a healing service in a Methodist church and claims she was healed. She has suffered no symptoms over a period of six years.

A victim of advanced tuberculosis, medically diagnosed by every known laboratory method, and bedridden for sixteen months, received Holy Unction from an Episcopal minister and was back at work in five days. His health has continued good for the seven subsequent years.

A child, paralyzed from the waist down as a result of polio, was carried into a Baptist healing service and walked unaided out of the church. This was four years ago, and he still has full use of his limbs.

A man with a heart hopelessly crippled from rheumatic fever received the laying-on-of-hands from his Presbyterian pastor, and fully recovered.

Overcoming skepticism

The immediate reaction of outsiders when confronted with alleged religious healings of this kind is complete incredulity. This was exactly my reaction when the phenomenon of spiritual healing came to my attention several years ago. In the first place, I had considerable scientific background, having worked extensively with private doctors and in hospital laboratories. In addition, as a magazine feature writer, I had specialized in scientific reporting. "Miracles," which imply the breaking of natural and scientific laws, obviously didn't make sense. Furthermore, I was an agnostic, and the claim that healings of supposedly incurable disease were the result of the direct intervention of the Holy Spirit seemed to me fantastically childish nonsense at best.

However, as the stories of healing continued to mount, my curiosity was aroused. Always on the lookout for a provocative article idea, it occurred to me that an exposé of the dangers and fraudulence of faith healing might make a good magazine piece. I therefore decided to do a little investigating. What began as a brief and cursory examination of the subject eventuated in several years of the most intensive research I have ever done.

I interviewed hundreds of people, including medical doctors, physicists, clergymen and laymen; I examined scores of case histories. As time went on, the cumulative evidence of genuine healing gathered. I procured medical substantiation (in the form of X-rays, lab and hospital reports, state compensation records and doctors' statements) for dozens of healings of organic and congenital diseases, including cancer, tuberculosis, and congenital bone deformities. Finally I had to admit that there seemed too many of such healings to ascribe to coincidence. Nor could the cured diseases be glibly written off as instances of wrong diagnosis, or casually dismissed as imaginary or psychosomatic.

Midway in my research my contemplated "exposé" was mentally drafted into a "report" on the phenomenon of non-medical healing. But while I could no longer deny that some sort of healing force was in operation, I continued for a long time to deny emphatically its connection with God.

In seeking the source of these religious cures, however, I ultimately found myself forced into a study of Christianity. Gradually, to my own considerable surprise, it began to make sense. I continued into a study of the early post-apostolic Church, which led me into an understanding of the theology which lies behind the healing ministry. I finally came to accept its validity.

The outcome of this exhaustive study and investigation resulted not in a skeptic's exposé, nor in an agnostic's report on a phenomenon—but in a book which is the story of an unbeliever's journey into faith: *A Reporter Finds God Through Spiritual Healing.*

What finally convinced me that these healings were of God, were the result of the direct intervention of the Holy Spirit? It was my gradual realization that when the body was so cured, there was an undeniable healing of the spirit. In lives profoundly changed after a spiritual healing, I recognized the Holy Spirit at work. In the deep spiritual regenerations I witnessed, I acknowledged the Hand of God.

Spiritual healing not new

There is nothing new about faith healing. It has been practiced in one form or another for thousands of years. Many were the sick treated, and probably helped, at the temples of Aesculapius, legendary Greek god of medicine. Many have been the sick treated and possibly cured by witchcraft. Many are the sick today, who by faith in an amulet, a well-phrased slogan, or their doctor, are physically improved.

But there is a vast difference between these kinds of "faith" healings, and today's revived healing ministry within the Church. Spiritual healing does not concern

itself with the curing of the body alone with no reference
to the spirit; nor yet is it the type of metaphysical healing
which affirms the spiritual at the expense of the physical.
Spiritual healing deals with the cure of the *whole* person
—body, mind, and spirit. Its goal and purpose is the seeking of a closer relationship with God—the soul's salvation.
When the *spirit* is healed through faith in and through the
power of the Risen Christ, healing of the mind and body
follows as an expected corollary.

The tremendously thrilling thing which is happening
today in churches all over the world is not from any new
concepts or revolutionary ideas. It is a reaffirmation of an
indisputable Christian truth: that the salvation Our Lord
came to bring us is *total* salvation. It includes the curing of
the body as surely as it does the healing of the spirit and
the saving of our souls from sin.

The prophets had foretold that healing would be a mark
of the New Age—the Day of the Lord—and it was. Jesus
confirmed the prophecy of Isaiah: "He will come and save
you. Then the eyes of the blind shall be opened, and the
ears of the deaf shall be unstopped" (*Isaiah 35:4–5*).

Why should we have so long overlooked Our Lord's emphasis on healing as an integral part of our redemption?
Why so long ignored the fact that nearly two-thirds of the
Gospel is devoted to His healing work? Again and again
we are told that none who came to Him remained unhealed, and that "as many as touched Him were made
whole." Of profound significance is the fact that He did
not intend that the healing of the sick, any more than the
preaching of the Kingdom, should be confined to His
earthly Ministry and should end with His life among men.
As He charged His followers to preach the Gospel to all
creatures, so did He charge them to heal the sick wherever
they went (*Luke 9:2–6*). The indivisibility of healing and
the Kingdom is made crystal clear as time after time we
see that "He received them, and spake unto them of the

Kingdom of God, and healed them that had need of healing" (*Luke 9:11*).

The story of the healing ministry of the Church begins in the Book of Acts, which records the prodigious healing work of St. Paul and St. Peter, to whom the multitudes flocked, "and they were healed every one" (*Acts 5:16*).

The history of the healing Church is continued in the writings of the early Christians known as the Fathers of the Church, who have given us eye-witness reports of the healing activity of the early post-apostolic Church, where for three hundred years after Christ physical healing was the rule and not the exception.

Then began controversy, growing disunity, diminishing faith. Gradually, healing within the Church ceased. She was forced to rationalize her failure to heal by claiming that the healing gift of the Holy Spirit had been withdrawn. It was then that the Church began unwittingly to "minimize His Holy Name."

New recognition of spiritual healing

Today's renascence of the healing ministry, then, marks the return to a fundamental part of Our Lord's teaching. It is a reacknowledgment of the nature and will of God as unmistakably revealed by His Son, the revelation disregarded for so many centuries.

Individual clergy all over the world have for two thousand years offered isolated instances of His healing power. The great Catholic Shrines have kept alive the knowledge that He heals today as surely as He did during His earthly ministry. But it is only recently that a rebirth of spiritual healing, as a part of the Church's official ministry, has taken place. This renascence is church-wide. There is probably no branch of the Christian Church which has not at least some churches practicing the healing ministry, and the number is increasing every day.

The present revival is still in its infancy, but it is already of such proportions as to have engaged the attention of many scientists. Healings of so-called incurable disease have led an increasing number of medical men to ask a cogent question: "Does a healing power actually exist?" More and more physicians of the caliber of Dr. Robert Laidlaw, chief psychiatrist of Roosevelt Hospital, New York City, find themselves in accord with him when he answers an unconditional "yes."

Dr. Loring T. Swaim, instructor at the Harvard Medical School for twenty years, comments that "A sick soul can thwart the best medical treatment." The American Medical Association recently put its stamp of approval on this point of view, by issuing to its membership a pamphlet dealing with the importance of religion in treating the sick. This leaflet discusses the vitally important role of religious faith in healing, and urges the close cooperation of clergy and doctors. It gives many examples of healings where faith in God, and prayer, were acknowledged by the attending physicians as decisive factors in the patient's recovery. With emphasis being placed on the desirability of "more fully correlating the body and spirit," medicine has officially recognized the importance of the spirit in the total health picture, and the role of God in healing.

As in medicine there is a growing belief that man is a trinity composed of body, mind, and spirit, so is there in all other branches of science an increasing tendency to accept, at least as a strong probability, the existence of spiritual forces operating in the world, even if as yet they can be neither weighed nor measured. A number of physicists agree with Dr. Henry Margenau, of the Sloane Physics Laboratory, Yale University, when he says: "I believe that the ultimate truth will not be found in physical science alone, but in the convergence of science and religion. The old view, that para-normal phenomena are intrinsically irreconcilable to the scientific viewpoint, is on its way out."

Dr. Margenau answers those who think, as I used to, that all religious belief is founded on blind faith, and all science is based on infallible reason and incontrovertible proof. "The most fundamental of scientific axioms," he observes, "are only postulates. Even the laws of arithmetic are not empirically true, but are based on hypotheses which today *seem* true, but tomorrow may be disproved. Accurately speaking, we must concede that a scientific commitment is based on faith as well as reason—just as religion is based on reason as well as faith."

Fifty years ago it was considered scientific heresy to maintain that man might be motivated by spiritual forces as well as mechanistic ones; that there might exist spiritual as well as natural laws. Today such a proposition is held eminently respectable. Research engineer Julius Weinberger, of the technical staff of RCA laboratories, makes a no-longer revolutionary observation: "The phenomenon of spiritual healing is an example of the operation of spiritual laws which are superior to, but do not conflict with, scientific or natural laws. In my opinion, research relating to the human soul or spirit is the most important job yet to be done by science."

The fact that spiritual healing is gaining the approbation of an increasing number of scientists may seem immaterial or even irrelevant to the believer. My reason for emphasizing the scientific viewpoint is the fact that I was able to verify medically scores of alleged healings of supposedly incurable disease. This convinced me of the validity of the healing phenomenon and flung wide my heart to Christ. I believe that *my* story is the potential story of countless unbelievers. To the faithful, believing is seeing. For me, and I know for many, seeing is believing. I have personally discovered that while faith is indeed the *heart's* cognition, it is the *mind's* knowledge which often plants the seed.

To the believer, God is responsible for *all* healing, whether or not He is acknowledged. As a famous French surgeon stated, "I bind the wounds, God heals them." The healing Church emphasizes that His healing power is not confined to any one method, but is dispersed through various channels, which include medicine and psychology as well as religion. The working together of clergy and doctors is vitally important in order that all the tools He has placed in our hands may be utilized. But when medicine has failed and God has taken over, we see those dramatic healings which to an increasing number of people are unmistakable evidence of the direct intervention of the Holy Spirit.

Tangible evidence of God's healing power

Like most writers, it is my custom to "walk away" from an assignment once it is completed, and get on with the next job at hand. This I have been unable to do with the subject of spiritual healing. One does not casually "walk away" from the tangible evidence of the power of God, from the exciting revelation that He lives.

If my research for *A Reporter Finds God* was arduous and painstaking, it is no less so today, although for different reasons. In the first instance, I was investigating to *disprove* a premise. I now investigate to *prove*. Those who believe need no such proof. Many unbelievers, regardless of evidence, will continue to disbelieve. However, I think that much harm is done the cause of spiritual healing by careless and fallacious claims of divine cure. So that fodder shall not be provided for the skeptics; so that the operation of the Holy Spirit shall not be prostituted into chicanery; so that the healing Church may be protected from all danger of hysteria and any hint of fanaticism, I am convinced that every effort should be made to confirm medically as many healings as possible.

Honest objectivity, to be sure, is as difficult to find in science as in any other field. The scientist who is unalterably convinced that all the answers can be found in physical science and refuses to consider any evidence to the contrary, has a closed mind. He is as guilty of irrational fanaticism as the religious who disdains all scientific progress. Nevertheless, the true scientist who is not blinded by materialism; who strives to make the theories fit the facts, can be a strong ally of the healing ministry. He may appear recalcitrant in acknowledging the power of God, but by his very slowness to capitulate; by his rational objectivity, he may help to safeguard spiritual healing from unthinking emotionalism, from a dangerous lunatic fringe, which could degenerate the great healing ministry of Christ into a fanatical cult.

A year or so ago, I attended a dinner, and found myself sitting next to the managing editor of a large city newspaper. We talked of many things, none of them to do with religion, for I knew he was an atheist. Suddenly, during a lull in the conversation, I heard a woman across the table mention a healing she had recently experienced. Immediately the subject turned to spiritual healing. Learning of my interest in it, the editor turned to me with a look of complete bewilderment. Because he had always thought of me as a down-to-earth reporter who had done considerable editorial work for his paper, he asked several searching questions. This marked the beginning of a conversation which extended far into the night. Neither of us made the meeting which the dinner had preceded.

At the end of the evening the newspaper man asked if he could examine my files. "If what you say is true," he said as we parted on the hotel steps, "this is the most convincing presentation of Christianity I have ever heard."

Within the next two months, after attending many healing services, this man was to say, "My whole life has changed. I have found now what I have probably unconsciously sought all my life—evidence of a living Christ."

And so it was with me. Six years ago, cynical and unbelieving, I scoffed at "miracles." My cynicism was to fall before the truths of the Christian faith, made intelligible to me by the healing ministry. My unbelief was to shatter before the irrefutable evidence of the power of the living God.

During the past two years, in traveling extensively over the nation, I have seen many wonderful healings. The phenomenon is no longer new to me, but my sense of excitement and awe has not diminished. This book is the story of what I have seen, of what I have learned, and of what I believe to be true regarding the healing power of God.

Today, more clearly than ever before, I see in the healing Church the unchallengeable answer to the agnostic belief that Christianity is mere legend, born of man's need; or only a philosophy, a way of life; or solely an historical event which occurred and was finished two thousand years ago, to be interpreted or misinterpreted ever since. To know the healing Christ is to see Christianity transformed into what it is meant to be: a dynamic, living and demonstrable reality.

God's Will for Us

OUR VERY FIRST step toward healing is to realize that God does not will our sickness. As the Author of good, not evil, He does not cause disease, nor does He inflict it upon His children as a means of punishment.

The unreserved acknowledgment of this tremendously vital truth serves as a stepping stone to spiritual healing.

In my case, and I believe in many other cases, it has also led to an acceptance of Christianity itself. My agnosticism was due in no small measure to the fact that I simply could not reconcile a God whom I was told to love and trust with the suffering I saw about me. I used to marvel then, as I still do, at the fortitude of those who, with complete resignation and apparently without rancor, could say, "This is God's will," as they watched a baby die of leukemia, or saw a child crippled with polio, or a young wife ravaged by cancer.

To me it seemed impossible, and it still does, to love or serve or even acknowledge, a Creator who is the perpetrator of disease, with which He cruelly and indiscriminately harasses mankind.

It was my study of the phenomenon of spiritual healing which was to lead me to the truth which is setting thousands of Christians free from the heresy which has so long shackled Christ's power in His Church and in our lives.

Healing the body leads the mind to God

It was in my first serious study of the Gospels that I was to discover that Christ has revealed to us, beyond the possibility of any misunderstanding, the true nature of God: a God of infinite mercy and boundless compassion, a Maker who so loved the world that He gave His only Son to suffer and die, so that we who crucified Him might be saved (*John 3:16*); a creator who knows and cares when even one of His countless sparrows falls to the ground (*Matthew 10:29*); a Parent to whom each one of us is as beloved, no matter what our deficiencies, as though no other child exists in the world.

Jesus said, "Be ye therefore merciful as your Father is merciful." These were not idle words, for His entire ministry is a demonstration of their truth. Again and again He reminds us that He and the Father are one: "He that hath

seen me hath seen the Father" (*John 14:9*). Wherever He
went, He healed the sick, in mercy and compassion. Working ceaselessly to fulfil the will of God, Christ banished
disease in His Father's Name, wherever He found it. He
"went about all the cities and villages . . . healing every
sickness and disease among the people" (*Matthew 9:35*).
It is unthinkable that as the multitudes followed Him and
He healed them all, that He was working against His own
will.

Jesus came to bring God to us—to save our souls. As the
Son of Man, He also knew the importance of our bodies.
He then, as now, often began His saving work with a physical healing which would result in spiritual change. Time
after time then, as it does today, the *visible* sign of the living God, turned those healed to their Lord.

Two thousand years ago a blind beggar received his sight
and "followed Him, glorifying God" (*Luke 18:35–43*).

A palsied man took up his bed "and departed to his own
house, glorifying God" (*Luke 5:18–26*).

The multitude "saw the dumb to speak, the maimed to
be whole, the lame to walk, and the blind to see: and they
glorified the God of Israel" (*Matthew 15:30–31*).

And so it is today. A steel worker, long deaf, receives his
hearing. He now leads weekly prayer meetings at the mill.
A business man, instantly healed of lung cancer, now devotes his spare time to witnessing for Christ. A hopelessly
crippled attorney walks again. He uses his oratory now to
teach a truth he has personally experienced: that Christianity is not a method for enduring illness; it is the means
by which disease can be triumphantly overcome.

Our Lord makes it abundantly clear that disease is part
of the structure of evil He has come to vanquish. He invariably speaks of sickness as something to rebuke, something
evil and therefore contrary to the will of His Father.

"And Jesus rebuked the devil; and he departed out of

him: and the child was cured from that very hour" (*Matthew 17:18*).

"He cast out the spirits with His word, and healed all that were sick" (*Matthew 8:16*).

To Jesus and His disciples, and to all the saints, Satan was a very real adversary. You may not believe in an actual devil, but you may concede that there seem to be a good and an evil force at large in the world, the latter continually opposing and hindering God's perfect will for us. This theory of Christian dualism, of God versus Satan, which has always been part of the faith, is one of the easiest of all Christian assumptions to accept. It does much to explain disease and suffering. It also helps to explain how, if God does not *will* disease, He appears to permit it.

God made the world, and He "saw that it was good." He also gave men free will. By the misuse of this great gift, evil came into God's creation, thus precipitating the battle between good and evil which has raged ever since. We are assured through Christ, however, that God *is* almighty and will achieve the ultimate and complete victory over sin, sickness, and death, which is assured us in the Resurrection. When this occurs, we will know in its full sense, the Kingdom of which He speaks. Meanwhile, we are catching a glimpse of it now through spiritual healing, as we witness with increasing frequency the conquest of the Holy Spirit over the evil that is disease.

Jesus commissioned the Church to heal

Our Lord leaves us in no more doubt of His Father's will concerning disease, than concerning sin. They are the two-headed enemy He labors unremittingly to overcome. The Gospels tell the story of His victory over both, a victory as unequivocal as His triumph over death itself.

But He never confined the conquest of sin and disease to His earthly ministry. He commissioned His Church to continue His work under the guidance of the Holy Spirit. He commanded His disciples to heal the sick with the same assiduousness with which they preached the Kingdom.

"He called his twelve disciples together, and gave them power and authority over all devils, and to cure diseases. And he sent them to preach the kingdom of God, and to heal the sick. . . . And they departed and went through the towns, preaching the Gospel, and healing everywhere" (*Luke 9:1, 2, 6*). Our Lord has left no room for doubt: the Kingdom of God and the realm of sin and disease cannot co-exist.

In traveling over the country and talking to hundreds of people about spiritual healing, I have encountered considerable confusion over the phrase "Thy will be done."

It is curious that over the ages these potentially comforting words should have developed a prevalent connotation that is far from comforting to many people. "Thy will be done" has long been prayed as a lugubrious accompaniment to hopeless situations, and the phrase seems to have become a natural corollary to disaster. We are so in the habit of using these words out of context that we have overlooked their real significance, which is fully explained in the Lord's Prayer: "Thy kingdom come, thy will be done *on earth* as it is *in heaven*."

And what is His will in heaven? That "there shall be no more death, neither sorrow, nor crying, neither shall there be any more pain" (*Revelation 21:4*).

For centuries Christians have been taught that the words "if it be thy will" are a virtually essential termination of all prayer. They have become an inevitable part of our prayer pattern. But while they certainly have their place, it is *not,* according to the teachings of Christ, in *healing* prayer. There are some areas in which we are not certain of His will, and must seek through prayer to learn it; but this is not true of sin and disease. Do we repent of our sins, concluding our prayer with "if it be they will"? Of course not. We *know* He wills our repentance. Likewise, on the authority of His Son, we are as certain that He wills our wholeness as we are that He does *not* will that we go out and commit a murder. We are as sure that He wills our body's health as that He wills our soul's salvation.

To pray "if it be thy will" is to limit the power of your healing prayer, for these are tentative, qualifying words, expressing doubt. They are the outward expression of an inward lack of faith in God's desire and ability to heal us. Such a prayer seems to indicate a lack of acceptance on our part of Christ's revelation of God in respect to disease; for Our Lord makes it clear that He healed always with the complete authority of one who *knew* the will of the Father. He spoke the word of power, unweakened by a qualifying phrase.

"Arise and walk," He said. "I say unto thee, arise." Without hesitation, with complete conviction, He commands, "Receive thy sight;" and "Be whole of thy plague."

So should we pray, not in submissive resignation, but in certain confidence: "I know that thy will for me is perfect health. Therefore I receive my healing in the Name of Christ, so that thy will may be fulfilled."

Resist disease; do not accept it

Most of us are probably all too familiar with the necessity of resisting temptation, and the results if we do not; but the idea of resisting disease as also evil, comes as a new idea to many of us. It's not always easy, in either case, and it requires considerably more faith and effort than sitting passively by and saying, "thy will be done." But if you believe that disease, like sin, is evil, you will find yourself compelled to combat the one as fiercely as the other so that His will may indeed be done. The result is often a miracle of healing, such as I saw not long ago in a southern town.

The parents of a six-months-old baby, hearing that I was in the vicinity, asked me to go with them to the hospital to pray for their desperately sick infant. This was not an unusual request. A great many people ask me to pray for their sick, feeling that my strong faith in God's healing power will be beneficial. Many ask also that I lay on hands, but this I have thus far refused to do, because I do not believe that I am a channel for healing. In acceding to the request of these distraught parents, I explained this and suggested that we ask a minister to accompany us to perform this sacramental act.

Their reply was: "Oh no, there's no use in that. We know that Sandy's case is hopeless, and that it is God's will that he die. We just want your prayers for his soul."

I was completely taken aback. There was no time for me to deliver a discourse on spiritual healing, as I was taking a plane out of the city within the hour; and I have never had the temerity to tell anyone how he should believe or must pray. It was obvious that the young man and woman were deriving a certain comfort, however small, from their resignation to the baby's fate. Dare I take it upon myself to interfere? Before I had actually made up my mind, I heard my own voice saying, "Look, there's every reason to think your baby is going to get well."

They both started. A sudden light flooded their eyes, then quickly receded. The father, belligerent in his despair, said, "How do *you* know? Do you know more than the doctors?"

"I only know," I said, "that it is not God's will that a six-months-old infant die. Will you just try to believe with me that He not only *wants* him to get well, but He has the power to *make* him well? We'll naturally pray for his soul, but let's pray for his body, too."

The young couple nodded, their eyes filled with tears.

We walked into the baby's room, and the three of us

knelt by the head of Sandy's crib. I prayed a brief prayer, ending with, "In the Name of Jesus Christ, Sandy, you are healed." The infant stirred, and I had the complete conviction that he would recover.

Before leaving the hospital, I begged the young couple to stop saying to themselves, "He's going to leave us, but Thy will be done"—and, instead, to offer prayers of faith and thanksgiving that His will *was* being done, and the child was recovering. Without comprehension, but with a new hope, they agreed. I found out later that to everyone's surprise but mine, the baby made a good recovery.

Coincidence? Perhaps, if this were one, isolated case. But I have seen many cases where as soon as an affirmative prayer replaced the prayer of hopeless resignation, recovery ensued. We must acknowledge a causative connection between the expression of our faith in God to heal, which constitutes the prayer of power, and physical healing.

"A thorn in the flesh"

But, you may say, if it is so obviously God's will that we be healed, what about St. Paul's thorn? If God refused to heal His apostle, how can we possibly think that He will heal us?

An increasing number of theologians, spear-headed by the Reverend Frank Uttley, entirely reject the hypothesis that Paul's thorn in the flesh referred to a physical ailment: "and lest I should be exalted above measure . . . there was given to me a thorn in the flesh" (*II Corinthians 12:7*). They have reverted to the theory, held by a number of early Church historians including St. Augustine and St. Chrysostom, that the thorn was actually the sin of spiritual pride. These clergymen point out that the figure of speech "thorn in the flesh" is used only three times in the entire Bible. As in the first two instances it does not refer to physical illness, they ask, with undeniable logic, why its use in

Paul's case should infer disease. They suggest, too, that the image of an invalid saint is not compatible with the Biblical picture of a titan missionary; a man apparently with the strength of ten, who endured shipwreck and persecution, imprisonment and stoning.

But the exact nature of the thorn seems relatively unimportant. What *is* important, is the fact that Paul was a man of overwhelming and unshakable conviction in the will and power of God to heal. His marvellous healing work, which included the raising of the dead, was as abundant as his preaching work, and was unequaled by any of the other apostles. In answer to prayer, God gave him strength for each day's needs—a strength with which any of us today would be well satisfied.

Whatever the thorn, whether disease or sin, Paul reaffirms the origin of both. He makes it perfectly clear that it was not placed in him by God, but sent by "the messenger of Satan to buffet me" (*II Corinthians 12:7*).

Occasionally I have wished that I could honestly believe that sickness is sent by God. Such a belief is an easy way out, and it is not difficult to see how Christians have for so long fallen into this line of least resistance.

In this connection, I remember a particular night several years ago when the whole concept of spiritual healing was still new to me. My husband was ill, and I had come home late from the hospital after a long and discouraging conference with his doctors. Completely exhausted, I threw myself on my bed, thinking how relaxing it would be to accept passively this illness as God's will, certain that there was nothing I nor anyone else could do about it.

I felt far too tired even to pray, but lying flat on my back, I leafed through the Gospels. When I had finished, I was more convinced than I had ever been before that sickness, like sin, is evil and must be fought to the finish, no matter how exhausting the battle. It seemed to me I could not say that my husband's sickness was God's will, without committing blasphemy; nor could I say "Thy will be done," and thereby wash my hands of the entire matter, without violating what I had come to believe was a fundamental Christian truth. I claimed, that night, His wonderful promise: "Whatsoever ye shall ask the Father in my name, He will give it you" (*John 16:23*). He honored my faith.

Suffering is not saintliness

As I have been unable to discover any Scriptural evidence whatsoever that God sends disease as chastisement, so have I failed to find any indication that He sends suffering as a means of spiritual regeneration. Indeed the Gospel evidence seems completely to the contrary. Is it rational to suppose that Jesus would have healed all who came to Him at the expense of their souls?

We should never forget the Cross in Christianity, but neither should its shadow obscure for us the joy of the Resurrection. While it is true that suffering is considered a part of the Christian vocation, it is also true that we must differentiate between redemptive suffering and purposeless pain. If we don't, we risk glorifying pain instead of the Risen Christ. But we don't have to make this difficult decision for ourselves. Jesus as already pointed the way.

Our Lord never said we didn't have to suffer. He healed the sick, but He warned us of persecution for His sake. He fed the hungry, but He said we who would come after Him must deny ourselves. He relieved the suffering, but He told us to take up our cross and follow Him.

He warned us of the pitfalls and temptations on the highway to His Kingdom, of the necessity for spiritual strength and moral stamina to complete the journey. Still He seems to make it clear that the battle against sin is an adequate testing ground for the soul, and the struggle toward holiness a sufficient crucible for the ennobling of the spirit.

As Christians we have tended to regard all pain, *per se,* as redemptive. For hundreds of years we have confused saintliness with suffering until the two have become synonymous in our minds; but, as the Reverend Dr. Leslie Weatherhead, prominent British Methodist, points out, it was not the suffering of the saints but their attitude toward it which determined their saintliness. Although their pain was not sent by God, they were able with His help to convert it to a holy purpose, offering their heroic endurance to His glory.

There are saints today. There is a woman in my city, declared by her doctors to be medically incurable. She has sought and received a magnificent healing of the spirit, but so far the healing of her body has not taken place. She is a tiny woman with a frail body, but she is a spiritual giant. All who come in contact with her feel humbled, strengthened and inspired. Having done all she can spiritually as well as medically, she has committed herself to God. She awaits His next step, not in submissive resignation, but in expectant faith and certain confidence that His love will ultimately free her from affliction. Meanwhile His grace is sufficient for her. She lives each day to His glory, offering to Him her patience, her serenity and her indomitable courage. His strength is made perfect in her weakness (*II Corinthians 12:9*). She transcends pain.

There are others like this woman whose suffering has tremendous redemptive power; but there are many more like the good churchman of my acquaintance who is ill from a duodenal ulcer.

For years he has felt a bitter hostility toward one of his office co-workers. His entire life, at home as well as at work, is colored by this continued resentment. Until his attitude changes, his ulcer will not heal; in fact, his doctor has implied as much. Yet this man piously declares that his illness is God's will, sent to strengthen him spiritually. Meanwhile, peevish and irritable, sick in both body and spirit, he makes everyone who comes within his range miserable by his complaining.

Now this type of suffering can no more be construed as redemptive than the stomach ache which follows the eating of too many green apples. There may be a certain *remedial* value in it, a warning to correct our faults—"for whom the Lord loveth he chasteneth" (*Hebrews 12:6*)—but there would seem to be little *redemptive* power in pain when it occurs as a direct result of our own unexpiated sins.

Redemption comes only when we tend our spirits as assiduously as our bodies; only when we are ready to correct, to change, to do His will.

The Reverend Edward Winckley, Associate Warden of the Order of St. Luke in South Africa, speaks from the vastness of his personal experience in the healing field abroad when he comments: "Unfortunately I have seen more illness used by the devil to further his own ends, than used for the glory of God."

Jesus suffered for us

There are those who argue that because Jesus suffered on the Cross, we, too, should suffer. In a sense this is true. Any sacrifice we make, whether it entails spiritual, mental, or physical pain, if suffered for Christ's sake, has redemptive power. But pain alone, simply because it is pain, does not, *ipso facto,* sanctify the sufferer.

Jesus never suffered for *suffering's* sake. He suffered to save us profitless pain. He "Himself took our infirmities, and bare our sicknesses" (*Matthew 8:17*).

He died for a cause, to free us from sin: He "who his own self bare our sins in his own body . . . that we, being dead to sins, should live unto righteousness" (*I Peter 2:24*).

As Anglican Father Winckley points out, Christian suffering is consequent upon trying to be a Christian; not suffering consequent upon disease. Therefore we must never confuse the issue by claiming that God sends disease for our spiritual benefit. This belief has caused thousands to suffer needlessly and die prematurely. As long as we think illness comes from God, we won't rebuke it; and as long as we think God has a purpose in our sickness, we won't resist it. As the Lambeth Conference on spiritual healing, held in England, reported: "In whatever way it [disease] may be overruled for good, it is, in itself, an evil."

Until the millennium there will be suffering which results from man's sin and ignorance, but this is a far cry from the idea of a loving God Himself sending disease.

The Reverend Richard Spread* makes the analogy of a human father who knows that his children will suffer. He certainly neither inflicts nor intends their suffering, but does all he can to teach them to avoid it. "You must fight against temptation," says the father, "no matter how hard the struggle, and no matter how much it hurts."

This human father does not first inject his son with cancer so that he may more effectively fight temptation. How, then, could we suppose that God could do so?—a God of whom Jesus says: "If ye then, being evil, know how to give good gifts unto your children, how much more shall your Father which is in heaven give good things to them that ask him" (*Matthew 7:11*).

Jesus came in the Name of this Father, to bring us total salvation. To save means to make whole, both physically and spiritually. The body's healing and the soul's redemption were never intended to be separated. They are concomitant, as Christ has shown us, and as the Holy Spirit is demonstrating today through His healing power.

There is much of which we are not sure, but of this we

Stretching Forth Thine Hand to Heal. London: Skeffiington & Son, Ltd.

can be certain on the authority of Jesus Christ: a maimed body is not a punishment, nor yet is it a prerequisite to the Kingdom of Heaven.

Disease is not the will of God, but the will of the enemy. It can be defeated at the Cross.

"I am the Lord that healeth thee." If you will believe that God wants you to be well, if you will pray the prayer of power, you will see that He has not changed.

God's Healing Touch

WHEREVER you are, whoever you may be, the healing power of God is available to you today just as it was two thousand years ago when "as many as touched the hem of his garment were made perfectly whole" (*Matthew 14:36*). On the basis of what I have seen, I am wholly convinced that there is no disease so "hopeless" that it will not respond to His almighty power, and no ailment so slight that it is unworthy of His healing love.

Once convinced that it is His will that we should be well, our next step is to release His healing power so that it may flow through us unimpeded. Successful spiritual healing depends primarily on love, faith, and repentance. These three factors are interdependent, but faith might be called the core of spiritual healing, as it is of all Christianity. It is only when we *believe* Jesus Christ was the Son of God that we can accept the reality of His resurrective power in our lives today. It is only when we *believe* what He told us of God that we can truly love our Creator. It is only when we *believe* what He told us of sin and its consequences that we can understand the necessity for repentance.

But no one knows better than I that this is easier said

than done. The simple, child-like faith which Christ demanded of His followers, and upon which He tells us depends our entry into the Kingdom of Heaven, is incredibly difficult for many of us to acquire in this day and age. I know it was for me; but I think now that had I known in the beginning what I have since learned, the road might have been less rough.

True faith accepts the evidence

Not long ago someone said to me: "I only wish I had your blind faith. But I'll never have that complete faith necessary for healing."

This woman couched her comment diplomatically, but I knew exactly what she meant. I remember when I, too, used to envy people their "blind" faith. Yet at the same time I felt distinctly superior that my intellect prevented my being so gullible as they. I have learned since that faith need not and should not be "blind." It is not a superstitious credulity in an intellectually untenable premise. It begins, to be sure, where the mind ends and the heart takes over, but the distance between the two is not impassably vast.

While it is true that faith is trusting in some things which cannot be proved by scientific formula—the "substance of things hoped for, the evidence of things not seen" (*Hebrews 11:1*)—it is also, as Dr. Weatherhead emphasizes, "loyalty to the trend of all *available* evidence." My faith, then, is an acceptance of the evidence that God lives. This abundantly available evidence is to be found in the restored bodies and recreated spirits of those He has touched with His healing hand.

There are some who do not believe because they *will* not. But to those who do not believe because they *cannot,* Our Lord reveals Himself today as unmistakably as He did when He appeared before His doubting disciples, and said: "Behold my hands and my feet, that it is I myself" (*Luke 24:39*).

Through the revival of the healing ministry we have been immeasurably blessed. We are living in a scientific era, but not since the time of Christ have so many been so sure that He lives. We are living in an age of reason, but not since the early post-apostolic Church have the tenets of the Christian faith appeared so eminently reasonable to so many minds.

My friend was also mistaken in her assumption that *complete* faith is necessary for healing. I think that there is actually no such thing as "complete" faith. If it were complete it would no longer be faith, but certainty. As an essential part of the man-God relationship, it must be by faith and not through knowledge, that we reach Him. "Thy faith hath saved thee," (*Luke 7:50*) Christ said. He says it still.

Faith is many things. It is our confidence in the integrity of Jesus Christ when He said that He was the Son of God. It is accepting as valid His promise when he said: "Ask, and it shall be given you; seek, and ye shall find; knock, and it shall be opened unto you" (*Luke 11:9*). It is placing our reliance on His assurance of a healing God. It is putting our trust in a Person, certain that He is worthy of it.

I have found that nowhere is it more clearly illustrated than in spiritual healing, that God rewards those who "diligently seek Him" (*Hebrews 11:6*). Jesus honors the desire to believe, as well as the fulfilment; the striving to accept, not only the achievement; the seeking and not only the finding.

Complete faith unnecessary for healing

Fortunately for most of us, our healing does not depend on the *amount* of faith we have. Our Lord assures us that faith as small as a mustard seed can move mountains (*Matthew 17:20*). It can also create healing miracles.

A young married woman was scheduled for radical surgery on a Tuesday morning about two years ago. A biopsy had revealed a malignant tumor in her left breast. On the Friday preceding her operation, she attended a healing service at her church. "You could have fitted my faith on a pinhead" was the way she expressed it. "I went to church fairly regularly but I had never before gone to a healing service. I really went this time only at the insistence of a friend."

During the service she felt a sensation "like electricity" streak across her chest, then center for an instant in her left breast. When she arose from the altar rail, she reports: "never in my life have I had such a feeling of indescribable well-being and joy. I knew that something wonderful had happened to me inside. My friend said I had been healed, but just then it didn't seem to matter whether I had been physically cured or not."

That evening the young wife told her husband what had happened. "He just laughed," she said, "until he looked for the lump and found it gone."

The next morning the couple went together to the doctor who after careful examination declared that the growth seemed to have "mysteriously diminished in size." At his suggestion, however, she entered the hospital on schedule for another biopsy. The report came back negative.

This woman's faith and that of countless others like her may have seemed less than a mustard seed, but it was enough for God to work through.

I have witnessed again and again Our Lord's merciful response to mankind's age-old and despairing cry: "I believe; help Thou mine unbelief." It was a father bringing his sick child to Jesus for healing who first uttered those words. A compassionate God extended His healing hand then, and He is no less merciful today.

A year ago an anguished father, whose small son was suffering from an inoperable brain tumor turned to God, offering Him what he had of faith augmented by desire and hope. It was enough. Week after week prayers were offered for the child as he received the laying-on-of-hands. His condition steadily improved. A month ago the doctors who had said there was no hope pronounced him completely well.

"Thy faith hath made thee whole" was the keynote of Our Lord's earthly healing ministry. From what I have seen I believe that faith in some form is always necessary for healing today, although I am well aware that occasionally some are healed who appear to have no faith whatsoever.

Take the case of a man scheduled for surgery for a severe stomach ulcer, who frankly admits that he attended a healing service merely to please his wife.

"Oh, I believed in God as an idea—an abstraction," he says, "but I had absolutely no faith in a personal God. Furthermore, I thought all this talk of 'miraculous' healing was absolute bunk."

Nevertheless, to his own stupefaction, the intense pain of his ulcer subsided as he knelt at the altar rail. A subsequent X-ray revealed that he was healed. No surgery was required.

Now this man himself may have lacked faith, but his unbelief was routed by the massed faith of the believing worshipers who knelt beside him in the church. Here, of course, is the tremendous value of the church service. There is inestimable power in corporate faith. The almost palpable aura of expectant trust which characterizes a healing service not only increases the faith of the believers but seems to "rub off," as it were, on the unbelievers. If miracles are created through faith, faith, likewise, is created by miracles. Those healed do not remain unbelievers. They go on their way, like the blind beggar, "glorifying God."

I saw a man healed of a crippling arthritic condition. Supercilious, scornful, in full accord with the Communist dictum that all religion is the opiate of the people and spiritual healing the apotheosis of crackpot-ism, this man attended a healing service out of a hostile curiosity. Unsought, unbelieved, complete healing came to this man. Why? Simply because the faith of the people around him was stronger than his doubt? Not entirely. It is cases like these which have led me to believe that one of the great purposes of today's manifestation of God's healing power, is conversion. This man and others like him are now among the Church's most dedicated workers, converting hundreds of unbelievers by their witness for the living Christ.

But the conversions wrought through spiritual healing are not confined to self-confessed agnostics. Like the man with the ulcer, there are thousands who have conceived of God purely as principle—an empirical hypothesis. Through their awareness of His healing Presence, they have a new and exciting sense of the reality of Jesus.

There are thousands more who have believed the theological Christ, but have never until now known and loved Him as their personal Saviour. These have discovered the power which is Christianity. It is in this conversion from a mere philosophy to a dynamic, power-filled faith that we see most dramatically illustrated the primary purpose of spiritual healing: the bringing of souls to God.

Physical healings, important as they are to the afflicted, are only corollaries to the healings of the spirit. A cured body is not an end in itself. To regard it as such or to seek it as such is to do violence to the entire concept of spiritual healing. As Dr. Michael Ash, Harley Street surgeon, comments: "The healing of the body is only a temporary cure between life and death; the ultimate cure is always of the spirit."

Repentance opens the door to healing

Jesus admonishes us to "seek ye the kingdom of God; and all these things shall be added unto you" (*Luke 12:31*). This is why faith alone is not sufficient. Faith unlocks the door to His power, but it is repentance which opens it.

"Preach ye the kingdom and heal the sick," Our Lord commanded. "He that believeth is saved." He also added that "repentance and remission of sins should be preached in his name among all nations" (*Luke 24:47*); for "except ye repent, ye shall all likewise perish" (*Luke 13:3*).

"But surely you don't believe all that ridiculous stuff," said an old friend whom I hadn't seen for years. "What on earth has happened to your reason?

"Yes, I *do* believe it now, and *because* of my reason.

No one understands better than I, who was myself a skeptic so short a while ago, the prodigious difficulty of believing what Christ said simply because He said it. But the healing ministry is based on this premise. Because I, with my own eyes, have seen the incredible power in His words believed, the astounding results of His promises claimed, it seems to me now a clear-cut case of cause and effect; a question of "By their fruits shall ye know them."

If we accept the validity of Our Lord's mission, and practice in so far as we are able what He tells us, we find the fruits of the faith. If we emasculate His teaching, selecting what we want to believe and rejecting what we would prefer to discard, we find ourselves left with a powerless ideology instead of a dynamic religion.

The subject of our own sin is one of those phrases of Christianity which most of us would probably like to forget, if not actively reject. But the destructiveness of sin and the salvation of His forgiveness, are the substance of Christ's teaching, the heart of the Christian Church and an inextricable part of the healing ministry.

"Thy sins are forgiven thee," Jesus said to the palsied man. "Arise, and take up thy couch" *(Luke 5:20, 24).*

"Confess your faults one to another . . . that ye may be healed," said James *(James 5:16).* Throughout the history of the Church healing and repentance have gone hand in hand.

It is through repentance that we draw close to God. It is through His absolving power that our souls are healed. During His earthly ministry, Jesus never refused His healing grace to a sinner, nor does He now. It is never the sin, only our lack of penitence which blocks us from God and His power. To deny our sin is to deny our salvation, for we cannot be saved from what we don't have.

What sin is

"But what *is* sin?" a friend said to me in genuine bewilderment. "I haven't *done* anything."

In his mind my friend, like a great many of us, associated sin with a concrete, nefarious act, like robbing a bank or committing a murder. In the sense of committing a penitentiary offence, he certainly hadn't "done" anything; but he had broken God's law. Just how he had done so was divulged during the course of our conversation.

Sin is disobedience to God, of which, in one way or another, we are all guilty. It is impossible to live a sinless life, but our salvation lies in the attempt.

Even in seemingly inconsequential things, such as eating too much or drinking too much, or smoking too much, which overindulgences might appear to concern only ourselves, we are breaking His Commandment to "Love thy neighbor as *thyself*"; for we are harming our bodies—desecrating, if you will, the temple of the Holy Spirit.

But as Bishop Austin Pardue of Pittsburgh emphasizes; "Although the sins of the flesh should not be minimized, the sins most frequently overlooked are the sins of the spirit." Hostility, resentment, anger, fear, jealousy—these are the things which most flagrantly violate the law of love issued by Our Lord. To break this law, is to commit an offense against God, and to suffer the consequences of physical disease as well as spiritual sickness.

My friend, for example, told me that he had suffered for two years from a painful kidney ailment, which despite treatment from one of his city's most eminent urologists, had grown progressively worse. His condition at the time we met was threatening to incapacitate him, and, as he put it, "If I have to stop working my family will starve. I'm ready to try anything, even God." This is certainly not an ideal reason to seek God, but it is not an uncommon one. Innumerable people have been healed as they learn just what "trying" God involves.

During the course of our luncheon my friend also told me of a bitter professional disappointment he had suffered two years before. He spoke with rancor of the rival who, by using distinctly unethical methods, had procured the job for which my friend had long worked.

Turning to me, his face flushed with unforgotten anger, he said, "You can see why I feel the way I do, can't you?"

Of course I could, but however understandable his resentment, if was not justified in the sight of God. He had broken the law of love, and appeared to be suffering the consequences.

With some embarrassment, not relishing my role of arbiter of someone else's "sin," I pointed out this possibility. He looked at me for a moment without speaking. Then he said; "You know, that may make sense at that. Only last week my doctor told me that anger could seriously aggravate my condition. He questioned me, but at the time I never thought of this incident I just told you."

"Whosoever shall smite thee on thy right cheek, turn to him the other also" *(Matthew 5:39)* may be considered poor business practice, but it is good health insurance.

The force of humility

A man who was a firm believer in the power of God to heal suffered what appeared to be a minor injury to his shoulder. He received a number of heat treatments from his doctor, but the pain, now radiating into his left arm, grew constantly worse. He then tried an osteopath, with no success. Finally he consulted an orthopedist, who, after X-raying him, concluded that the pain was caused by pressure on a nerve in his neck. It was recommended that the patient be placed in traction. The patient agreed to be hospitalized immediately upon his return from an urgent business trip which could not be postponed.

By his third day away, the pain in his arm, no longer controllable by codeine, had become insupportable. He took the morning off to attend a healing service at a local church.

"As the minister prayed and laid on hands," he relates, "something came to me in a flash of enlightenment. I suddenly realized that I felt tremendously resentful toward a newcomer in my office who I felt was threatening my position. At almost the same instant, and I can't tell you *why* I did it, I found myself praying for this man and asking God to bless him. As I prayed, I felt a sensation of burning heat race down my arm. The pain seemed to seep out my fingertips, along with the heat. I haven't had a twinge since that moment. Incidentally, that man in the office and I have become close friends!"

The saints all put their finger on pride as the great spiritual culprit. As the most common of the sins which beset us, and the most dangerous because it is so insidious and far-reaching in its effects, it might not be too inaccurate to say that pride is actually behind and responsible for all sin. It leads to the exaltation of our own egos to the point where we worship ourselves and our achievements instead of the Creator of both. This tendency leads us into the greatest sin of all, a willful separation from God.

Pride has nothing to do with the self-respect which Our Lord surely meant us to have and to maintain, or He would never have issued His Second Commandment. Pride means the sort of self-aggrandizement which precludes humility. Humility is the very basis of our relationship with God.

Without humility we cannot have true faith, for faith presupposes complete confidence in someone other than ourselves. Without humility we cannot love God, for love is a humble desire to please the loved one. It is lack of humility which makes us deny our need of penance. It is lack of humility which makes it so difficult, not only to seek out our faults, but having discovered them, to confess them. Whatever other virtues we may possess, if we do not have humility, we are lost; whereas, however grave our faults, if we are humble enough to confess them, we can be saved.

A housewife, a veritable "pillar of the Church," suffered from seriously impaired vision from hardening of the arteries in the eyes. Her ophthalmologist declared that the damage done was irreversible, and his prognosis was eventual blindness. The patient, however, refused to accept this verdict as final. She knew too well the marvelous power of God to heal.

For some six months she sought spiritual healing through prayer and the sacramental healing rites of the Church, with no result, physical or spiritual.

"I couldn't understand it," she said. "I felt that there was a definite block in me which was hindering God's power, yet I couldn't put my finger on it. One day I sat down and really tried to think it through. *I* didn't smoke or drink like Mrs. S, who did both. *I* never missed a Sunday in Church, and Mrs. X missed at least once a month. *I* gave twice as much to the Church in time and money as did Mrs. T.

"Suddenly, as I went on in this vein to myself, I had the answer. It was my smugness; my self-righteousness; my intolerance; my *pride* which was the trouble.

"Next day I went to the healing service, and for the first time in many years of church-going, I had a real sense of the sin I was asking to have forgiven. I received the laying-on-of-hands with the first *honest* humility I think I had ever felt. Kneeling there at the altar rail, I felt His Presence as I never had before."

Slowly but surely this woman's vision improved. Today, four years later, it is normal.

"As many as received Him, to them gave He power," *(John 1:12)*. And again and again it is being demonstrated that we cannot receive Him if the door to our heart is closed by unrepented sin. But in our desire to open it, so that His healing power may be freed, we must guard against a neurotic overemphasis on our shortcomings as Christians. To remain perpetually on our knees in penitence, is to have misunderstood the act of contrition, which is in two parts. For it is as important to be able to *accept* His forgiveness, as it is to *ask*. While it is true that "If we say we have no sin, we deceive ourselves," it is no less true that "If we confess our sins, He is faithful and just to forgive us our sins, and to cleanse us from all unrighteousness" *(I John 1:8, 9)*. It is not, therefore, in an unhealthy state of continual self-condemnation that we will find healing. It is in our joyful acceptance of His absolving grace.

Love fulfils the power of God

If faith evokes the power of God in our lives, and repentance releases it, it is love which ultimately fulfils it.

Wherever I have seen the healing ministry at work, I have observed the limitless power of love in action. Through today's manifestation of the Holy Spirit, many of us worship for the first time what we know to be the living God. We no longer have to struggle to love a disembodied Spirit or an Infinite Mind. We know Him now as He has been revealed in the Gospels. We have felt the touch of His gentle Hand, and we have known the comfort of His undeniable Presence. Through our knowledge, then, of the living Christ, we have learned to truly love the Father. As our love meets the love of God, from which all love derives, miracles are wrought.

Time and again, in telling me of their healings, people have said in surprise: "You know, I wasn't even thinking of myself. I was praying for the person next to me, when I was healed."

The experience of a middle-aged woman who had suffered a serious heart condition, is typical of His love, reflected however palely in our own actions.

"As I knelt at the altar," she said, "I could see that the woman next to me was in obvious pain. I was so anxious that she be healed that I forgot to pray for myself and prayed for her instead. While I was praying, I felt such peace and joy flood my entire being as surpasses description. I found myself almost running home and suddenly realized that I wasn't short of breath."

A few days later this woman had another X-ray and cardiogram made of her heart. She had been healed.

In mentioning healings of this sort to a clergyman with a great deal of healing experience, he commented: "Yes, that's why when I lay on hands or administer Unction, I like to have other loving members of the family present to pray with me. I have seen patients literally *loved* back to life."

You may find the healing Christ at home, through daily

devotions; or at church, through the healing Sacraments; or through the intercessory prayers of others. But whatever the method, the road to Him will be the same—a highway opened by faith, cleared by repentance and illuminated by love. Thousands have traversed this road before you, daring to claim His magnificent promise: "Verily, verily, I say unto you, He that believeth on me, the works that I do shall he do also; and greater works than these shall he do" *(John 14:12)*. He has honored their faith, and He will honor yours.

There is much we have to learn of the operation of the Holy Spirit, but these things we know: if we confess our sins, however inconsequential they may seem, to Him who has promised us forgiveness; if we try to meet His love with ours; if we offer our lamp of faith to Him, however dimly it may seem to burn, He will fill us with His healing grace. On this earth we may not see His Face, but as we step into the light of His healing Presence, we can know the end of darkness.

The Healing Sacraments

GOD's healing power is not limited to any one church, nor is its channeling confined to any one method. However, today's healing Church has discovered the tremendous effectiveness of the Sacramental healing rites used in the early post-apostolic church: the laying-on-of-hands and Holy Unction.

Not long ago a member of a non-sacramental church who was unfamiliar with the healing ministry asked whether I thought there was actual healing power in the rites themselves.

My answer was, of course, "no" in the sense that I knew

she meant. They are not black magic or a church-instigated form of sorcery. Of themselves, they have no weird healing properties. Essentially, they serve as channels through which God's healing power may flow. They are the means by which we can more easily receive a power infinitely greater than ourselves. As outward and visible signs of God's healing grace, they are an invaluable psychological aid in inspiring faith and arousing hope. For those too weak to pray, they are of incalculable comfort.

A woman who had suffered from a medically diagnosed abdominal cancer recalls: "I couldn't concentrate on prayer, and the effort of summoning up an 'active' faith was just too much. All I could do was 'receive.' When my minister laid on hands, I could virtually feel God's healing peace flow through my body. The pain left, and I fell into a natural sleep within minutes."

This patient was operated on the following day. Although there were clearly discernible evidences of the ravages of cancer, no trace of the malignancy was found. She is today in perfect health.

For those whose conscious minds cannot be reached, such as the insane, the unconscious, and young infants, the healing sacraments have again and again proved of inestimable value.

I recently saw a clergyman anoint an infant reportedly dying from collapsed lungs. The baby was deathly pale and even with the help of oxygen was breathing laboriously. As the minister ended his prayer, the infant stirred. I watched the color creep slowly but unmistakably into her ashen cheeks. The shallow, rapid breathing perceptibly deepened and slowed. She made a complete and rapid recovery.

About six months ago, a minister was called to lay hands on a man in his fifties who had suffered a cerebral hemorrhage. The doctors had warned his family that he could not be expected to regain consciousness before he died. Before the clergyman had lifted his hands from the patient's head, the man opened his eyes in full consciousness, and smiled. Except for a scarcely discernible dragging of his left leg, the patient's recovery has been complete.

A schizophrenic under restraint, whom the doctors called incurable, was anointed at the request of his family. As the clergyman made the Sign of the Cross on his forehead with the consecrated oil, the patient visibly quieted. His restraints were shortly thereafter removed, and his doctor now offers hope of complete recovery.

Mere chance, you say, that these results should coincide with the administration of the healing rites? I used to think so too, but I have seen too many such cases to write them off as mere coincidences.

The healing work of the Sacraments

So many healings of this sort raise the interesting question as to whether the healing sacraments serve always as mere symbols, mere psychological aids. Could so many seemingly miraculous recoveries be ascribed to a symbol whose meaning a tiny baby, or an unconscious man, or a schizophrenic beyond reason, could not possibly comprehend?

Many theologians of all churches are now in agreement that the sacraments appear to have actual healing power, not of themselves, but according to, and dependent on, the attitude of the person who receives them. Here again, it is a question of faith, somewhere. Obviously patients like the three just mentioned, are incapable of believing anything at all with the conscious mind; but the faith of the Church, or the clergyman, or the attendant family or friends, can supply that belief which is necessary to convert a symbol into an active agent of transforming power—an energy which frequently appears to penetrate into the unconscious or subconscious mind.

Dr. John Ellis Large, who is conducting a notable healing ministry at the Church of the Heavenly Rest in New York City, casts considerable light on the function of the sacramental rites when he says: "I believe that this is a Sacramental universe and that pure spirit is utterly without meaning unless it is incarnate. Even the handshake, the kiss, the pat on the back, takes pure spirit and translates it through our physical bodies."

As the handshake, then, is the physical act by which friendship is expressed, the Sacraments are the physical means by which God's power is conveyed.

These sacramental rites are not essential for healing. It is by simple faith that we reach God, and by earnest prayer that we receive His power in our lives. However, as the Reverend John Gaynor Banks, founder of the Order of St. Luke, has so often emphasized, God is a respecter of *conditions*. Whatever your feeling concerning the actual power inherent in the sacramental acts, it is undeniable that for many they help immeasurably in providing the *occasion* for healing; that they seem to create peculiarly favorable conditions for the operation of the Holy Spirit.

No one church is wholly responsible for the present revival of spiritual healing, but from the beginning the Episcopal Church has led the way. The Reverend Richard Rettig, of St. Peter's United Church of Christ, Pittsburgh, who is himself conducting a remarkable healing ministry, says: "We all owe a tremendous debt to the Episcopal Church, which has demonstrated how the healing ministry could and should be made a part of the normal ministry of every church. As more and more churches are following her lead, Divine healings are no longer exceedingly rare occurrences, but can be *expected* as the result of obedience to Our Lord's Commission."

Clergymen of all denominations have noted the effectiveness of the Episcopal Church—a sacramental church —in the healing field and have eagerly studied her methods. They find them to be based on those of the primitive Church, where healing of the body was considered as vital a church function as the forgiveness of sins. In recognition of the fact that the laying-on-of-hands and anointing are New Testament-authenticated healing techniques, most non-liturgical churches have adopted these same sacramental rites with outstanding results.

Several ministers of non-ritualistic churches to whom I have spoken have expressed concern as to how their congregations, not raised in the sacramental tradition, would accept the sacramental healing methods. A glance at the backgrounds of the communicants attending Episcopal healing services has reassured them; for at most such services members of non-liturgical churches outnumber the Episcopalians. These laymen, as well as their clergy, apparently have no difficulty in accepting the historical precedent of the Sacraments. They recognize in them methods instituted by Our Lord Himself.

Points of contact with God

Spiritual energy, like electric power, is released at a point of contact. The Sacraments seem to serve as extraordinarily strong points of contact with God, through which His divine energy is released in our lives. They make the connection which releases a spiritual light so bright that it may illuminate the soul of a mere bystander who happens to be within its arc.

Take the case of a friend of mine, a newspaper reporter. Last year during Lent he attended a noon service at a downtown church, which, to his surprise, was followed immediately by a healing service.

"I didn't have to be back at my desk for another half

hour," he said, "so out of curiosity I decided to stay to find out what this was all about.

"I had never heard of the laying-on-of-hands, and when those who sought healing either for themselves or others, were invited up to the altar rail to receive this rite, I sneaked up to a front pew so as to see better how this, to me definitely peculiar, thing worked. I knelt in the pew so as not to be conspicuous, and watched out of the corner of my eye as the cleryman laid his hands on each head, saying over each supplicant a brief prayer.

"He was only half way down the line when there suddenly rushed through me the strongest conviction I have ever known of the actual Presence of God. For the first time in my life I *knew* beyond the shadow of any doubt that Jesus Christ *was*. This was so profound and exciting an experience that I was unable to return to work. I went home instead to tell my wife what had happened. Since then we've both joined a church for the first time in our lives."

When the Episcopal Church reactivated her healing ministry, dormant for centuries, but always an official part of her ministry, she followed explicitly the healing practice of the primitive Church. Not only does she emphasize the sacramental approach, but, as was also the custom of the early Church, she permits authorized laymen with the gift of healing recognized by St. Paul, (*I Corinthians 12:28*) to work under her supervision. The inspired interdenominational work of such outstanding lay healers as Episcopalian Agnes Sanford and Methodist Louise Eggleston has served to stimulate, encourage, and advance the healing ministry everywhere.

The effectiveness of this combination of charismatic and sacramental healing has been remarked by the clergy of all denominations. As the Reverend Dr. Dixon Rollit, who is conducting an outstanding healing ministry at Pittsburgh's Church of the Ascension, comments: "It is more than mere coincidence that as the use of these New Testament methods increases among our churches, so does the frequency of New Testament-like miracles of spiritual healing." This does not mean that every minister with a healing ministry uses the sacramental rites. There are some, like the Presbyterian pastor, William Holmes, who are conducting most effective ministries without their use.

The laying-on-of-hands

The Reverend Robert Young, also Presbyterian, is more typical of today's healing clergy, when he says: "I always lay on hands. It is a technique authenticated by Our Lord —one that He enjoined His disciples to use."

Mr. Young refers to the fact that the Church derives her authority for this rite from Jesus Christ, who repeatedly laid on hands to heal. "He laid His hands on every one of them, and healed them" *(Luke 4:40)*. "And He laid His hands on her: and immediately she was made straight" *(Luke 13:13)*. Not only did He use this method Himself, but He charged His disciples to do likewise: "And these signs shall follow them that believe," He said. "In my name shall they cast out devils. . . . They shall lay hands on the sick, and they shall recover" *(Mark 16:17, 18)*.

As His hands were the channels of divine healing power, so were the hands of His apostles *(Acts 28:8)*, and so are the hands of our healing clergy today. This rite has actually been in continuous use through the centuries as a means of conveying spiritual grace. Not only is it used in Confirmation and Ordination, but at every church service throughout the year; for the outstretched hands of the minister when he pronounces the benediction represent the imposition of hands, which in the early Church was individually administered to each communicant at the close of the service.

Holy Unction

While the laying-on-of-hands is a sacramental act, it may be used by certain spiritually-gifted laymen for healing. Holy Unction, however, is in a slightly different category. Not a sacrament in the sense of the two great Sacraments of Baptism and Holy Communion ordained by Our Lord, Unction is, nevertheless, an official Sacrament of the Church. As such it can be administered only by an ordained minister and received with some degree of preparation. This rite is also a New Testament-authenticated method which obviously had Our Lord's sanction, for under His direction the apostles "cast out many devils and anointed with oil many that were sick, and healed them" (*Mark 6:13*).

St. James actually initiated the format of today's healing Church when he said, "Is any sick among you? Let him call for the elders of the church; and let them pray over him, anointing with oil in the name of the Lord: And the prayer of faith shall save the sick, and the Lord shall raise him up; and if he have committed sins, they shall be forgiven him" (*James 5:14–15*).

In the early days of the Church, Unction was the Sacrament specifically intended for the healing of the body. It was as a result of the Church's growing failure to heal that the meaning of Unction changed from a healing Sacrament to the rite of Final Absolution.

In an attempt to explain her diminishing healing power, the Church began to teach what Dr. Weatherhead refers to as the "Will of God heresy." This is that God no longer willed to heal and was inflicting suffering and disease as a punishment for sin. As a result, Unction gradually lost its relevance to physical cure and became associated entirely with the forgiveness of sins. Early in the ninth century it became the Extreme Unction of the Roman Church. Dur-

ing the Reformation the Anglican Church officially restored the original use of Unction, but only on paper. It
remained an unused and virtually unread portion of the
Prayer Book until just a few years ago.

As a better understanding of spiritual healing has developed, and Unction is gradually losing its wide-spread connotation of death, more and more clergymen are reverting
to its use. Not only Episcopal priests but a growing number
of non-liturgical clergymen report that they regularly use
consecrated oil in their healing work. Even the Roman
Church has, in individual ministries, re-established the
original meaning of the Sacrament, with outstanding healing results.

Some ministers use the rite interchangeably with the
laying-on-of-hands, and others use it exclusively. However,
most clergymen with very large healing ministries attended
by diverse denominations, prefer to administer it only
when requested. They think that the meaning of Holy
Unction is not yet sufficiently well understood to attempt
its use in large, mixed groups. Methodist Dr. Albert Day,
who has only recently retired from one of the nation's most
outstanding healing ministries, voices the opinion of a
number of ministers, when he says: "I found that when
Unction was indiscriminately administered to people with
no understanding of the Sacrament, it tended to be more
of a distraction than a benediction. For this reason, I
anoint privately those who desire it."

Both the laying-on-of-hands and Unction have proved
to be enormously effective channels for the healing power
of the Holy Spirit. However, a good many clergymen report instances of healing which follow anointing, after the
imposition of hands has apparently failed.

A man suffering from tuberculosis, for example, had
sought healing for many months. While his condition did
not worsen, and spiritually he seemed improved, there was

no marked change in his physical condition. He finally asked for Unction, and was anointed one morning at ten o'clock. That afternoon was the first in over a year that his temperature did not rise. It remained normal, thereafter; his disease was declared arrested, and he returned to work in an unusually short time.

Another case was that of a woman whose gradually failing eyesight finally resulted in total blindness. Her doctors told her it was hopeless to expect any sort of cure. Believing in Christ's healing power, she received the laying-on-of-hands a number of times, with no apparent result. She was anointed at the altar, at her request. On her way home from the church, she suddenly regained her vision.

Confession

It may well be that the large number of healings which appear to result from Holy Unction are a result of the fact that the rite is so often preceded, at the clergyman's request, by confession. This, too, follows the custom of the early Church, where Unction was the Sacrament for physical cure, while the Sacrament of Penance was intended specifically for the healing of the soul.

The Roman Catholic Church has obligatory Confession; the Episcopal Church offers Sacramental Confession for any who desire it, in addition to the general confession which is provided by every Protestant denomination. As the healing of the body and spirit are interdependent, there seems little doubt that the efficacy of either healing rite is increased by confession, in whatever manner your church provides or your conscience dictates.

God is the healer

One of the great dangers in spiritual healing is the tendency of the patient to identify his healing with the healer instead of with God. The healing then becomes a "faith" cure instead of a spiritual one. This is a particularly great hazard of evangelistic ministries which the sacramental approach helps to avert.

The priest or minister has no personal power. He needs no healing "gift." His only "power" lies in the Holy tradition he represents. He is the dispenser of the Sacraments of the Christian Church purely by virtue of his priesthood and through no virtue of his own. Because his personality does not intrude between the supplicant and God, the true Source of healing is not easily misconstrued.

When the concept of spiritual healing is new to us and someone we know is healed under a particular ministry, even in the church, it is human nature to place great faith in that ministry. I remember, for example, how upset a friend was when the clergyman who had administered to my husband for a heart ailment was unavailable when her own husband suffered a similar illness. But as our understanding of the Sacraments increases, as we feel through them the Power that is "nearer than breathing; closer than hands and feet," we find ourselves gradually "growing out" of faith in a healer into faith in God.

But if the sacramental method helps us to place our eyes on God and not the healer, it can, conversely, lead us into the error of mistaking mere ritual for the road to heaven. The healing rites, indeed Baptism and Holy Communion, can be worthless gestures, meaningless symbols, blind superstition. It is only when they are received with some degree of comprehension, sanctified by faith and activated by prayer, that they become valid, power-charged instruments of the living Christ.

It may be that the sacramental way seems artificial or complicated to you. If it does, don't use it; for it certainly isn't essential. I have confirmed marvelous healings under evangelistic ministries. I have seen wonderful healings occur in churches without benefit of the Sacraments. I have also known remarkable healings to occur at home through prayer. God is always as close to us as the air we breathe. We know the verity of His promise, "Lo, I am with you alway." Yet within His healing Church there is concentrated unprecedented spiritual power. Here most of us can more easily reach out our hands and touch the hem of His garment. Christ came to give us life. Through His body, the Church, and through His arteries, the Sacraments, there is mediated to an extraordinary degree the healing power of the Risen Christ, which throughout the Gospels He has promised us.

Through the ancient rites of healing, used first by Our Lord, our sense of expectancy, our awareness of His love upon which our healing depends, are quickened. Through them our souls and hearts become receptacles for the grace and healing of Jesus Christ. He does not fail to fill them.

Healing for You and Yours— Preparation

HEALING for you and yours is there for the asking. Our Lord said, "Whatsoever ye shall ask the Father in my name, He will give it you" (*John 16:23*). Dare to claim that promise, and you can know its fulfilment.

That there is power in His words believed is not mere surmise. It is a fact as incontestable as that the world is round. You are not treading an unknown way, nor does any burden of proof lie with you. Just as you do not need to prove the efficacy of the wonder drugs, neither do you have to prove the healing power of God. Thousands before you have already done so.

Everyone is worthy of God's healing

A woman said to me the other day: "But who am I to claim His promises? I'm just not good enough to be healed."

Individual worthiness has nothing to do with it. Jesus came to save sinners, not saints. Your healing is not a reward for good behavior; it is a fulfilment of His will. No one can actually be worthy of the redemptive power of Christ. "By grace are ye saved. . . . It is the gift of God." (*Ephesians 2:8–9*). It is a free gift, rendered us according to our need, by a God "whose property it is always to have mercy."

If you are a Christian, you must believe that Christ came to redeem mankind. If you really believe this, you won't find it difficult to believe that if He still has the power to save your soul from sin, He also still has the power to heal your body.

No one knows better than I the difficulty of acquiring the sort of faith which will enable you unreservedly to believe the words of Our Lord. Yet it can be acquired, and nowhere else in the realm of human experience is the struggle so worth the goal. "And He will reward those who diligently seek Him" is one of the great understatements of the Christian faith. We are all the children of an infinitely loving and compassionate God. He "came not to judge the world, but to save the world" (*John 12:47*). He plays no favorites, but "maketh His sun to rise on the evil and on the good" (*Matthew 5:45*).

A blueprint for action in illness

A short while ago someone asked: "I believe in the will and power of God to heal, but this is all so new to me. Exactly what do you *do*, in the event of illness, especially when the best medical care seems unavailing?"

This is so common a question that to answer it I will blueprint a course of action which has proved enormously effective in scores of cases.

If you are physically able, attend healing services at a church. No matter how slight your knowledge or how small your belief, your presence in a church is a demonstrable act of faith on your part which Our Lord will honor. It is no longer necessary to travel to one of the great shrines, such as Lourdes, for *every* healing church is now a shrine, consecrated by the prayers of the faithful and hallowed by the presence of the Holy Spirit. In the fellowship of believers, in the atmosphere of expectant trust which pervades the healing church, you will find your own faith fortified and sustained, and you will grow in grace and understanding.

But the healing power of Christ is by no means confined to the altars of His Church. If you are physically unable to go to church, contact several churches with healing ministries, asking each one to pray for your healing. The illimitable power of corporate prayer is not conjectural, it is established fact. Although all prayer is beneficial, the prayers of those, clergy and laity alike, who uncompromisingly believe that God can and will cure the sick, have a unique healing power.

Next, if you or the patient is familiar with, and sympathetic to, the healing sacraments, ask for the laying-on-of-hands or Unction. If it is possible, notify a prayer group at what hour the sacramental rites are to be administered. Their prayers, offered simultaneously with yours and those of the officiating clergyman, will have tremendous power.

This power was demonstrated in the healing of a man with a carefully diagnosed stomach cancer. The patient's wife had been told by his doctors that one-third of his stomach would have to be removed. She had also been warned that owing to a serious heart condition her husband's chance of survival was extremely slim.

It was arranged that the patient receive the laying-on-of-hands an hour before surgery. A healing prayer group was so notified, and their prayers requested. The patient was wheeled to the operating room, serene and unafraid.

The surgeon found no trace of cancer. All evidence of the heart ailment had disappeared. "Only a Higher Power could have caused this healing," was the comment of the doctor. This healing occurred four years ago, and there has been no return of any symptoms.

If a patient is unfamiliar with the healing rites and might be either antagonistic to or frightened by their administration, the laying-on-of-hands may be received by others with special intention for the sick one. Such was the case of a physicist with a lung cancer diagnosed by X-ray, sputum analysis, and bronchoscope. Prayers for his recovery were offered by many different churches, and at least one novena was made.

On a certain Thursday morning at ten A.M. an entire prayer group attended, as a body, a healing service, receiving the laying-on-of-hands on behalf of the ill scientist. "Within an hour of this service," the erstwhile patient reports, "something strange happened to me. I was suddenly flooded with an ecstasy of joy. I felt a keen awareness of the actual Presence of God in my room, accompanied with a conviction that I would recover."

The anticipated surgery in this case was never undertaken, for all subsequent laboratory tests proved negative. The patient was able to resume work in a week, and has had no recurrence of symptoms after a period of three years.

Healing depends on you

But as important as are corporate and intercessory prayer, and as effective as is the receiving of the healing rites, the release of the full power of the healing Christ in your life depends on you and your ability or at least your attempt to meet certain conditions. Spiritual healing is filled with paradoxes. Miracles are wrought by faith, yet faith is often born through miracles. Spiritual regeneration effects physical healing, yet sometimes the physical healing occurs first. The spiritual change immediately follows as a result.

Some people are healed by faith alone, with no prior preparation; yet there is a great fundamental truth of spiritual healing which cannot be over-emphasized. Indeed, if there were but one key to God's healing power, this might well be it. It is your willingness to remain unhealed physically, if you can only know God. Nowhere is it more clearly illustrated than in spiritual healing that "Whosoever will save his life shall lose it: but whosoever will lose his life for my sake, the same shall save it" (*Luke 9:24*).

This is not an easy concept. To one who is in pain, the cessation of pain may seem to take precedence over everything else. When a loved one appears to be hopelessly ill, his physical recovery can seem the only thing that matters. Your belief that the soul's salvation is more important than the body's healing, can be acquired only by the help of God through prayer. If you are like most of us, it will be impossible for you continually to sustain this conviction. It will most probably come to you as a sudden revelation. It may not last, but that flash of truth is sufficient to cause a miracle.

It did in the case of a West Pointer doomed to live out his life as a cripple in continual pain from a shattered leg which repeated surgery had failed to heal. "As I received the laying-on-of-hands," he said, "I suddenly knew that the only thing that really mattered was that I find God. All at once the pain in my leg and the fact that my doctors had told me I'd never walk again without crutches, didn't seem to matter at all."

Within two days after this experience, he was completely without pain and was walking unassisted on the injured leg. He walks today with no sign of a limp. "This healing is the work of God," reports his stupefied orthopedic surgeon.

The wife of a business executive reports a similar experience. "I had been told by my husband's doctors that he could not recover from a grave kidney ailment. My husband didn't believe in spiritual healing, so I'd wait until he was asleep at night, then gently lay my hands on him and pray. My own faith was very weak, and all that seemed to matter was that his death somehow, some way, be staved off. Then one morning at about two A.M. I had a sudden flash of revelation that both he and I were closer to God than we had ever been before. I knew, for just a split second, the complete joy of standing on what seemed the threshold of His Kingdom. I experienced a sense of total conviction that death could never separate my husband and myself.

I slept then, and awoke for the first time in days without fear. My husband's condition dramatically changed for the better. Today, three years later, he is in perfect health."

Time and again it has been demonstrated that our best assurance of healing lies in the fullness of our realization that God's greatest gift to us is Himself. Unless we seek Him for His own sake, and not for His healing power, we may well be denied both.

Trust in God casts out fear

A woman with a seriously ill child remarked to me not long ago, "Everywhere in the healing ministry I hear people referring to the 'prayer of faith.' I wonder precisely what they mean. I believe that God can heal my little girl, but if I'm supposed to pray without fear, I might as well not pray at all. I can't *help* being afraid."

Neither can countless others who worry needlessly that fear will block the inflow of God's healing power. If human fear impeded healing, there would be today very little evidence of the operation of the Holy Spirit. While obviously we should have that complete trust in God which would cast out all fear, few of us do have it. But as Our Lord in His mercy understands our struggle for faith, so does He in His compassion comprehend our anxiety for those we love.

As for the "prayer of faith" it is a simple thing. It is talking to God as you would talk to your own earthly father, with implicit trust in His love for you and unfaltering confidence in His personal concern for your welfare. It is knowing in your heart what you say with your lips.

It is generally conceded that faith and the intellect have nothing to do with one another. Yet I have found that, for most of us, or minds must be reasonably satisfied with the concept of the healing Christ before we can take that final step which leads to our heart's acceptance of Him. The prayer resulting from the reconciliation of our mind's belief and our heart's faith is the means by which His power is set free in our lives.

Reconciliation with God

How can you effect this reconciliation? Give Him just thirty minutes a day of your time, and He will do the rest. He is only waiting for you to take that one step, however tentative, in His direction. His outstretched Hands are ready to clasp yours.

Select a time and place where you can be relaxed and undisturbed. At night, in bed, is a particularly good time, for then the subconscious can take over when you sleep.

Begin by reading one of the accounts of healing in the Gospels (listed at the end of this book), for this is one of the surest methods of discovering and believing the healing Christ. "Faith cometh by hearing, and hearing by the word of God" (*Romans 10:17*). Listen well, so that you may know exactly what it is you seek. In our anxiety to acquire faith, we often confuse faith with its object, mistaking the means for the end. We speak of "healing by faith," but it is not faith which heals. It is Jesus Christ. No one was ever healed by his own laboriously achieved belief.

As you read, note how clear a distinction Our Lord makes between involuntary sickness and disease, which He so often refers to as "works of the devil," and voluntary suffering, or the bearing of the cross for His sake. You cannot help seeing the emphasis he places on physical healing. The implication of healing with the Kingdom and the interrelationship of the two cannot escape you.

"And He sent them to preach the kingdom of God, and to heal the sick" (*Luke 9:2*).

"Heal the sick . . . and say unto them, The kingdom of God is come nigh unto you" (*Luke 10:9*).

"And as ye go, preach, saying, The kingdom of heaven is at hand. Heal the sick, . . . raise the dead, cast out devils" (*Matthew 10:7–8*).

'If I with the finger of God cast out devils, no doubt the kingdom of God is come upon you" (*Luke 11:20*).

Reflect for a moment on these statements. Has God changed His mind about what constitutes the kingdom? If so, then He is a changeable God, *not* the same yesterday, today, and forever. Has Jesus, the Christ, lost His desire and capacity to heal? If so, then He has withdrawn His commission to His Church to "preach the Gospel to every creature . . . lay hands on the sick, and they shall recover" (*Mark 16:15, 18*). I think you will agree that this is a highly irrational assumption.

How to banish doubts

At this point, if you have any lingering doubts as to God's will to heal you, bring them out in the open and face them. Ask yourself what may seem an irrelevant question: Do you believe in doctors? Haven't you always tried to obtain the best medical care for your family and yourself? If your answer is in the affirmative, and at the same time you question God's will to heal you, you have presented yourself with an irreconcilable inconsistency. Do you honestly believe that you are going against the will of God when you consult your doctor? Do you really believe that all hospitals, doctors, and nurses are flouting His will in their battle against disease and suffering? In the obvious answer to this question, I believe you will find your answer to what God wills for you.

Now consider some of the many promises He made you: "He that believeth on me, the works that I do shall he do also; and greater works than these shall he do; because I go unto my Father" (*John 14:12*). "If we ask any thing according to His will, He heareth us" (*I John 5:14*). "Ask, and it shall be given you; seek and ye shall find; knock, and it shall be opened unto you" (*Luke 11:9*).

Consider whether you believe *anything* that Christ said in the Gospels. If you do, why should you disbelieve the promises He made you? Remind yourself how unthinkingly you place your trust in those around you. If your bank promises three per cent interest on your savings, don't you believe it? If your grocer promises delivery of your order in time for dinner, don't you believe him? If a friend promises to do an errand for you, don't you assume that he will keep his word? Is Jesus Christ less reliable than your banker or your grocer or a casual friend?

Shut the door of your mind now, and silently repeat: "Be still, and know that I am God" (*Psalms 46:10*).

"They that wait upon the Lord shall renew their strength" (*Isaiah 40:31*).

"All things are yours" (*I Corinthians 3:21*).

Rest now for a moment in the comfort of the greatest of all His promises, which you are already beginning to realize: "I shall never leave thee nor forsake thee. . . . Lo, I am with you alway, even unto the end of the world" (*Matthew 28:20*).

Don't worry about your faith, or try to compute it. If you have come this far in an effort to find the healing Christ, you are already within His touch; for "ye shall . . . find me, when ye shall search for me with all your heart" (*Jeremiah 29:13*).

The door of your soul is opening. God is entering in.

You are ready now to pray your healing prayer.

Healing for You and Yours— Healing Prayer

WALK with firm steps to the throne of God. Ask for your healing, not hesitantly nor shyly, but boldly and positively. Remember that you are aligning yourself with God against the forces of evil. You are affirming His will. Do it in a strong, courageous manner.

If you pray for yourself, ask forgiveness for those sins of which you are guilty. Make as certain as you can that your contrition is honest, that you are sorry, not because your sin is hurting you by blocking you from God's benefits, but because your sin is hurting Christ.

Praying for others

If you pray for another, quietly repeat the name of the

person for whom you seek healing. It is important that you visualize the patient entirely well, completely whole, vibrant with His life. If your prayer is for a loved one, ask that Christ's power cleanse the patient of resentment, hostility, hatred, false pride and all other sin.

Visualize Our Lord in the sick room, laying His Hands on the patient; or, if you prefer, mentally hold the patient up to God for healing.

"Let Your healing Light flood every organ of this body; your Love permeate its every cell," might form the basis for your prayer. "Fortify my faith, Oh Lord, strengthen my trust in thee. In the Name of Jesus Christ, I ask and claim this healing."

Use any words you wish. The important thing is to ask and to be confident of His will, for by confidence your faith is released. Ask, expecting the healing, for by your expectancy, His power is liberated.

Whatever else you do, make sure to end your prayer with thanksgiving for the healing, believing it already accomplished. This conviction of victory, even before it is ostensibly realized, is the essence of all faith and prayer, and the root of Christian healing. "As thou hast believed, so be it done unto thee" (*Matthew 8:13*). Jesus has left us no room for speculation on this point, which He so dramatically illustrated at the tomb of Lazarus. You recall His great prayer of faith while Lazarus *still lay dead:* "Father, I thank thee that thou hast heard me" (*John 11:41*).

Our Lord did not wait until Lazarus was restored to life before He prayed His thanks. As certainly as He gave us the Lord's Prayer, so did the Son of God give us the key to healing when He said, "What things soever ye desire, when ye pray, believe that ye receive them, and ye shall have them" (*Mark 11:24*).

To believe you have received before you see the evidence is the crux of faith. It is one of God's conditions, not only for healing, but for all His blessings.

This sort of faith is progressive. It can be cultivated through prayer. It increases as your awareness of the reality of the healing Christ grows. Conversely, your awareness of Him quickens through increased faith—a faith which gradually accepts the promise that "with God all things are possible"—and goes courageously forth to claim it.

Conclude your prayer with praise for the victory, "being fully persuaded that, what He had promised, He was able also to perform" (*Romans 4:21*). Thank God, knowing that you are healed.

Pray your healing prayer. Then commit the patient to God, convinced of His healing will and loving care. A common tendency, when we are worried about someone close to us, is to repeat endlessly: "God, please heal him." Prodding God's memory with parrot-like repetition is not necessary; it does not constitute a power-filled healing prayer. Pray your prayer once a day, and leave the patient in God's Hands.

To believe that you have received healing before it is evident does not mean that you should stop praying. In all but one of the recorded New Testament miracles, the healings were instanteous. I have seen many marvelous instant healings, but today the majority are gradual. The faith of the Church as a whole is still weak, and the spiritual stature of most of us is still small. If you are not healed at once, continue your daily devotions. Attend healing services faithfully, and receive the sacramental healing rites at regular intervals. As you grow in understanding, and as your spiritual perception quickens, you can expect your physical ailment to respond to His great healing power.

Jesus said that "men must always pray and not give up" (*Luke 18:1,* Goodspeed). I have on file many cases like that of a World War II veteran who, according to medical opinion, had been hopelessly and permanently crippled by a landmine explosion. He began to attend the weekly healing services in his local church seven years ago. It was nearly four years before his physical healing was complete.

God hears all prayers

A great many people say that they find it difficult, if not impossible, to pray for themselves. A man suffering from extreme hypertension put it like this: "I feel guilty praying for myself, there are so many worse off than I am." This is a typical reaction which all of us may share to some extent. Being human, we tend to limit God. We're afraid that if we "bother" Him by asking healing for ourselves, we'll cheat others who may need Him more.

But the greatness of God cannot be confined to our human concepts. His Presence and power are limitless and indivisible. To each one of us who seek Him, He is *wholly* there in His full majesty and power. When we accept Him in our hearts, we receive the full God. We are depriving no one else. Just as television brings simultaneously to millions the same picture, the same personality, the same voice, so is God present simultaneously to every individual in the whole world.

Therefore, in the case of our own illness, we should attempt to pray for ourselves as best we can.

Bishop Austin Pardue comments: "I feel very sorry for anyone who does not consistently seek help from the Lord. The person who does not pray for himself is missing contact with the source of all power."

We will find additional help in asking the prayers of others. Most of all we will be aided by attending healing services. We will discover at the altar of our church that it is no more difficult to receive the sacramental rites for our physical healing than to receive Holy Communion for our spiritual regeneration.

Fasting

Numerous people wonder about fasting in connection with healing. Fasting and prayer have always gone hand in hand. Jesus used it in His healing work (*Mark 9:29*), and there is frequent reference to fasting in connection with the healing ministry of the early-post-apostolic Church. The value of fasting in today's healing ministry has been demonstrated again and again. As an act of faith which quickens us spiritually, it makes us vastly more receptive to the Holy Spirit. It is certainly to be recommended before attending a healing service.

A young woman whose father (a medical doctor) suffered a serious ailment of his left eye decided to accompany her prayers for his recovery with an all-day fast. Prior to this decision both she and her father had prayed and attended healing services with no discernible physical result.

Late in the afternoon of the day she was fasting she was seized with an intolerably severe pain over her left eye. "It got so bad," she relates, "that I vowed I'd never fast again. At the end of an hour I was ready to give up and get something to eat, convinced that hunger was causing the headache. Then suddenly the pain stopped."

Unknown to her, at the time of the onset of her pain, her father was sitting in an ophthalmologist's office, awaiting a final examination before surgery on his eye. Suddenly he felt his diseased eye begin to water copiously. When the eye was examined twenty minutes later, no sign of the ailment remained.

Share the glad tidings

Because I believe that one of the great divine purposes of today's manifestation of the healing power is conversion; because I have seen the first faint glimmerings of faith so often fanned into flame by the witness of those healed, I believe that it is incumbent upon those who have felt His healing touch, to bear witness.

"And the things that thou hast heard of me among many witnesses, the same commit thou to faithful men, who shall be able to teach others also" (*II Timothy 2:2*).

But witness with care. Don't make careless claims of divine healing. Don't talk incessantly of what God has done for you, or you place yourself in the same category as the bore who talks of nothing but his operation. With dignity and circumspectness, do as He asked: show "how great things God hath done unto thee" (*Luke 8:39*).

Probably through the witness of others you yourself found the healing Christ. Don't withhold the great truth you have discovered.

"If ye continue in my word, then are ye my disciples indeed" (*John 8:31*). As such, and with deep concern for the spiritual welfare of others, share the glad tidings.

The power of Jesus' name

A few months ago a woman asked me: "Suppose someone is taken suddenly and violently ill, say, with a heart attack. Suppose that you believe in the power of God to heal, but know practically nothing of spiritual healing, and are in no way prepared to pray a powerful prayer of faith. What can you do?"

I answered her with the story of a woman whose husband had recently suffered a coronary attack. It was his second attack, and because of the severe heart damage resulting from the first, suffered three years before, the cardiologist had predicted that another such attack could well prove fatal.

"Tom woke me about three A.M. gasping for breath, sweat pouring down his face from the awful pain in his chest and elbows. I was much too frightened to pray a real prayer; but while I was waiting for the doctor, I knelt by my husband and placed my hands lightly on his chest. Then I seemed instinctively to make the Sign of the Cross while I repeated the words; 'In the name of Jesus, let him be healed.' Almost at once his pain diminished and he grew less fearful. By the time the doctor arrived a few minutes later, Tom seemed remarkably like himself. The doctor sent him to the hospital where oxygen and emergency medication would be at hand. The next day heart X-rays and a series of cardiograms were ordered. Not only did the new lab tests indicate no additional damage—there was no evidence of the original infarction!"

So many cases of this nature have given rise to the question: "Is there actual power in the Name of Christ?" In the middle of the twentieth century this seems a fantastic idea. Yet so impressive has been evidence of this power that a group of scientists in England, headed by several eminent British doctors including a well-known Roman Catholic surgeon, have engaged in experimental studies in which they claim to have demonstrated that when the Name of Jesus Christ and the Sign of the Cross are used in healing, a marked and instantaneous difference in the radiations emanating from the patient's body can be detected.

That there should be actual power in the Name of Christ is not so incredible as it appears at first glance, when we realize that today's healing ministry is based so closely on the New Testament and early post-apostolic Church methods, with many of the same results. We are told by St. Luke that "the seventy returned again with joy, saying, Lord, even the devils are subject unto us through Thy Name" (*Luke 10:17*). In the writings of the Church Fathers in the second and third centuries, there is repeated reference to the "power in the Name"; the fact that "The Name of Jesus taketh away disease" (*Origen*).

To anyone who has closely observed the healing ministry at work today, this same power is clearly discernible.
Obviously it does not lie in meaningless repetition of a
word which may induce a sort of hypnosis. Nor does it re-
side in the vain reiteration of a syllable, utilized as a kind
of magic incantation. The power in the Name is in its use
as an outward expression of our inward (and perhaps subconscious) acceptance of Him as the source of all love, all
life, and all power. All the spiritual preparation I have
suggested is that you may know this truth with your heart.
This is all you need to know to find the healing Christ.

The stones in the structure of your faith are your conviction that God wills your health; that physical healing is as
much a part of Our Lord's ministry of salvation today as
when He walked the earth; and that God's promises are
meant for *you*. Their realization depends only on your
courage to claim them for yourself.

Remember that "All things are possible to him that believeth" (*Mark 9:23*).

Remember that it is in your quest for God, and your
hunger for His Kingdom, that you will find the healing
Christ.

Above all, remember this: You were saved by Our Lord
on the Cross. You have only to receive and claim that salvation. He, long ago, made you a promise: "If ye shall ask
anything in my name, I will do it."

Ask now, in the Name of Jesus, for your healing. He will
honor your faith.

How to Stay Well

IT IS AN infinitely wonderful thing to be healed by the
power of God, but it is even more wonderful to remain
well.

Most of us tend to seek God's healing power only when we and our doctors are at the end of our ropes. This use of the healing ministry makes it a ministry of desperation, of last resort, which it should not be.

As far as physical healing is concerned, you should seek God's help at the onset of illness. You should not hesitate to call your clergyman when sickness strikes, any more than to call your doctor. Time and time again there have been remarkable results when the medical profession and the clergy work concurrently—not only in cases of dire illness such as cancer or tuberculosis or a severe coronary, but in less dramatic ailments.

Take, for example, the case of a young man with a severe stomach ulcer, whose doctor had prescribed two weeks of hospitalization, and six months of drastically curtailed activity. Immediately after the diagnosis of ulcer was made, the patient received the laying-on-of-hands with prayer. After six days in the hospital, X-rays showed the ulcer completely healed.

Or take the case of a woman with a torn muscle in her arm, whose orthopedist placed the limb in a cast for two weeks, advising that at the end of this time, an intensive program of therapy, exercise, and massage would be necessary. Prayers were immediately held, and the laying-on-of hands administered. When the cast was removed, the arm was healed, and no further treatment was indicated.

Healing of nervous and emotional difficulties are also greatly expedited by the cooperation of medicine and clergy, as in the case of a young woman suffering from a profound nervous exhaustion, who was literally too tired to raise her arms to comb her hair. Her neurologist's prognosis: recovery would take at least a year of rest and treatment. The outcome after attending four healing services with a friend: a complete return to her former energetic self within a month.

Mistaken medical prognosis? Sheer coincidence? Doctors familiar with spiritual healing no longer think so. "We are beginning to realize," says Dr. Burnett Rae, "that spiritual healing is not an additional form of therapy to be tried when all else has failed, but is central to the whole problem of health and healing."

Spiritual healing not for sick alone

Because the ministry of healing is essentially spiritual in character, it is not just for the sick. It is for all who seek an inpouring of the Holy Spirit; for all who want to know Christ better and to love Him more; for all in search of peace of mind, and that rare spiritual treasure, peace of soul; for all who seek that abundant life He came to bring us.

Countless seekers have found the object of their search at the altar of the healing church. Just why there should be so vivid an awareness of the reality of Christ through the healing sacraments is a phenomenon that defies explanation. Yet that He is overwhelmingly present in the healing church is apparent to even the unbeliever.

Not long ago while walking with an electronics engineer, we passed a church well known for its healing ministry. I asked him to go in with me for a moment. He was a complete skeptic, but he reluctantly agreed.

No service was in progress, and the church was entirely empty. We sat in a back pew for a few moments, in silence. Then the man turned to me and said, with excitement in his voice: "There's some strange power in here. I can feel it, like electricity. What is there in this church?" The answer to that question? Christianity.

So impregnated with power is the healing church that it is not at all unusual for healing to occur while a patient prays in an edifice devoid of minister or congregation, but full of the Holy Spirit.

If a healing of cancer or diabetes can occur in an empty church by virtue of the Holy Spirit, it is not strange that our nervous tensions, anxieties and fatigue are successfully dissolved by this same recreating power so abundantly in evidence during a healing service.

Healing services strengthen faith

For most of us, the battle for faith is a continuing one—the price we pay to reach His throne. I remember when a clergyman with an outstanding healing ministry said to me: "You know, for months after I had started healing services, I had to fight for faith. Even now, although I have seen many miracles of healing, my subconscious and conscious minds still occasionally war. But each time I lay on hands, I feel again the full impact of His Presence."

In my own case, even after I had seen with my own eyes and had had verified such marvelous evidence of God's healing power, I would often go home and feel the faith literally drain out of me. Often it was not fully restored until I went again to a healing service. It is through the inspiration of the healing church and the massed faith of believers that our own faith is inevitably strengthened and rekindled. Indeed it is even born, if the desire for faith is there.

But the healing ministry does more than revive our faltering faith. Because of the tangible evidence it provides that God lives today; because of the demonstrable proof it offers that He is a God of mercy and love, who relieves our suffering whether mental, physical, or spiritual, the teaching of His Son acquires for us a new relevance and validity. We gain a new and thrilling insight into all the aspects of His ministry. We are aware at last of the vast difference between knowing *about* Our Lord, and knowing *Him*. The historical Jesus has become for us the living, pulsating Christ, who metamorphoses our lives.

Illumined by new knowledge, the Gospel of Our Lord is revealed in all its power. We recognize, as surely as did the apostles and the early Christians, the good news brought us by the Son of God: that He came not to save bodies and not to save souls, but to save men. We know the truth at last, and the truth has indeed set us free.

Because the radiance of the healing Christ has cast a new light of comprehension over all of Christianity, we are able to receive the *full* faith, through which we are assured we may inherit all His promises (*Hebrews 6:12*).

Healing power in Baptism and Communion

Take, for example, the tremendous healing power inherent in two great Sacraments ordained by Our Lord, Baptism and Holy Communion. Our awareness of the living, healing Christ has transformed these often casually received rites into instruments of breath-taking regenerative power—physical as well as spiritual.

We find that "Be baptized . . . and ye shall receive the gift of the Holy Spirit" is not an idle promise of indiscernible spiritual benefit. We note that scores of adults have received healing after the administration of this Sacrament.

The Reverend Edgar Sanford, with a healing ministry of long duration, has baptized many critically sick infants, for whom no hope of recovery was held. Not one of these baptized babies died.

So many healings have followed the administration of the Sacrament of Holy Communion, although it is not a specific healing rite, as to suggest that it may actually be the greatest of all healing Sacraments. When the Lord's Supper is received with a fuller understanding of the healing Christ and the totality of His redemptive mission, it takes on a new and profound significance. It becomes fraught with the power of His redeeming Presence—the power which heals both body and soul.

Our Lord's assurance that "He that eateth my flesh, and drinketh my blood, dwelleth in me, and I in him" (*John 6:56*) takes on a new trenchancy as we realize that through Holy Communion we and His whole Church receive not only the "remission of sins and all other benefits of His passion" (*Book of Common Prayer, page 81*), but His Incarnate Life.

Our personal relationship with God is the most vital of all our relationships. It demands much the same expenditure of time and effort on our parts as the establishment and maintenance of our human relationships. To *make* friends, for example, we must spend time with people so that we may learn really to know them. To keep friends, we must exert the effort to visit with them, or we lose contact and our sense of closeness with them. So it is with God. The aim and purpose of spiritual healing, is to build our lives in harmony with His will. Prayer and meditation are the means by which we learn to know God better and achieve this harmony.

Prayer maintains health.

How, through God, can you remain well? How can you be free from physical disease and free from the tensions and harassments which beset most of us in these times? If prayer is a vital factor in healing, it is equally vital in maintaining full and vibrant health.

Donald Robertson, M.D., writes in a recent article in *The Christian Century*: "Prayer promotes maturity and eliminates neuroses and neurotic behavior. When we surrender our lives to God, the old physical machine can turn off its defenses. Blood pressure drops, digestion is re-established, tensions dissolve, and normal sleep returns. That is why I, as a physician, assign such an important place to prayer in relationship to the problem of health."

Many of us have long dismissed the "practice of the

Presence of God" as a spiritual exercise indulged in only by the cloistered religious. But no matter how religiously illiterate you may be, when you have once felt this Presence at a healing service, you will no longer be content without it. The Kingdom has already been planted in your heart.

Meditation will no longer seem the pastime of a few religious, but the means of bringing Him into your life so that you will know the exaltation of His continued nearness.

Daily prayer will no longer consist of a hasty ritual, mumbled before you fall asleep. It will be the treasured means by which you can learn to know and experience God—the means by which His power is released in your life, and by which He enters in.

What, you may wonder, will be the factual results of His Presence in your life? Here are some: you will never again know loneliness; your fears and your anxieties will disappear, for they cannot coexist with the living Christ. In Him and through Him, you will find as He promised, the "peace which passeth all understanding."

Praying effectively

How do you meditate and pray? There is no single way, but here is one which is simple and effective:

The first thing to do is to delegate a portion of time each day for quiet devotions. Whether it is fifteen minutes or an hour or two, observe it every day.

Start with a comparatively short period every day, increasing it as you may desire. This is better psychologically than to set aside a large segment of time, and find yourself gradually decreasing it until you may omit it altogether.

For the sake of convenience, divide your devotional period into two sections, one of meditation and one of prayer.

Begin the first part by relaxing comfortably in a chair.

Close your eyes, and try to realize that you are in God's Presence. Repeat, aloud or silently, one or more of the following texts: "Be still my soul" or "My strength is in thy might" or "I shall not fear" or "Lord, increase my faith" or "My peace I give unto you." Say these words slowly, thinking carefully about what you are saying.

Now read one chapter from the New Testament. Read consecutively so that in time you will have read the entire New Testament. In this way you will learn to know better the mind of God.

Read slowly a psalm such as the Twenty-third, which will increase your inner peace; or the Ninety-first, which will add to your trust. Throughout your reading, stop at intervals, and contemplate His nearness to you, remembering His words: "If a man love me . . . my Father will love him, and we will come unto him, and make our abode with him" *(John 14:23)*. Let the sense of His abiding presence wash over you.

Realize that you are always in the presence of God, for God is everywhere. Nevertheless you will have to *know* that you are in His presence before His power becomes available to you. This meditative, contemplative approach helps you to know; therefore devote as much time as you can to it, but not so much that your attention begins to wander. Even the few minutes spent as I have suggested, if persisted in daily, will increase your consciousness of God to the point that you know that He *is,* and that Christ dwells in your heart. Your spiritual perception will be quickened, and that spark of the divine which is in you will be released with remarkable results in your life.

Much as I dislike the word "technique" in connection with prayer, it is undeniable that there is a technique that when followed achieves results.

In addition to the Lord's Prayer (which should be said every day) there are other specific kinds of prayer. The prayer of faith for healing is not the same as the prayer for guidance, through which we strive to learn His will. The prayer of worship is different from the contemplative prayer in which we attempt to enter the Presence.

A framework for prayer

For those who want to pray, but are not sure how; or for those who have prayed for years but would like to pray more effectively, I suggest the following framework, which includes the five essential points of prayer. By daily adherence to this general pattern, you can realize in your life the illimitable power of prayer.

1. ADORATION: Begin your prayer by a recognition of the Holiness of God. A great physiologist says: "The most ignored mental activity which gives strength to personality, and power to prayer, is a sense of the Holy: this God so approachable to him who knows how to love is hidden from him who knows only how to understand."

All prayer should begin, as does the model prayer, in an atmosphere of reverence and love. To worship and to love is an instinctive human need. You will not find it difficult to worship your God. "Hallowed be thy Name." Repeat this phrase slowly. Then follow it with "Praise ye the Lord" or "Praise the Lord, O my soul, and all that is within me" or "Holy, Holy, Holy, Lord God of Hosts. Heaven and earth are full of thy glory."

2. CONFESSION or PENITENCE: You are in the Presence of God, of complete holiness. Ask Him, with humility, for forgiveness and believe that you receive it. You have been told on good authority that a contrite heart is the only requisite for absolution.

3. INTERCESSION: Intercessory prayer has been called the purest form of prayer. Bishop Everett Jones aptly terms it, "Love on its knees." Here you are holding up to God, for His help and healing, those who are sick or op-

pressed. Pray for those close to you whom you love, and ask that they go their ways, continually surrounded and protected by the might and love of Christ.

Then pray for the sick in mind, body, and spirit all over the world, asking that the healing hands of Christ be unfettered by the power of believing prayer. Pray that this power shall be realized in its full glory, unimpeded by doubt and unweakened by skepticism, touching all who are in need. End your intercession with a prayer for the belief of the unbelieving Church. For when the full faith of the whole Church is universally restored, the Kingdom will be clearly discernible, and we will know a foretaste of heaven.

4. PETITION: We come now to the time when we may voice our own needs to God. For many of us, this has been the first and last prayer we have ever learned. While there is, of course, a definite place for our personal petitions, if we make this our *only* prayer, perpetually bombarding God with our personal demands, the result tends to be negative. When we keep our petitionary prayer in its proper context as one of the points to be covered in the prayer pattern, but not the only one, then it has power. When we pray carefully, certain that what we ask is not in conflict with His will and confident that Christ knows and understands our needs, whether they be physical, material or spiritual, we may expect fulfilment of our requests.

5. GRATITUDE: Express now, as well as upon awakening and upon going to bed and continually throughout the day, your gratitude to God for those countless blessings He has bestowed upon you. Your wife, your husband, your children, your sight, your hearing, your health, a good meal, a lovely day. There is never a time that you cannot find something for which to be grateful. Even if things seem to have piled up on you and you feel depressed wondering what on earth you have to be thankful *for,* you can at least offer thanks that things are not always so bad!

Let your gratitude be the underlying theme of your life. Let your thanksgiving for God; for His sacrifice for you on the Cross; for His forgiveness; for His intercession for you and yours, be the keynote of your worship.

St. Paul says: "In everything give thanks: for this is the will of God" (*I Thessalonians 5:18*). If you *do* make sincere thankfulness a way of life, you will find that something wonderful happens. You will have set in motion an infallible law of prayer. Your blessings will be added to in direct proportion to your gratitude for those already received. "Metaphysicians have discovered," writes Charles Fillmore, "that words that express thanks, gratitude, and praises, release energies of mind and soul; and their use is usually followed by effects so pronounced that they are quickly identified with the words that provoke them." Say these words with your lips and mean them in your heart, and you will prove the verity of this statement.

End your devotions with a short period of silence. For prayer is communion with God, not a monologue. You have talked to Him; now let Him speak to you. You are likely to find that you have never heard Him until now, not because He hasn't spoken, but because you haven't listened.

Your formal daily devotions are over, but your prayers are not. "Pray without ceasing" is the injunction of St. Paul. You will find that brief mental invocations throughout the day, such as "Holy, Holy, Holy" or "I laud and magnify thy Holy Name," or "Thanks be to God," are sufficient to hold you in His Presence. Say these or similar short prayers on the bus, or in the office or at home, bearing in mind that this is not to remind God of *you,* but you of *God.*

You will find, as have so many others, that you will grow into prayer by praying, and come into the Presence through practice.

The actual words you say are immaterial. All that really

matters is what is in your heart. God recognizes your slightest impulse toward Him through prayer, and honors it. Your attempt, however feeble it may be in the beginning, to link yourself with His inexhaustible power will result in the restoration of your spirit and in the strengthening of your body. You will know at last, from personal experience, the full meaning of these words: "They that wait upon the Lord shall renew their strength; they shall mount up with wings as eagles; they shall run, and not be weary; and they shall walk, and not faint" (*Isaiah 40:31*).

Physical benefits from prayer

The spiritual benefits of prayer have long been known but it is largely through the healing ministry that we have become aware of its physical results. As long as there is sin in the world, there will be sickness. It is interesting to note, however, the improvement in health and the unusual maintenance of good health enjoyed by those associated with the healing ministry, either as laymen or clergymen. A Presbyterian attorney who became interested in the healing ministry some two years ago, voices the experience of innumerable people when he says: "I had all my life been subject to severe colds, throat infections, and sinus trouble during the winter months. I am convinced that it is more than coincidence that during the past two years I have not been indisposed, even for a day."

The experience of a mother with three youngsters is also typical. "For years I have been nervous and tired," she says, "and also terribly apprehensive about the children's health. But not any more. Through the healing ministry I have an entirely different concept of God. I know now that He wants them to be well, and that if they do get sick, He will heal them. The result has been that they have turned into the healthiest youngsters on our block, practically never have even colds. As for me, the days aren't long enough to do all I want to do. I sleep like a top and have forgotten what 'nerves' mean."

Realization of the healing Christ transforms our lives. It eradicates our fears, for we know that in His mercy, He will protect and heal us. It dispels our anxieties, for we know that in His compassion, He will guide us to a solution of our problems. It dissipates our tensions, for we know that we can unequivocally trust Him.

Confident of His love for us, we can rest and relax in the greatness of God. At last we have learned the joy of Christianity. "Joy to the world, the Lord has come," is no longer merely the opening line of a familiar hymn. It is a reality imbedded in our hearts. Joy invariably induces a salubrious physical reaction. Couple it with a sense of security in a God who cares; confidence in a God who heals; assurance in a God who protects; and jittery nerves, worry, and fear will be a thing of the past.

"I was almost a psychotic 'worrier,'" a business man told me. "But no more. My affairs and my whole life have taken an almost incredible turn for the better since I have learned to commit them to Him with perfect trust."

"Fear," a woman remarked to me, "is hell on earth. For years I was afraid of life. Finally, in my effort to escape it, I became an alcoholic. Two years ago I was instantly healed by the power of God. I am free at last. I have put my hand in His, and I can never be afraid again."

There are very few of us who will not find ourselves recipients of the fringe benefits of the Christian faith—health and joy—if we follow the simple prescription consisting of two ingredients: daily devotions and, if possible, weekly attendance at a healing service. For the Church, which is the Body of Christ and the extension of the Incarnation, is as indispensable as your private devotions.

Christianity is a communal affair. It is not the individual worshiping God alone, in his own way, although it is that, too. It is also joining in corporate worship; the refilling of your spiritual cup from the continuous spring of Christ's power so uniquely present in the Church. At a healing service you will be spiritually irradiated; exquisitely aware of the Presence who extends a personal and perpetual invitation: "Come unto me . . . and I will refresh you."

Bringing comfort to the comfortless, hope to the despairing, and the living Christ to all who seek Him, the healing Church is the shrine which welcomes, in His Name, the sick and the fearful, the sinful and the sorrowing, the weak and the spiritually hungry. You will find its altar the point of contact which electrifies and recharges your entire being, flooding your life with the incandescence of the Holy Spirit.

A Healing Ministry in Every Church

THROUGH the healing ministry I have seen those starving for the Bread of Life fed. Their hunger has been forever assuaged by the demonstrable evidence of the living God.

The scores of clergy with whom I have talked are in unanimous agreement that the healing ministry is the most dynamic and thrilling phase of their work. Many have confessed that it was in their administration of spiritual healing that they felt for the first time the undeniable Presence of Christ. Why, then, has not every church a healing ministry?

After talking to many ministers who are interested in healing, but have not yet begun services, I believe that their reluctance to enter the healing field personally is due more frequently to a misunderstanding of spiritual healing than to disagreement with its theological premise. I have noted that when the clergy more fully understand the healing ministry and that when they observe first-hand the administration of spiritual healing and its results, more and more institute healing services.

Faith healing not spiritual healing

Typical of these clergymen is one who a year ago objected that in spiritual healing too much emphasis is placed on physical healing. His protest is a common one, due to a prevalent misconception of spiritual healing. He was confusing it with faith healing, which, although the terms are often used synonymously, is not at all the same thing. The latter, accurately speaking, does not necessarily have anything to do with Christian healing. It need not be, and indeed it frequently is not God-based.

Dr. Alexis Carrel has noted that "extreme acceleration of the processes of organic repair can effect so-called miracles of healing." This acceleration can be caused by faith in anything—a healer, a doctor, a bottle of tonic. When a physical cure appears to result from this type of belief, the spirit is left untouched and unhealed. When cure comes as a result of prayer through the clergy who serve as channels for the healing power, and is accompanied by spiritual regeneration, it becomes the spiritual healing practiced by the Church.

The ministry of healing, with its roots in the Incarnate Christ, is above all a spiritual ministry. The term "spiritual healing" means far more than physical healing achieved by spiritual methods. It means a healing of the whole nature of man by the power and grace of Our Lord. When the soul and the spirit are healed, so usually is the body. Those who have been so healed have known the presence of the Lord in a special and wonderful way. Surely no clergyman who understands this can object. There can be no over-emphasis on the healing of sick souls and ailing spirits, for such has been the mission of the Church since the time of Christ.

When the clergyman I mentioned thoroughly understood the intent of the healing ministry, he instituted healing services. A few weeks ago he said to me: "I have learned that spiritual healing is a very, very spiritual ministry. If not one physical cure had resulted, which fortunately is not the case, I would institute a healing ministry wherever I was because of the extraordinary spiritual blessings it imparts, both to the minister and laymen."

Church support for healing ministries

Because healing is at once the newest as well as the oldest of the Church's ministries, it is necessarily the most immature. Handling the power of God is not a responsibility which can be lightly undertaken. We should be aware that the healing ministry is fraught with danger, as is every aspect of religion; but as we do not eschew the Christian faith because of its fanatics, neither should we shun spiritual healing because we fear its inevitable lunatic fringe. We must remain alert to the threat that the body's health may be over-emphasized to the exclusion of the spiritual, which could result in the perversion of the healing ministry into heresy. But the potential hazards inherent in spiritual healing constitute the most valid reason—the extreme necessity—for keeping the healing ministry within the Church where it belongs; where the theological aspects of health and wholeness may be continually impressed.

The New Testament preaches a Gospel of physical as well as spiritual redemption (*Romans 8:23*). To keep that Gospel in its proper proportion, it should be preached in the organized Church. If it is not, people will go where it *is* preached, and too often over-emphasized.

Jesus mediated His healing power to the Church. By fulfilling His commission in its totality—"Preach ye the Kingdom and heal the sick"—and by correlating the healing ministry into the total life of the Church, spiritual healing can be protected from distortion.

As the promulgator of the Christian faith and the fountainhead of the Holy Spirit, it is the Church which must safeguard the healing Power from degeneration into chicanery, and the operation of the Holy Spirit from prostitution into either psychic or "faith" healing. It is the Church which must serve as the perpetual reminder that it is the soul's conversion which is the greatest of all miracles, the one to be most avidly sought and the goal of true spiritual healing.

Vocation unnecessary for healing ministry

Two years ago I talked with a clergyman who voiced a misapprehension shared by many of his fellow theologians. "I firmly believe in spiritual healing," he said, "but I have no healing gift, no vocation."

No minister refuses to preach because he has no "vocation" for speaking. He does not refuse to counsel because he has no "vocation" for guidance. He does not refuse to organize fellowship groups because he has no "vocation" for organization. All these activities are part of his entire vocation to the Church's ministry. So is spiritual healing. No minister needs a special healing vocation, for every ordained man, by virtue of his ordination, has the power and authority to heal in the Name of Jesus Christ.

I saw this same clergyman a short while ago. He told me that soon after our first talk a woman came to him and asked to be anointed for healing. "I told her frankly that I knew nothing of the service, and had never seen Unction administered. She was so persistent that I finally told her

218 God Can Heal You

that if she would bring me a copy of the service the following week, I would borrow some consecrated oil."

The woman procured a manual from the Order of St. Luke, and received Holy Unction on the appointed day. She instantly healed. "At that moment," the minister commented, "I knew exactly what St. Peter meant when he said: 'Ye men of Israel, why marvel ye at this? . . . as though by our own power or holiness we had made this man to walk?'" (*Acts 3:12*).

Healing is only one of the ministries of the Church, but it is a vital one upon which the fruitfulness of the entire ministry seems to depend. More and more of the clergy are recognizing that, if the Christian faith is to be imparted in its entirety, healing must be restored as a normal part of every ministry.

The Reverend Albert Baller, a Congregationalist pastor trained in psychotherapy, speaks for many of today's clergy when he says: "My recently acquired knowledge of spiritual healing has caused me to do some careful revising of my thinking about the purpose of the Church and where the pastor's greater efforts should be placed. I am quite certain that we will be led, in the not too distant future, to make the spiritual healing services an important part of every church's total program."

Spiritual healing and counseling

Some ministers are concerned over what they believe to be the time-consuming element of the healing ministry. "I'm so busy already," said one, "that I simply can't undertake the extensive counseling I understand is necessary for spiritual healing."

Some healing churches emphasize counseling more than others, but many ministers have come to believe that in the effort to prepare patients for spiritual healing, the counseling aspect of this work has been over-emphasized. The

Reverend John Maillard, Anglican priest highly instrumental in the recovery of the healing ministry in England, states that no more and no less counseling is required for spiritual healing than for Holy Communion.

There is no indication that Jesus used the psychiatric approach in His healing ministry; likewise, many today who seem impervious to medical treatment are healed by the direct intervention of the Holy Spirit without benefit of counseling—healed not only of physical disabilities, but of mental and nervous disorders as well.

A homosexual, for example, who was unsuccessfully treated by psychiatry over a period of years, finally consulted his pastor. After two brief sessions, in which were explained the purifying, healing power of God's love, the patient began attending healing services. Within a few weeks he was completely well, and is now happily married.

Or take the scores of instantaneous and complete healings of alcoholism, which are taking place under the ministry of healing. Many of these cases have spent thousands of dollars on unavailing psychiatric care and futile hospitalization. Suddenly they respond to His healing touch. As one said: "I hadn't been inside a church for years. At my wife's pleading I went, with tongue in cheek, and received the laying-on-of-hands. Then and there I felt the real Presence of Christ, and at that precise moment I lost all desire for alcohol. That was five years ago. I haven't had a drink since, and what is even more wonderful, I haven't even wanted one!"

The clergyman, it should be understood, is a physician of souls, not of minds and bodies. He should no more be expected to psychoanalyze than to perform surgery. It is interesting that those with the largest and most notable healing ministries are forced to limit strictly the time they devote to counseling. St. Paul said: "I determined not to know anything among you, save Jesus Christ, and Him crucified" *(I Corinthians 2:2)*. This often proves to be all that is necessary to know today for healing.

Christ's power to heal unchanged

A Methodist minister states that he was taught in seminary and had for years unquestioningly believed that "miracles" were confined to the New Testament. "But in view of what I see happening," he says, "I am convinced that Christ is healing as surely today as He did during His earthly ministry."

There are many people, clergymen and laymen alike, who still honestly believe that Christ's healing ministry was not meant to continue into our time. It seems to me, however, that if this contention is followed to its logical conclusion, it must result in two things: first, a categorical denial of the historicity of the early Church, which was a healing church; and, second, a violation of what I understand to be a basic Christian tenet: the immutability of Jesus Christ, who is the same yesterday, today, and forever. If He is not the same today as He was yesterday, then He has changed—and change must be for the better or worse. Either Jesus was not perfect and has changed for the better; or He was perfect, and has changed for the worse. In either case, He could not be the perfect Son of God upon which our religion has been predicated.

"It was only recently that I realized this," remarked a young Presbyterian minister. "If His command to preach the kingdom and heal the sick was valid two thousand years ago, it must be equally valid today. If He has retained the power to save souls, it is hardly likely that He would have lost the lesser power to heal bodies."

Concerning the theological aspects of the healing ministry, the Reverend Richard Winkler of Chicago comments: "If a minister thinks spiritual healing theologically "wrong," let him step into a church where there is an active healing ministry and observe the saved souls and healed bodies that come about as a result. The practical effects are far more convincing than any theological arguments which may be expounded."

No failures in spiritual healing

Probably the most prevalent deterrent to the institution of healing services continues to be the fear of failure. Again and again the question is asked: "But what happens to a person's faith if he is not healed? Won't he then turn completely from God?" The answer is an unequivocal "No," as anyone with a healing ministry will testify. But this is something which can only be learned, and believed, after personal experience.

The Reverend Don Gross, who has had extensive experience in the healing field, speaks for the healing clergy, when he says: "We pray, expectantly and with the conviction that God intends health. Sometimes the people we pray for die, or the disease remains; but people who have undertaken prayer for spiritual healing do not become discouraged or rebellious. Knowing His yearning to bestow life and health, their love for God abundantly increases, and their faith is invariably strengthened through their prayers for healing."

Those who have earnestly sought spiritual healing are never left unhealed. If the body is not healed, the spirit is.

Take the case of a young nurse who discovered that she had an inoperable cancer. She attended a number of healing services, with no discernible physical improvement; but her serenity and obvious happiness were an inspiration to those who knew her. When weakness and pain finally forced her to bed, her minister administered Holy Unction twice a week. After the second week, her pain left; and, to the amazement of her doctors, she was able to discontinue the use of morphine.

The day she died, three months later, she said to her minister: "Neither God nor His Church has failed. I have had a revelation of His Kingdom. I know now that this is only the beginning of a fuller life."

Joyfully and confidently she went into the outstretched arms of Christ, having been blessed by a gift from God not often given to those on earth. His power had transformed her faith into knowledge, her hope into certitude.

Not only are there no "failures" in true spiritual healing, but many of the clergy consider it the most universally successful of all their ministries. As an Episcopalian priest comments: "When I think of the word failure in regard to my work, I never couple it with spiritual healing. I think of Baptism, for the country is filled with baptized pagans; or I think of Confirmation, for my parish is filled with lapsed communicants. But in spiritual healing, spiritual grace is *always* received. Where physical healing does not result, it is received to an extraordinary degree."

Experience indicates that there appears to be no basis for the fear on the part of those unfamiliar with the healing ministry that a patient who does not receive physical healing will be psychologically harmed; will tend to blame himself, or doubt the sincerity of his own faith. He realizes that as so-called failures to heal are not the fault of God, neither are they necessarily his. He knows that an unhealed body is no more the will of God than a sinful world, and that both are the result of human weakness, of corporate faithlessness, and mass disobedience. The gloom of centuries of unbelief cannot be instantly and universally dispelled; the thunder of man's doubt and misunderstanding cannot be immediately and wholly silenced.

Total health is the will of God

Nevertheless, the healing clergy, convinced that total health is the primary will of God and believing that Jesus is the Saviour of our bodies as well as our souls (*Ephesians 5:23*), are not relaxing their efforts to determine the cause of the physical failures of spiritual healing. Meanwhile they emphasize that while some unknown, alien factor may have hindered the healing of the body, nothing can impede God's healing of the spirit. Experience testifies to the magnificent truth, that none who turn to Him remain unhealed.

Never have I seen this more convincingly demonstrated than in an Episcopal Church where I happened to be speaking a few months ago.

After the service a pale, obviously ill man came up to me to tell me of his illness from which the doctors had given him one chance in a million of recovering.

"I have attended healing services for two months," he said, "and I've grown continually worse. What can I do?" Without waiting for an answer, he asked the question uppermost in the minds of all who are very ill. "Have you ever heard of a case like mine being healed?"

To know that someone has been healed of the same ailment from which we suffer is, understandably, a tremendous faith-booster. Happily I could give him an affirmative answer, as has been the case whenever this question is asked, for I believe that every disease known to modern man has responded to the healing power of God.

As I detailed the healing of a case similar to his, I saw the despair in his eyes replaced by hope. I observed that what appeared to be a purely intellectual assent that God could and would heal seemed now to tremble on the brink of emotional acceptance of that fact.

The result was that, after asking to make a sacramental confession, the first in his life, the patient was anointed at ten-thirty that night at the altar of a church filled with the power of the Holy Spirit. A spiritually transformed man walked down the altar steps at the conclusion of the service. The expression in his eyes, the indefinable but unmistakable radiance about him must have been remarked by even the most skeptical. To the believers there seemed no doubt that he had been touched by the healing Hand of Christ.

"I've never felt such peace and joy," he said. "It doesn't matter now whether my body is healed or not. I've found something better than physical health."

When I left the city that night I had no idea whether or not his disease had been cured, but I knew that he had been marvelously healed. I have learned since that this man has completely recovered his health.

Only a few years ago, a religious healing was a rare occurrence. Today the statistics offered by the Reverend Alex Holmes, English Congregationalist, are, as nearly as I can ascertain, typical. This great young leader of the healing ministry in the Free Churches in Britain, states that forty per cent seeking help under his ministry, are completely healed, forty per cent greatly benefited and the remaining twenty per cent, although not physically helped, are spiritually aided to an outstanding degree.

God lives in the healing ministry

As the healing ministry expands, and the faith of the whole Church quickens; as the discordant voices of doubt diminish, and more and more Christians turn to Our Lord, daring to claim His promise that all who ask in His Name shall receive (*John 14:13*), we see that complete healings are occurring in ever-increasing number. Those long deaf now hear His voice with unprecedented clarity; and those long blind perceive with new insight the meaning of His words: "He that believeth on me, the works that I do shall he do also; and greater works than these shall he do" (*John 14:12*).

All men everywhere have longed for the definite assurance, the concrete evidence that God lives. We have it now in the healing ministry which has made the good news of the Gospel a reality.

We are fully aware that "blessed are those who have not seen and yet have believed." But we remember, too, that Our Lord did not withhold from His doubting disciple the proof of His identity. "Reach hither thy hand, and thrust it into my side," He said to Thomas, "and be not faithless, but believing" (*John 20:27*).

And so, today, a merciful God has had compassion on us of little faith. He again offers us the evidence of His mighty acts, "that ye might believe that Jesus is the Christ, the Son of God; and that believing ye might have life through His name" (*John 20:31*).

Through this evidence I have seen countless unbelievers brought to God. I have seen the passive belief of thousands of nominal Christians blaze into flaming faith. Wherever the healing ministry is in effect, I have seen the spiritual life of the community immeasurably strengthened; the spiritual power of the Church inestimably enhanced.

Because of these things, it seems to me that it is the holy obligation of the Church, and the sacred duty of the believing laity, to create a universal awareness of the healing Christ—an awareness before which a troubled, searching world must fall to its knees, echoing the words of Thomas, "My Lord and My God."

"When Two or Three Are Gathered Together"

OUR LORD promised us that, when two or three are gathered together in His Name, He will grant their requests.

Thousands of prayer groups, not only in the United

States but all over the world, are claiming this promise with magnificent results. These groups are part of the growing laymen's movement to strengthen the Church's ministry. They are translating the Sunday Gospel into a meaningful seven-day-a-week way of life.

Roberta Fletcher, a pioneer in the healing field, and one of the most outstanding and inspired leaders in healing prayer group work, says: "The corporate prayer work of laymen is a God-given commission as certainly as the healing ministry is the privilege and responsibility of the clergymen of our churches."

Laymen today are striving to fulfil this commission. The fruitful results of their efforts have done much to hasten the restoration of the Church's healing ministry.

All prayer has power. As a world-famous surgeon has commented: "It could not happen that any man or woman could pray for a single moment without some good result." Yet it is through corporate prayer, when minds and hearts are united in unselfish love and complete faith, praying in His Name with a single, common purpose, that we realize so frequently the unlimited power of God.

The protective power of prayer

That prayer is an actual, palpable force will not be denied by any who have experienced its effects. Among the most dramatic demonstrations of the protective power of prayer are the wartime experiences of so many men. Instance after instance is recorded of those saved by prayer from situations of desperate danger. An Englishman reports that every man in his regiment carried with him at all times a printed copy of the Ninety-first Psalm, which he prayed as continuously as possible. Not one man was lost from that regiment in four years of combat. In view of what we now know about the actual power of prayer, it no longer seems purely coincidental that so many parishes with active prayer groups report that they lost not a single boy during the Korean War.

My first personal experience with prayer as an almost physically discernible power came not during danger and not during illness, but during my first speaking tour on the subject of spiritual healing. I was nervous about talking on a subject which was still comparatively new to me and wholly foreign to all my previous training and experience.

As I stood for my first address, looking apprehensively over the large and well-filled church, I suddenly and distinctly felt what can best be described as a wall of protection completely surrounding me. So actual and concrete a thing did it seem that I had the impression that if I reached out my hand, I could touch it. My nervousness was immediately and wholly dissipated—and I proceeded with my talk.

Later that evening I mentioned this experience to a member of the church. "Yes," she said, "That's understandable. You see our prayer group joined together in prayer for you as you stood to speak. We have made arrangements with other groups so that you will be prayed for twenty-four hours a day as long as you are in our State."

I felt the impact of those prayers throughout my visit. Time after time since then I have experienced the same phenomenon, as have many others. This cannot be written off as "imagination" or "wishful thinking." The conviction frequently occurs, as it did in my case, when the subject knows nothing of the prayers being offered in his behalf.

Take another typical example. At six o'clock one evening not long ago, a friend telephoned to tell me, hysterically, that she had just received a medical verdict from her doctor: cancer of the uterus.

Immediately I called the leader of a prayer group, and

asked that as many members as possible be requested to pray for my friend at 7:30 that same evening. I stopped by the patient's home about nine P.M. ostensibly to cheer her up, and found her confident and serene—a far cry from the hysterical woman to whom I had spoken a few hours before.

"The strangest thing happened," she said. "I was so upset and frightened I just went all to pieces. Right in the middle of drying the dinner dishes I suddenly felt a sense of complete security and peace come over me. I don't know how to express it, but I felt a physical sense of protection, as if I were inside some sort of protective barrier."

Dr. Alexis Carrel saw a cancer shrivel to a scar before his eyes while he was at Lourdes. He knew then that the physical results of prayer were neither imaginary nor coincidental. "Prayer," he was later to say, "is the most powerful form of energy that can be generated. It is a force as real as terrestrial gravity. It is the only power in the world that seems to overcome the so-called 'laws of nature.'"

An increasing number of his colleagues are beginning to agree with him; for so often does either a complete healing or dramatic improvement take place either at the exact time of prayer or immediately afterward, that the results of prayer are no longer universally dismissed as accidental.

Take the case of a patient suffering severe pain from a ruptured disc. A prayer group prayed for this patient at 7:30 one evening. At 8:30 he reported that he was suddenly free from pain. The scheduled surgery was subsequently canceled, and over a period of more than three years he has remained symptom free.

Or take the case of a man whose one remaining kidney had ceased to function. After he was rushed to the hospital, his wife was told that he was dying from uremia. She immediately telephoned her minister, who promptly called a special prayer meeting. From that hour on the patient began to improve. His recovery was rapid and complete. "Miraculous" was his physician's comment.

Medical cooperation with prayer groups

Not only are doctors beginning to ascribe the healing of medically hopeless cases to a Higher Power, but some of them are actively cooperating with prayer groups by joining such groups themselves and by enlisting their aid in the treatment of patients.

One such doctor tells of a four-year-old child brought to him for treatment. The little boy had never taken a step in his life and was blind, deaf, and dumb. The physician called the leader of a local prayer group and requested prayers for the wholeness of the child. A few weeks later the small boy was brought back to his office. He walked in, went to the window, pulled open the blind, and laughed aloud. This is the power of God released by prayer.

Some doctors regularly call in local prayer groups in the case of critically ill patients. I saw this type of cooperation in action not long ago.

While I was discussing prayer with a group leader in Texas, her telephone rang. It was a doctor from a local hospital asking that she and three other members of the prayer group report as quickly as possible to the hospital to pray for a critically injured accident victim who had just been brought to Emergency. Within ten minutes she had contacted the other members of the group. In less than an hour they were at the hospital, kneeling in prayer at the patient's bed while a clergyman laid on hands.

Group prayer is in the great tradition of the Christian Church, instituted by Our Lord on the night of the Last Supper when He led His disciples in prayer (*John: 17*), and carried on by the apostles and their converts as they met in secret upper rooms. "When two or three are gathered together, there am I in the midst" has become today, as it was in the early Christian Church, a demonstrable truth.

Healing prayer circles are considered by clergymen to comprise a vital and indispensable part of their healing ministries. "Were this ministry not supported and strengthened by the believing prayers of our group," says the pastor of one church, "I would not have undertaken it." Many ministers attribute the effective results of their healing ministries to the fact that each service is attended by at least five members of the healing prayer group, all offering prayers for the sick.

Prayer groups a source of healing ministries

A number of clergymen consider the formation of a prayer group the initial step toward the institution of healing services in the church. In more than one instance (and this should be of interest to any layman who would like to see the healing ministry revived in his church) it has been the tremendously effective work of a group of dedicated, praying laymen which has induced a formerly hesitant minister to institute healing services in his church.

An outstanding example of this is found in North Miami, Florida, where the work of the prayer group organized and led by Mrs. Adele Miller resulted in a revival of the healing ministry, not only in her own church, the Church of the Resurrection, but also in several other churches in the vicinity.

Four years ago Mrs. Miller was seriously ill physically, mentally, and spiritually. After her name was placed by a relative on the prayer list of St. Stephen's Church in Philadelphia, she found her health improving. Through reading literature on spiritual healing, and through the help of her rector, Father Charles James, and the Reverend Ben Schumacher, she completely recovered her health. Anxious to pass on her new knowledge of the healing Christ, she formed a prayer group of interested women, beginning with only five members.

One of their first prayer results was the healing of a man desperately ill of tuberculosis. This was followed by the healing of a chronically sick woman, who learned through prayer group work to forget herself and pray for others.

This small prayer group, which now forms the local branch of the Order of St. Luke, then went to Father James and requested that he institute healing services. Observing the work and methods of the group, he readily acquiesced. Each weekly Communion service at the Church of the Resurrection is now immediately followed by the laying-on-of-hands.

As the laymen's movement grows, more and more prayer groups are being formed. Many are interdenominational. Working harmoniously together in love, unity, and understanding, the members are demonstrating for all to see the power of the healing Christ which is the heritage of all Christians, regardless of church affiliation. They have accepted their responsibility as Christians to be "Disciples of His Words." They have recognized that salvation of one's own soul is not the only obligation of the Christian; and that it is very often in our attempts to save others that we ourselves are saved. Like the disciples gathered with one accord in one place, the "fellowship of the concerned" is witnessing to the power of the risen Lord in human life.

Prayer transcends distance

As there is no limit to the power and love of God, so is there no spatial limit to the power of intercessory prayer. People in Europe have felt the beneficence of prayers offered by groups in California. Nor is the influence exerted by interdenominational prayer circles confined to the curing of sick souls and ailing bodies. Their example of concord, unselfish love, and a unity of faith in the healing

Christ is doing much to bridge the chasm which divides various denominations.

The often far-reaching results of group prayer is typified by an instance which occurred several years ago.

A young girl suffering from a brain tumor was prayed for simultaneously by several groups, including one in Lincoln, Nebraska and one in Dallas, Texas, shortly before she went into the operating room. When her skull was incised, the surgeon was flabbergasted to find no evidence of the tumor which had been so clearly visible in the X-rays. Her recovery was complete and permanent. But this healing did not end with the patient. An entire community was made thrillingly aware of the healing Christ. Prayer groups were started in the locality where the patient's family lived, and a longstanding schism between two churches was healed.

Prayer is the means of unleashing the greatest force on earth. It is the means of releasing God's power into our lives and affairs. If every one of us were to live perpetually surrounded by the prayers of others, neither sin nor sickness could penetrate that protective armor.

If prayer were more widely understood and generally practiced, it would recreate the world, for the power of God for good can destroy all evil. Helen Shoemaker, who is one of the country's great leaders in the general prayer group movement, says: "It is my conviction that the people of prayer hold the real balance of power in the world. It is only when we begin to pray as Christ taught us to do that we can hope to lift the dark cloud of evil hanging so heavily over the heads of us all."

Jesus assured His apostles that "Ye shall receive power, after that the Holy Ghost is come upon you" (*Acts 1:8*). As we grow in spiritual understanding, we find that this power is equally available to us. It is being thrillingly demonstrated by those small bands of people who meet together in prayer, striving to fulfil His words.

How to Start a Prayer Group

IF YOU would like to start a prayer group and are not quite sure how to go about it, the experience of others may be helpful.

The logical place to begin is within your own church, where you are apt to find like-minded people, and where your minister will be able to help you.

A typical group got its start in Pittsburgh three years ago when a young man and his wife discussed the matter with their clergyman and procured from him the names of several other couples who he thought might be interested. They subsequently invited four couples to their home one evening, and from this meeting evolved a group of eight people who were eager to grow together in spiritual experience. Weekly meetings were established, and within a year the group had expanded to the point where it was necessary to subdivide it into three separate circles.

From the original group there also evolved a neighborhood women's group which meets one morning a week. This prayer fellowship continues to expand, and one of its original members, Mrs. Patricia Naugle, comments: "We all find our lives tremendously enriched spiritually. Learning more of how to pray and discovering something of how the Holy Spirit works in our lives has enabled us to find answered prayer in the form of problems solved, needs met, and physical and spiritual healings. We know a peace and joy not of this world."

If your minister is unable to help you in your prayer group efforts, contact a few people on your own. Ask them to your house and talk the matter over with them. Don't let lack of numbers deter you, for many prayer fellowships have begun with only two or three members meeting for study, discussion, and prayer.

An extremely effective group was started in Dallas, Texas, a few years ago by Mrs. Lella Whiteman. She reports that in the beginning there were many weeks when only she and her husband attended the scheduled "meetings." But they persevered, and gradually the group expanded. Known now as the Upper Room Prayer Group, this circle is an impressive witness to the power of prayer, as was demonstrated in the healing of an acute alcoholic. The patient underwent surgery and was found to be suffering from advanced cirrhosis of the liver. The surgeon estimated that he would not live over thirty days, and these under the influence of strong narcotics to alleviate the intense pain. A relative asked prayers for the critically ill man. The patient went into a deep sleep that same afternoon and awoke free from pain. From that time on no narcotics were necessary, as there was no recurrence of pain. He was, at the same time, instantly healed of alcoholism—and today, years later, he is medically certified a well man in every respect.

Starting a prayer group

Prayer group studies have resulted in the conclusion that the ideal size for a prayer circle is not fewer than six or more than fourteen persons. Nevertheless, don't be discouraged or fail to meet because your group may still be limited in size to three or four members. There is a new group which meets in an Episcopal Church once a week directly before the healing service begins. On numerous occasions only three of the group has turned up. Yet this tiny circle has dramatically demonstrated the promised power when two or three are gathered together in His Name. More important than the number is that each member of the group is making a sincere effort to grow spiritually. The most effective prayer groups, regardless of size, are those whose members all engage in daily meditation and prayer.

When you have discussed your proposed healing prayer group with your clergyman, and have contacted a nucleus of individuals interested in the project, your next concern is where to meet, how often, and how to conduct the meetings when they are underway.

Some groups meet in the homes of members; some in churches; some in library rooms. Probably for a beginning circle, which is usually small, a private house is the best answer. How often you meet is up to your membership. Generally speaking, the most active and effective groups meet once a week, for it has been found difficult to establish and sustain the rapport between members, so vital to corporate prayer, with less frequent meetings.

Experience indicates that in order to assure unity and power in your group prayer, you must meet regularly, always planning your meetings in advance so that they will not be haphazard. The meetings should be limited to approximately one hour. Above all, the members of your group must be in love and fellowship with one another. If there is any anger, hostility, or resentment present, the prayer power will be non-existent.

Before your first scheduled meeting, appoint a leader. It can be either the host or hostess, if you are meeting in a home, or you can appoint a leader to serve by the month or whatever term is agreeable to your group.

Outline for prayer group meetings

The following outline for a meeting is used, with minor variations, by many groups. It can be adapted to suit the preference of any particular circle.

1. Have your group sit in a circle. If the group is sufficiently small, members can sit around a table.

2. The leader opens the meeting with a prayer, which can be either spontaneous or taken from the Book of Common Prayer or any other prayer manual. Spontaneous prayer is always to be encouraged, but don't force it in the beginning. Let the members grow into it.

3. A selected reading from Scripture.

4. A brief period of silent meditation. There is great power in united silence, but don't allow the silent period to persist too long, for the attention tends to wander. Close the meditation with a short prayer by the leader.

5. This is the time of "witness," obeying the injunction of Our Lord to "Go and tell." Let the members relate recent experiences of answered prayer, sharing with the others personal spiritual experiences.

6. Study period. This can consist of reading on the subject of spiritual healing, either one chapter from a book or a magazine article or pamphlet. The Order of St. Luke can supply you with material suitable for your group.

7. A short discussion period on what has been read. Here the leader should take a tactful but firm hand to prevent rambling irrelevancies.

8. Announcement of next meeting and lesson assignment, if any.

9. Intercession. This fifteen-minute period can be opened by the leader with a prayer of praise and thanksgiving. Then the first names of those on the prayer list (which was earlier submitted to the leader) will be read aloud, and prayers offered for them. These names may include any members of the group who are themselves in need of healing. Your intercession might well be concluded with prayers for the healing church and the whole world; with special prayers offered for any national or international problem current in the news. Many groups hold hands during this entire period of intercession.

10. The leader now closes the meeting with a prayer of

general thanksgiving, ending with repetition of the Lord's Prayer.

Your prayer group is now ready to adjourn. Before going home, you may want to enjoy some social fellowship with your prayer circle, for as Mrs. Naugle points out, "Friendships made here, not with just a social background, but with true concern and love for one another, far transcend the ordinary sort."

Time will disclose the most feasible and effective way for your group to function. Your circle may decide to pray daily at home for those in need, at a stipulated time, so that your prayers will be offered in unison. Or, in addition to your weekly meetings, you may want to attend healing services as a group, praying for the sick. Or you may prefer to function more informally, appointing a telephone committee which will relay to other members the names of those desiring prayer—no specific time for prayer being set, except in cases of emergency.

When your group expands sufficiently, you may decide to function as does the Prayer Healing Fellowship at St. Stephen's Church in Philadelphia—dividing into teams, each praying for a specific half hour, so that prayers are being offered almost around the clock.

Prayer lists

As time goes on, you will probably find your group confronted with various questions. How long, for example, should the same names be carried on a prayer list? Experience has proved that you will find it advisable to set a definite time limit. Some groups carry names for as long as a month, others for only a week, depending on the circumstances of the particular need.

The prayer chain affiliated with St. Peter's Episcopal Church, Brentwood, Pittsburgh, handles this matter in a fairly typical way. Here prayers are offered for those on the so-called "active" list, for a period of ten days. If continued prayer is requested, the group continues for another ten-day period.

A "permanent" list is also kept of those requiring prayer for a month or longer. This list is renewed at monthly intervals, if requested. This renewal process is necessary in order to keep in touch with those who are requesting prayer.

Then there is the question of how many names should be prayed for by one group. Some feel that the list should be limited in number. The Bishop of Coventry, England, for example, feels very strongly on this point. Practically, however, this seems virtually impossible to do; for no one can, in good conscience, refuse to pray when asked. It is interesting to note that Dr. Rettig and his Prayer Band pray for many hundreds, and a remarkable number of healings result. As Dr. Rettig comments: "To limit the number of people on our prayer list seems to me like limiting the power of God. We have to remember that it is God, not we, who heals—and His power is without confinement or 'limitation.'"

St. Stephen's, too, carries an enormously long prayer list. These names are as often prayed for as a group as individually. We are all aware of the healing results of this fellowship.

However, if your group feels, as so many do, that more power is attached to prayer when personal concern and attention can be focused upon the particular individual in need of help, try to divide your list of names so that each member has only as many as he can handle.

Should a disease be named?

Whether to name the *disease* of the patient you are praying for is also a question which arises frequently. There is so wide a divergence of opinion on this point that it would seem advisable to discuss the matter with your group, and do whatever the majority decide upon.

There are those who feel that prayer concentrated on the specific ailment has greater power than a more generalized prayer for the "health" of the patient. Others feel that we are so conditioned to fear certain diseases such as cancer that negative thoughts may subconsciously intrude into our prayers. The possibility of unwittingly and unconsciously enveloping a patient with fear is one that must be reckoned with. What you decide on this matter depends on your group. I have seen spectacular healings result from both methods of prayer.

Very much the same problem prevails in regard to prayer groups visiting and praying for patients medically termed "hopeless." Some, like the group I have previously mentioned, have achieved wonderfully effective results from this method. Others feel that they can pray more effectively for such patients if they do not see them. I can readily understand this attitude, as I remember so well my first experience with prayer for a so-called "hopeless" case.

I had been asked by the doctor in charge to go to the hospital and pray as a clergyman administered Holy Unction to a patient desperately sick with cancer. Now I had previously witnessed and verified many healings of so-called terminal cancers. I was completely confident of God's will and power to heal. Yet, when I walked into that hospital room and saw the unconscious patient, my heart sank. For a moment my faith faltered. It took every effort of which I was capable to envision that still figure on the bed as a completely whole and well man, which is so necessary a part of the healing technique.

Since that time I have found it considerably easier to eradicate any vision of illness, whether near or apart from the patient. I have learned to enter a sickroom, not with the disease on my mind, but rather with what God has to give that patient and anyone else who will receive in faith. Nevertheless, it is understandable how many prayer groups can function more effectively at a distance, just as some can function more effectively if they do not know the nature of the disease which afflicts those for whom they are praying.

If at all possible, find out what has happened to those you pray for. Some groups ask that this information be telephoned or written in. Others which function on a larger scale, such as the Society of the Nazarene, under the leadership of Mrs. Ethel Banks (who is magnificently carrying on her clergyman husband's work), send out cards at intervals, asking that they be returned, filled in with the pertinent information concerning the patient's progress, whether continued prayer is desired, etc.

Beware of pride in successful healings

For any healing or improvement reported to you, give thanks; but be constantly on guard that a feeling of pride does not develop. As Helen Reagan Smith, leader of an Oklahoma prayer group points out: "Let us begin to feel, '*We* did that with *our* prayers,' and all power immediately evaporates from the group."

As we witness, with a wonder akin to awe, the power of the Risen Christ released in our lives by group prayer, we tend to overlook the fact that prayer itself cannot heal. Rather does it serve as a window through which His light may shine. It is our longing for God, our humility in seeking Him, our earnest efforts to follow more closely in His footsteps, which enable that window to transmit His radiant energy. The exact manner in which your fellowship elects to work is immaterial. All that matters is that each member is seeking a closer relationship with God; striving to release to others in need and to a sick world the healing power of Christ.

"Prayer," says Helen Shoemaker, "is the bridge that we throw across the space between our weakness and God's strength—a bridge over which He can walk into the lives of men and nations."

Every layman has a part in the construction of this bridge—a bridge conceived in faith, built on love, and dedicated to the living Christ. Your prayer group is one of its girders.

The candles lit by small groups of praying laymen will gradually expand the circle of His light until it illumines every corner of the earth. All darkness will then be dissipated. His light will suffuse the world.

The Power of Prayer: The Story of Robert Byers

Not long ago a desperately ill boy made a remarkable recovery. The young man's family and friends and many inhabitants of the New England village where he had lived and gone to school believe that it was a miraculous healing. The consensus of medical opinion on the case is that regardless of the medical aid rendered the patient, without the healing power of God released by prayer, recovery would have been extremely unlikely. This is the story of that healing.

When Robert Byers, aged twenty-one, complained of fatigue on Thursday, July 11, 1957, his father, a lusty construction foreman, thought little of it. Young Bob, a junior at Grove City College, Pennsylvania, was not used to physical labor, and the construction work he had undertaken in Newfoundland as a summer job, was strenuous to say the least.

The following day, however, Bob was more than tired; he began to have trouble walking and moving his feet. Late that afternoon he was half-carried home from the job. The local doctor was unable to diagnose the trouble. Later that night, when Bob appeared to be growing paralyzed, a second doctor was called who proved equally bewildered. The next morning, completely unable to walk by now, the boy was taken to the Naval Dispensary, where, after a lengthy examination, he was ordered to remain overnight while further tests were conducted.

By noon Sunday his condition had drastically worsened. A consultation was held at the Dispensary, and a tentative diagnosis made: polyneuritis (Guillain Barre Syndrome), a sister disease to polio, with an adult death rate of two out of three.

As the Naval hospital lacked facilities to care for such a case, the doctors urged the patient's immediate return to the United States. Arrangements were quickly made by telephone for his admission to a Boston hospital. A Navy plane was ordered to be ready in two hours, equipped with oxygen and other emergency equipment. Meanwhile Bob's condition was growing progressively and rapidly worse, and it was necessary to perform a tracheotomy shortly before he boarded the plane.

At midnight on July 14 two doctors, the pilot and co-pilot, and Bob on a stretcher, accompanied by his parents, took off for the Boston airport. The Superintendent of the Naval Dispensary had telephoned Boston to have the custom and immigration men, as well as the ambulance on the field when the plane arrived.

For the first two hours after the Newfoundland take-off, the doctors worked frantically over Bob to keep him alive. Meanwhile his parents sat in their seats, frozen with fear. It was at this time that Monte Byers, the tough construction man whose sole claim to fame was that he could "swear louder and knew more curse words than anybody else" began to pray for, as he said, the first time in his life.

"Dear God, please hear the prayers of a sinner," he entreated. "Don't let Bob die. He's so young and so afraid, please give him a few more years. I don't even know how to pray, but please give me the knowledge."

A few minutes later the big, rugged pilot came back through the plane. He put his hand on the distraught father's shoulder. "We're praying, too," he said.

"This," said Mr. Byers, "rather startled me, because he didn't look any more like the type that prayed than I did. I wondered how he knew I was praying."

The plane was met by an ambulance with two attendants and two doctors. The family were quickly checked through customs and immigration, while Bob was transferred to the ambulance and rushed to the hospital.

By the time his parents arrived by taxi, the boy was ensconced in a private room outside of which were gathered thirteen doctors. In groups of four, they proceeded to enter the sickroom and examine the patient. At the end of an hour, the initial tentative diagnosis was confirmed: polyneuritis.

The doctor in charge explained to the Byerses that it was touch and go with Bob. His respiratory muscles were failing, and it was necessary to place him at once in an iron lung. The doctor went on to explain that the large group of doctors in attendance were house doctors who were being briefed on Bob's case so that in event of emergency all of them would know exactly what to do. Two of these doctors were assigned to sleep in the room next to the patient, with an oxygen therapist across the hall.

Within a few hours of his admission to the hospital, Bob was completely paralyzed from his feet to his eyes; even his eyelids could close only partially. His mental faculties and his power of speech were all that remained unimpaired.

Beds in the seldom-used hospital solarium were set up for the stunned parents. A vigil began which was to last for over four months.

"We lost all track of time," relates Mr. Byers, "even lost track of the seasons. The days and nights seemed almost the same."

Friends began sending the Byers religious pamphlets. "One of our friends," says Mr. Byers, "was the librarian at Wickford, Rhode Island, who sent me a book called *A Reporter Finds God Through Spiritual Healing*. For awhile I was too nervous and upset to read it, but I kept handling it and carrying it from place to place, along with a pamphlet containing the Gospel of St. Luke. I tried not to let anyone see these for fear they'd think I had become a religious fanatic in desperation, or say, 'The old sinner is scared and now he wants God to help him.' That was exactly the case, but I didn't want them to know it.

"One day I started to read *A Reporter Finds God* and was impressed by the writer's own early reactions towards religion. Apparently they were the same as mine. The title said she had found God. I wanted to know how, and there wasn't much time. I knew I had to have His help before it was too late.

"I'd read a few paragraphs; then some emergency would occur in Bob's room. A lot of doctors would appear, go in and revive him, and then I'd try to read a little more. Finally as I read, I began to feel that if only I had enough faith, God would guide the doctors and Bob would get well. My prayer now became, 'Dear Father, give me more faith.' "

The Byerses now made it a habit to stop by the hospital chapel at least three times a day, on their way to the cafeteria for meals. They asked any friends or relatives who came to the hospital to join them in prayer. On a table in the solarium Mr. Byers kept a pamphlet always open to a

Bible verse: "He giveth power to the faint; and to them that have no might He increaseth strength" (*Isaiah 40:29*).

"I kept reading this over and over hundreds of times," he said. "It seemed to describe Bob exactly, because he certainly was faint, and it promises that He increaseth strength. I'd read this and pray, and then go down to see if Bob looked any better."

The often-repeated and always heartbreaking plea of his son, "You won't let me die, will you, Dad?" echoed and re-echoed in the father's ears during the endlessly long, wakeful nights. "When I couldn't stand it any longer," he recalls, "I'd go to the men's room where nobody could see me, and get on my knees on the floor and pray."

One Sunday morning in August it looked as if Bob could not last out the day. His sister and her husband were hastily summoned from Rhode Island, escorted to and from the airports by state police. At this time many different prayer groups in and around Wickford had been alerted to the situation. Both Protestants and Catholics met in churches and in homes to offer prayers for the boy they all knew.

By midafternoon on that Sunday Bob seemed less exhausted than in the morning, but another serious crisis developed; he had pneumonia. Fluid had developed in his lungs by the following day, and it became necessary to tap his side. During this operation his right lung collapsed, and two tubes were inserted in his chest, while air was pumped into an incision in his throat to enable him to breathe. Months later the chest surgeon on the case remarked: "The night I put those tubes in Bob's chest I never expected him to be alive the next morning."

But although he was alive, he was in critical condition. In the late afternoon he went into shock, and the doctors worked over him all night.

Relatives summoned from Pittsburgh and other members of the family gathered in the hospital. They spent most of the night praying in the solarium.

"We must have been a rather strange looking group gathered in that room," recalls Mr. Byers. "We would all get together and pray silently for a little while. Then, a few at a time, would slip down to Bob's room and watch him. Then we would get together again, and someone would say, 'Let's have another prayer.'

"We were all scared. I can't describe how scared we were. We got the hospital chaplain to pray with us, but I had the distinct feeling that he didn't think Bob would pull through; that he was praying for *us* so that we wouldn't go to pieces when we lost him."

The next day the boy was in very poor condition. The doctors who had stayed with him twenty-four hours a day told his parents that they had done all they could, but that he was slipping fast.

"We felt so helpless," Mr. Byers said, "and we continued to question the doctors, longing for a ray of hope. When they couldn't give it to us, we'd say to them; 'All we can do, then, is pray.' To my surprise, every one of the many doctors on the case without exception replied in all sincerity: 'That will help.' "

By dint of transfusions and other emergency measures, Bob continued to hang on, barely alive, through August and September and into October. Much of this time his condition was so critical that six or eight members of the Byers family virtually lived at the hospital.

"As I look back now," remarked Mr. Byers, "I begin to realize how wonderful it was for this big institution to allow a family to practically move into it with a patient. We must have been pests to those busy doctors and nurses, always waylaying them and asking questions, but they were always courteous and kind, taking time to explain."

In the middle of October another blow struck. Bob's right lung had been severely damaged by the pneumonia and ensuing complications, and double surgery would be necessary. The first operation would involve the removal of one rib in order to insert a larger drainage tube; to be followed by a second in which the lower lobe of his lung would be removed. Only too well aware of their son's already extremely precarious condition, the boy's parents were terrified by the thought of this surgery. It was at this time, the week-end of October 19, that Mr. Byers called relatives in Glenshaw, Pennsylvania, asking them to contact Kathryn Kuhlman, the Pittsburgh evangelist mentioned in the book *A Reporter Finds God*.

"I wanted her to come to Boston," Mr. Byers said, "to conduct a healing service for Bob; and I wanted it made clear that, whatever the cost of the trip, I would pay for it."

Two days later Bob's cousin called from Pittsburgh. "Our minister has talked to Kathryn Kuhlman," he reported. "She says there's no need for her to go to Boston, for she can't heal anyone, only God can. And she can pray as well in Pittsburgh as she can in Boston. Now here's what she told us to do. Do you have a pencil? Write this down."

The boy was very excited as he relayed the message:

"This is important. Miss Kuhlman and her people here, and there are hundreds of them, will pray for Bob on Tuesday, Wednesday, and Thursday nights. On Friday at one o'clock, they will have a healing service for him. They will fast from Thursday midnight until Friday sundown, and she said all of you at Boston should also fast.

"Tell Bob all about it. She wants him to be aware of all that's going on. You are to keep praying as you have been, only here is the prayer everyone is to say: 'that God's power will work in Bob.' Don't pray for him to get well, just ask that God's power work in him.

"Tell Bob not to be afraid, no matter how or what he

feels. You and Aunt Adria are to be with him on Friday at one o'clock, and it is important that all of you keep repeating this prayer. Uncle Monte, be sure to tell Bob about my calling. We've both always been kind of skeptical about things like this, but tell him I said this is the greatest thing I have ever heard—that this is *real.*"

The boy's excitement and conviction were contagious. Mr. Byers' hopes rose. He read to his wife the instructions he had written down, and later to Bob. After he left the room Bob asked for his mother: "Why is Dad doing all this? Can't the doctors do any more for me?"

She replied: "It isn't that, Bob. Your Dad is just trying to get you well."

They followed Miss Kuhlman's instructions. On Thursday night, so strong was their faith that they had their son's clothes pressed and shoes shined in the event that he would be able to leave the hospital after the Pittsburgh healing service.

At one o'clock on Friday, October 25, a number of the Byers' family and friends, all of whom were fasting, knelt in the Church at Wickford, saying the prayer. Mr. and Mrs. Byers were in Bob's room repeating it with him. A few minutes later in the middle of the prayer, Bob suddenly fell asleep. Curiously enough, his parents almost immediately followed suit. It was two weeks later that Bob's sister reported that she, too, had suddenly fallen asleep in the Wickford Church, sixty miles from Boston. "That sleep," they agreed, "seemed almost a supernatural thing. We all felt strangely peaceful and rested when we woke up."

When Bob awakened, still repeating the prayer, he said in disappointment to his father, "Nothing happened, Dad." To which his father replied: "Don't be discouraged, son; we don't know. God works in mysterious ways."

Three days later another X-ray of Bob's chest was made.

The Byerses were told that the removal of his rib was not going to be necessary. In view of a clearly discernible change there now seemed a possibility that he might not have to undergo lung surgery of any kind.

The next day Bob, who had until now been fed entirely by tube, remarked that he was starved and asked for food. After disposing of the orange juice and cereal brought him, he promptly said, "What's for dinner?" When told the hospital was serving roast beef, he demanded some. The doctors at first adamantly refused, but at his insistence they finally gave permission. A roast beef dinner was served him that evening, and he ate every morsel.

X-rays continued to be taken at intervals. Each report was better. His lung healed completely, and he improved daily. In a short time he could be taken off the respirator for an hour at a time. One night he turned off the machine himself for eight hours. The doctors were horrified, but he apparently suffered no ill effects. He was warned, however, to take it slowly. Gradually his time out of the machine increased until by the end of October he was out more than half the time. In early November the respirator was no longer needed. Meanwhile, as his father expresses it, "The paralysis had just rolled off him like rolling back a rug; first his face, then his arms and chest and legs."

On November 3, he was allowed to sit up and dangle his legs over the side of the bed for five minutes. On November 7, after four months of total paralysis, unable to move even a finger, he rolled himself out to the solarium in a wheel chair. A short while later Bob went home.

Today he is well, able to walk and drive a car. The only reminder of his illness is the physical therapy he is still undergoing to strengthen his long-unused muscles. When one of his doctors saw him a short while ago, tears ran down the man's face. "I never would have believed this possible," he said.

To Bob and his parents, the promise of St. James is an unquestionable reality. "Is any sick among you? Let him call for the elders of the church; and let them pray over him. . . . And the prayer of faith shall save the sick" (*James 5:14–15*).

"To us," says Mr. Byers, "Kathryn Kuhlman and her people were the elders of the church. Through her and the others all over the country who were praying with her, Bob got well. She must be a wonderful person. In June we're all going to Pittsburgh to thank her and her people personally for their prayers."

As is so frequently the case in spiritual healing, the story of Bob Byers has not ended with his own cure. Because of this evidence of answered prayer, because of this visible demonstration of the power and mercy of God, the spiritual perception of the Byers family and close friends, and of hundreds of others has been quickened and deepened. These people have been converted to the healing Christ.

For some a new and exciting awareness of His presence has replaced the former prosaic acceptance of a remote God; for others, a lip-service religion has been galvanized into a flaming faith; for many, prayer has now become a way of life.

Men and women who until Bob's sickness had really never prayed at all now kneel side by side each night. Prayers for the sick, spoken now with a new conviction that God's will is health, are already bearing fruit. Families whose Bibles have long lain gathering dust have opened them again and read aloud each day. In Wickford, many of the school children who prayed for their alumnus, Bob, and saw with their own eyes the answer to these prayers, will bear on their lives forever the imprint of a knowledge not to be found in textbooks.

"Bob is the living proof of a miracle performed by God," asserts his father. "It's just impossible to describe how your life changes when something wonderful like this happens. There is one thing I know: mine can never be the same again since Bob was healed and since I've learned that Christ is actually right here, ready to help anybody who turns to Him."

Many of those connected with this healing have expressed this same thought. In them is vividly apparent the peace, the joy, and the strong sense of security which inevitably accompany a regenerated faith.

Bob Byers and his family express their gratitude to Kathryn Kuhlman as an instrument of God's power, and to all who offered prayers. But many of those who prayed are even more grateful; for in Bob's healing they have felt for the first time the touch of God upon their own lives. Through fasting and prayer they, as surely as the boy who was healed, have come to know the living Christ.

Medical Recognition
of the Healing Phenomenon

INCREASING scientific acknowledgment of the reality of spiritual healing has lifted that phenomenon from the realm of suspected crackpot-ism into that of impeccable respectability. The extent of the growth of the healing ministry can be measured by the amount of scientific curiosity it has aroused, and by the research it has engendered.

Just a few years ago, mere mention of "miraculous" healing evoked scathing derision from the medical profession. This situation is slowly but surely changing. While doctors are rightly cautious concerning alleged non-medical cures, an increasing number are beginning to agree with Dr. Howard Craven, of Washington, D.C., who said to me not long ago: "If we are to be honest, we have to face the truth that a large number of remarkable healings appear to be taking place without medical or surgical intervention. Many of these cannot be categorized as purely psychosomatic. Experience seems to justify the belief that spiritual healing completes the chain that welds the patient into an integrated, whole, happy, well, unit."

Five years ago the almost universal chant of doctors, when confronted with medically inexplicable healings, was "wrong diagnosis." Today many of these same men, now familiar with the healing phenomenon, believe that the continued affirmation that the medically-diagnosed disease never existed in the first place constitutes an unwarranted indictment against modern diagnostic methods and medical skill, and is neither an honest nor a realistic approach to the subject.

The Trinity of Body, Mind, and Spirit

Dr. Albert Reissner, Brooklyn psychoanalyst, expresses the new attitude toward illness held by many of his colleagues when he says: "More and more of us are becoming convinced of two things: first, that man is a trinity composed of body, mind, and spirit; and, second, that the underlying cause of most disease is spiritual. We have observed that unless a healing of the spirit takes place, the cure of the body or mind is not apt to be either complete or permanent."

This concept is perhaps not so scientifically revolutionary as it may appear at first glance; for actually the step is not long between the medically accepted fact that sick emotions breed sick bodies, and the dawning awareness of the relevance of the spirit to physical, mental, and emotional well-being.

In June, 1955, the American Medical Association held its annual convention at Atlantic City. The incoming president of the Association urged that his fellow-physicians "take more into the sickroom than your medical skill. . . . Unless we are willing to give of ourselves and our faith, our science will avail us little."

A recent article in the Journal of the American Medical Association, emphasizes that the old concept of the "godless" doctor is rapidly being stamped out. Medicine and religion are now working together more closely than in any other period of modern times. Studies to correlate more fully the body and the spirit are already under way—studies, interesting enough, suggested and initiated by the medical profession.

It was at the request of numerous doctors affiliated with the Houston, Texas, Medical Center that a pioneering venture was undertaken not quite two years ago. Here an "Institute of Religion," under the auspices of five Protestant denominations, was established to function as an integral part of the medical center. The purpose was to foster a closer cooperation between clergymen and the medical profession, in order that "healing of the *whole* patient—body, mind, and spirit—may result. As one doctor puts it: "We believe that total health depends on healing the man who has the disease, not merely the disease the man has."

Here at Houston is the beginning of what promises to be a new era in the practice of both medicine and the Church. We find the clergy, functioning no longer as mere consolers, but as healers, working side by side with doctors, who are no longer only scientists, but practicing Christians as well.

Dr. Claude Forkner of Cornell University comments: "We do not know what it is that brings about recovery of a patient. I am sure, however, that often it is faith which is a most important factor."

The Faith of the Doctor

When a doctor, as well as his patient, has faith in the healing power of God, an astoundingly effective medical practice results. One of the nation's most eminent heart surgeons, who is associated with the Methodist Hospital in Houston, is a case in point.

This surgeon performs, with an extraordinary record of success, delicate and intricate heart operations on patients who come to him from every state in the Union. He conducts his work in an atmosphere permeated with faith. Himself a firm believer in God's healing power, he carefully screens each member of the four medical teams which work under his supervision. He accepts for duty only those doctors and nurses who avow their belief in God and in the power of prayer. The doctor, like his co-workers, never operates without first going to the hospital's interdenominational chapel to pray. He asks his nurses and his patients, who occupy some four floors in the hospital, to remain in prayer while he is in surgery. He is a highly skilled surgeon, but he reminds his patients that faith and prayer are vital factors in their complete recovery.

In talking to the wife of one of these patients I learned that her husband, who required an aorta transplantation to save his life, had been referred to this surgeon by their family physician, two thousand miles away.

"I was in a strange city," she said, "worried to death over my husband's precarious condition, but I shall always remember the heartwarming and inspiring experience of my association with that hospital. It was a marvelously strengthening thing to know that my husband was continuously surrounded by an atmosphere of almost palpable faith and prayer. The surgeon's highly successful record is not difficult to understand. I only wish there were more hospitals run along these lines."

There *are* other such hospitals. The Good Samaritan in Los Angeles is one, and there will soon be more. A symposium of physicians and clergymen in New York City has recently proposed that hospitals and medical schools inaugurate "departments of religion" in order to promote a better understanding of the spiritual needs of the sick. Just a few weeks ago a group of physicians from Johns Hopkins Hospital in Baltimore met in conference to determine the best and quickest means of establishing a religious center to function in connection with the hospital.

"We want our patients," said one of these doctors, "to be assured the maximum benefit which can be derived only from *total* healing treatment. We believe that cure of the body, if it does not take into account the spiritual aspect of every patient, comprises only a partial cure."

These physicians commented that they now refrained from using the word "terminal" in reference to any condition. Why? "We have seen too many so-called 'terminal' cases perfectly healed by the power of God" was the answer.

Psychiatry, too, has recognized the interdependence of science and religion in the complete healing of an individual. Where mental illness is concerned, a growing number of modern psychiatrists, in opposition to Freud, but in the footsteps of Jung, agree with Dr. Reissner that a vital factor in the patient's recovery is his return to religion. Concrete evidence of this change in thinking can be found in the recent opening of the Lutheran Medical Center in Brooklyn, New York. Operating under the direction of Drs. Paul Qualben and John Kildahl, this Center was founded and is staffed by trained psychiatrists who are also ordained ministers. These men are uniquely qualified to render both psychological aid and spiritual treatment to their patients.

When I first began my research on spiritual healing a

few years ago and sought to procure medical confirmation of the alleged cures, I was met with uncompromising hostility by virtually every doctor I contacted. However, in traveling over the country during the past year, I have found the picture rather drastically changed. I have been asked by many doctors to go with them to the hospital to pray for critically ill patients. A no longer unique experience was one I had recently in the Southwest.

During an interview with a prominent physician on the staff of a large city hospital, he said to me: "No one knows better than I the power of God to heal. Time after time I have seen medically hopeless cases literally raised from the dead through prayer and the laying-on-of-hands. I consider the ministrations of the healing clergy just as vital to my patients' welfare as the medical treatment I can render them—and I can assure you I do not stand alone in the medical profession in this conviction."

As I sat in the doctor's office, his telephone rang. He gave some rapid instructions, ending with, "I'll be at the hospital in ten minutes." Turning to me, he excused himself. "A patient is sinking. I have to leave at once."

On his way out he paused at his secretary's desk to ask her to contact a clergyman from a nearby church. "Ask him if he will meet me at the hospital as soon as possible to lay on hands."

The minister his secretary called was an Episcopalian with an outstanding healing ministry. The doctor was a Presbyterian, and the patient a Methodist.

Studies in the science of spiritual healing

During the past three years there have been held a number of seminars in Rye, New York, where, for the first time in history, doctors and psychologists, physicists and clergymen have met to discuss and attempt to fathom the now-acknowledged phenomenon of spiritual healing. A few of these doctors have gone on to Dr. J. B. Rhine's parapsychology staff in an endeavor to learn more of the phenomenon. Others are working with physicists on the theory that electric and magnetic fields are somehow involved. In this connection, a number of scientists are attempting to devise a method by which the "healing power" can be scientifically measured.

Under the auspices of the Laymen's Movement for a Christian World, a committee of sixteen has been appointed to explore the subject in all its aspects. This committee includes six medical doctors, of whom Dr. Frank Sladen, Consultant to Medical Service, Henry Ford Hospital, Detroit, and Dr. Robert Laidlaw of Roosevelt Hospital, New York City, are two. Among its other scientists is Julius Weinberger of the R.C.A. research laboratories.

Concurrently, an objective study of spiritual healing is being conducted by the American Foundation of Religion and Psychology, with which Dr. Smiley Blanton is actively associated. A group of California scientists is presently engaged in an exhaustive research program. In addition to these formal research groups, numerous individual physicians, their interest whetted and curiosity piqued by what they have learned, are privately studying and researching the phenomenon.

All of this investigation indicates medical recognition of the type and number of spiritual healings being reported. Whether it will eventuate in a conclusive report is open to conjecture by a number of both doctors and clergymen. Nevertheless, even if the power of Christ cannot be accurately analyzed in a laboratory and the healing of the human spirit defies the X-ray machine, the value of scientific exploration cannot be overestimated. As products of our mid-twentieth century culture, it is natural enough that we demand a scientific approach.

If for no other reason than to inspire faith in those who

disbelieve, scientific confirmation of healings seems vitally important. As a man wonderfully healed of a so-called "fatal" kidney ailment said to me the other day: "You know, if I hadn't known of Dr. Alexis Carrel's experience of seeing a cancer instantly healed before his eyes, I could never have taken spiritual healing seriously." Yes, I knew; for if I hadn't been able to medically substantiate scores of claimed healings, I would have quickly written off the whole subject as superstitious fanaticism.

The last survey on spiritual healing, severely limited in scope by lack of funds, was conducted in 1954 by Dr. Charles Braden of Northwestern University, under the auspices of the then Federal Council of Churches. The findings revealed that sixty-four different types of disease had reportedly been spiritually healed. The largest percentage of healings had occurred in cancer cases, while heart healings followed as a close second.

In some cases these cures were apparently effected as a result of close cooperation between doctors and clergymen. In others, the reported healings had occurred after the doctors had apparently failed. When several outside physicians were asked to comment on the latter group, however, they claimed that the diagnosis had been in error.

Regardless of the documentary evidence of disease and cure, unless a physician has a personal knowledge of the case involved the results of any scientific investigation may well be inconclusive. Doctors frequently differ in their diagnosis of a disease. As one doctor points out, there are few medical men engaged in practice who will accept another's X-rays or laboratory findings. This will hold doubly true when one attempts to compile irrefutable evidence of non-medical cures.

Medical testimonies to instantaneous healings

In cases of instantaneous healings, unless a doctor is on

the spot or personally familiar with the case, he will understandably find such cures difficult to credit. Take the case of a woman in Cleveland who suffered a third degree burn on her right hand. The doctor treated and bandaged the injury in his office. On her way home, she attended a healing service at Emmanuel Episcopal Church, where the Reverend Laurence Blackburn laid his hands lightly on the bandage. As he prayed, the pain in the patient's hand ceased. She felt she had been healed, and returned to her doctor for examination. There remained no sign of the burn except a faint pinkness of the skin. The physician was astounded. He called it a miracle. But would any other, who had not seen the injury just before and just after?

Then there was the woman in Texas who was suffering from an abdominal swelling caused by a tumor so large that it had increased her weight by approximately fifteen pounds. She attended a healing service a few days before she was scheduled to enter the hospital for surgery. When she arose from the altar, her abdomen was as flat as a board. Upon reaching home, she stepped on the scales and found that she had lost over fifteen pounds since early that morning. She went immediately to her doctor, who found no evidence of the tumor. "A higher power has healed you," he said. Would medical investigators be able to accept this type of statement as incontrovertible scientific evidence?

Because of the nature of the subject it would seem that positive findings must come from the increasingly large group of doctors who are actually at the scene of action when medically inexplicable healings occur. The religious-medical combine such as is functioning in Houston may well provide the means for this sort of research. Here the cumulative evidence can be studied and evaluated; for, as one physician says: "It is the massive *cumulative evidence which is so impressive.*"

This is illustrated in St. Peter's Church in Uniontown, Pennsylvania. The Reverend Larned Blatchford, who practices a healing ministry there, reports that nineteen members of the parish underwent major surgery during the past twelve months. In each of these cases malignancy was strongly suspected by the attending physicians. In not one case, however, was malignancy found, nor did any operation prove as serious as had been previously indicated. In every instance a remarkably quick and uneventful recovery took place.

Doctors are increasingly disinclined to dismiss this sort of thing as purely coincidental, just as they are becoming loath to write off as mere coincidence the fact that so many critically ill patients take a dramatic turn for the better at the exact time that prayers are being offered in their behalf.

Cooperation of Doctors with Healing Ministries

Physicians who a short while ago scoffed at the mention of spiritual healing are now working in close cooperation with the churches' healing commissions and clinics. The Healing Commission of the Diocese of Los Angeles, for example, includes a substantial number of doctors; while the Order of St. Luke, an interdenominational healing mission founded ten years ago by the Reverend John Gaynor Banks, includes twenty-five doctors as active members.

Many Christian doctors are now members of prayer groups affiliated with various different churches. St. Stephen's Episcopal Church in Philadelphia numbers half a dozen medical men in its prayer circle, which, divided into groups, prays for the sick at half-hour intervals twenty-one hours a day. In Toledo, Ohio, a powerful healing prayer group has been established and is led by four of the city's leading doctors.

In some areas where the healing ministry is strong, it has

become common practice for physicians to send, and sometimes to accompany, their patients to healing services. Occasionally instantaneous healings occur. Frequently the healings are gradual, but doctors report that only rarely does the patient fail to derive obvious benefit from the services. Two doctors to whom I have spoken report that they themselves have been healed instantaneously—one of what had been considered incurable deafness; the other of an incompletely healed fracture where surgical intervention had been distinctly indicated.

Most doctors have conceded that the religious attitude of a patient was an important factor in his recovery. What many are now beginning to understand for the first time is that the *physician's* faith in a healing God can be of immense importance in his healing work. As Dr. William Reed of Bay City, Michigan, observes: "Today there is a new awareness that in the close cooperation between the church and medicine lies a new, great kind of care of illness which brings Christ into His proper place in the thinking and activities of both groups. We are learning through spiritual healing that Christ has a message for physicians which must be listened to."

If I have given the impression that all, or even most, doctors now accept the validity of spiritual healing, I have been in error. Many physicians (but significantly those who know the least about it) react as did a doctor I talked to a few days ago. One of his patients had been diagnosed by means of internal examination, supported by vaginal smear and biopsy, both positive, as having cancer. A complete hysterectomy was scheduled. Before her operation date, she attended several healing services. Convinced that she had received healing, she requested that another smear be taken. It was, and returned negative. A week later another biopsy was performed with the understanding that, were it positive, the hysterectomy would be performed while she was still under the anesthetic. The biopsy was negative; no operation necessary.

When I asked her doctor how he explained this, his answer was typical of nearly all doctors several years ago, but far fewer today: "It's perfectly obvious that she never had cancer," he said. When I asked how he could be so sure in view of the laboratory findings, he replied: "I'm sure, because if she had had cancer, it would still be there. It was all a mistake." It is this sort of reasoning which makes the procurement of medical confirmation both difficult and time-consuming.

It has been my observation in talking to physicians that much of their initial hostility to spiritual healing is due to their mistaken idea that those who believe in spiritual healing don't believe in doctors. Nothing could be further from the truth. The advocates of spiritual healing believe medicine to be a divinely instituted profession. They concur with Dr. Norman Vincent Peale when he says: "The combination of the physician who treats and God who heals is no less a religious process than the cure of souls."

Fully recognizing that the complete healing art comprises three indivisible parts—medical, psychological, and spiritual—those who conduct healing ministries not only urge but insist that those who attend services remain under the care of their doctors. I have noticed that when a physician thoroughly understands this, his antagonism usually diminishes. I recently had occasion to interview two doctors, both eminent men in their fields, in connection with a medical article I had in preparation. I had interviewed these same men several years ago in regard to spiritual healing and had found them unequivocally hostile to religious healing of any sort. However, since that time, both had done some investigating. One now voluntarily offered me cases from his files which, he said, "must be termed 'miraculous' as they are medically inexplicable."

The other commented: "Since talking to you last, I have seen many healings of diverse organic and chronic diseases which defy medical explanation. When these healings come as a direct result of prayer, they must, in my opinion, be accepted as miracles."

Dr. Paul Tournier, internationally known French physician, states in his *A Doctor's Casebook* that there is a hierarchy of the person, in which the body is subject to the spirit. With this contention an ever-growing number of physicians, such as Dr. Evarts Loomis of Southern California, agree. "I have noted repeatedly in my practice," he says, "that the extent of a physical healing seems to depend on the change in the spiritual life of the patient which goes with prayer and meditation. On several occasions when a patient was not making satisfactory progress, I have prayed with him either verbally or silently, whether he be Catholic or Protestant, in office or hospital room. Almost invariably, improvement has followed."

Dr. Charles H. Mayo, who conducted an investigation on spiritual healing several years ago, reported: "Christian healing has passed beyond the stage of experiment, and its value cannot be questioned. Spiritual healing no longer is the hope of the few, but the belief and practice of a large and rapidly increasing number of persons."

A steadily growing number of doctors, now familiar with the results of the revived ministry of healing, concede that this is a factual statement.

There is little doubt that we are standing on the threshold of a new era in the treatment of disease—an era of real Christian faith, which, when coupled with scientific techniques, may well make the *non*-healing of any disease more remarkable than its healing.

It is toward this end that so many dedicated doctors and clergymen are now working. Both use the same text as a basis for their efforts. While the Church fully concurs that

"God hath given men skill. . . . With such doth He heal men and taketh away their pains," the doctor, with increasing frequency, asks that his patients "Pray unto the Lord, and He will make thee whole" (*Ecclesiastes 38:6–8*).

PART II HEALING MINISTRIES

Modern Apostles

A FEW YEARS AGO, the institution of a healing ministry was a somewhat perilous undertaking. It required the preparation of a congregation probably unused to the idea of spiritual healing.

Today, however, with a widespread general knowledge of the subject, the task of instituting a ministry of healing is far easier. Many clergymen are finding it possible, as did the Reverend Earl Walker, United Lutheran pastor of the Hebron Church in Pittsburg, to begin healing services without prolonged preparation. In his own words: "I just began. I delivered two or three sermons on the healing power of Christ, and then I combined our regular Sunday vespers service with a healing service. My sermons here are based on the Bible and excerpts from various books on healing. After a period of quiet prayer for the sick, I invite any who wish to receive the laying-on-of-hands to come to the altar."

The greatest activity in spiritual healing is usually found in those communities where a leading churchman, of whatever denomination, is keenly interested in the subject. The enthusiasm and support of Bishop Austin Pardue of Pittsburgh, for example, is largely responsible for the leading role this city is playing in the renascence of the healing ministry. Once a ministry has set a precedent, it is easier for others in the locality to "just begin."

The Reverend Harry D. Robinson, Jr., pastor of the Bellmore Methodist Church in Bellmore, Long Island, began his healing ministry by the formation of a healing prayer group. He then sent out a letter to the general church membership in which he asked that they join with him in seeking from God, through group prayer in the church, health and strength for themselves and those they loved. "A prayer group can be as real a tool in God's hand as is the modern hospital," stated the letter. "So I invite you to put another tool in the hand of God: Come and join yourself to a praying group before the altar of our church; come if you are curious, and would like to learn what can happen; come if you are not well, and seek to be well; come if you would help another by your prayers; come and bring someone else who longs for health and wholeness."

Mr. Robinson's weekly healing services include hymns, a message from the Bible, and prayer. Those who wish it receive either the laying-on-of-hands or Holy Unction. Although this is a ministry of only a few months, it has produced many remarkable results.

The Reverend Laurence Blackburn, D.D., Episcopal rector of Emmanuel Church in Cleveland, initiated his notable healing ministry with a mission consisting of a series of eight weekly lectures. He delivered six of these himself and procured two guest speakers well known in the healing field for the remaining two. Each lecture was followed by a question period, and intercessions. The result was a congregation highly literate on the subject of spiritual healing. Services with the laying-on-of-hands were begun the week following the final lecture. Within two months attendance at these weekly services represented thirty-three different churches and nine denominations.

A healing mission is a splendid way to precede the institution of a healing ministry, for it provides a more concentrated and effective "education" in spiritual healing than is possible by an occasional Sunday sermon. If the minister of a church does not feel himself qualified to conduct such a mission personally, he can arrange with someone outstanding in the healing field to deliver the lectures. Where a particular church is small and unable to support such a mission, clergymen of different denominations have cooperated in bringing a missioner to their area. This has proved a fruitful method, for healing ministries have been instituted in as many as five different denominational churches as a result of one series of lectures in one community.

Sunday sermons on healing; the organization of prayer groups; the sending of letters to church members; missions —all these are possible and valuable methods of instigating a healing ministry. Exactly how to begin depends on the individual church. The important thing is to begin.

The Reverend Robert Young of North Presbyterian Church, Pittsburgh, says: "I am ordained, as are all Christian clergy, to preach the Truth, which includes healing. I was called by my congregation to obey God and to lead them in His Holy Ways. I can see no more reason for reluctance in starting a healing ministry than for hesitancy in administering Holy Communion."

The Reverend Young has discovered, as have so many others, that the ministry and their congregations alike can grow in understanding of the healing Christ only after a healing ministry is already functioning, not before it has begun.

Over the past two years, I have seen the beginning of many new ministries of healing. I have watched increase, not only the spiritual stature of the participating laymen, but the spiritual power of the officiating clergy. These men are indeed today's apostles, handling the power of God as surely as did His first disciples—and with much the same results.

The stories of the individual ministries which follow, are the stories of just a few of the many which are influencing today's revival of spiritual healing. They have been chosen at random. Some are well known; others are not. All, however, are representative of the healing ministry as it functions in various communities and churches over the nation. As each is, in essence, the story of every healing ministry to date, so does each constitute the potential story of every ordained minister in Christendom; for anyone who is authorized to Baptize or to administer Holy Communion or to perform the Sacrament of Marriage is "ready" to undertake the vital ministry of healing which is so inherent and inseparable a part of the Church's whole ministry.

Some of the following clergymen have an undeniable healing gift; others have not. It is perhaps significant that none was aware of this gift until he began his healing work. But the absence or presence of a charismatic gift is immaterial. The clergy cannot, nor does it ever profess, to heal. It serves only as a channel for Christ's healing power, as it is mediated through the Church.

A glance at these healing ministries makes it clear that God mediates His power under varying circumstances and in different surroundings. As the Reverend William Holmes, well known for his healing work in New Mexico, confesses with admirable candor: "It took me a long time to realize the foolishness and egotism of trying to bottle up almighty God in my own limited and conventional thought molds. But at long last I have learned no longer to distrust or disdain the manifestations of spiritual power and healing which come outside my own familiar path."

All of us who believe in the healing Christ owe an incalculable debt of gratitude to our twentieth-century apostles of healing. They are the spokesmen for Christ who are not only eloquently re-articulating, but reaffirming with "signs" the tremendous truth that God loves us and that nothing, not things past or things to come or even we, ourselves, can separate us from His love. Through the working of the Holy Spirit they are leading the way to a new era in Christianity—a rebirth of its pristine power, founded on a vibrant faith in the living God.

The Reverend Alfred W. Price

(EPISCOPAL)

ONE HAS only to step inside the beautiful old church of St. Stephen, in the heart of Philadelphia, to recognize it as a true sanctuary of healing, a center of living faith, filled with the presence of the Holy Spirit.

The inspired leader of this "powerhouse of the love of Christ" is a six-foot-four ex-marine, holder of a Purple Heart from World War I, and for many years the national chaplain of the Military Order of the Purple Heart. As gentle as he is strong, as compassionate as he is huge, Dr. Alfred W. Price is a true apostle of faith and love, whose healing ministry has exerted an immeasurable influence on churches of all denominations.

It all began for him in 1942, shortly after he had assumed the rectorship of St. Stephen's Episcopal Church. Searching for a way to help more effectively the many who came to him in mental, spiritual, and often physical distress, he providentially came across a small leaflet which, as he says, "was actually to precipitate me into the healing ministry."

This pamphlet contained a description of the revived emphasis on physical healing which fell within the province of the historic ministry, and related the success of several ministers in the laying-on-of-hands. As he finished reading it, Dr. Price recalled that when he was a student theologian, he had heard Dr. Richard Cabot, of Harvard

Medical School, contend that ministers could be doing three-quarters of the healing work of physicians, and doing it better.

Still pondering the matter the next morning, Dr. Price went into the church to pray for guidance. He opened his Bible to James 5:14: "Is any sick among you? let him call for the elders of the Church; and let them pray over him, anointing him with oil in the name of the Lord."

The words he had read so many times before were now fraught with new meaning. When he arose from his knees, he had made his decision.

From his pulpit the next Sunday Alfred Price invited anyone interested in healing to attend a special noon service the following Thursday. Thus began a ministry of such spiritual power as to attract the attention of both clergy and laity across the nation—a ministry which has served as an example for churches everywhere.

Early in his healing ministry, Dr. Price learned that when the Sacrament of Holy Communion was used at the healing services of a large city church such as St. Stephen's, it tended to keep members of other faiths, or of no faith, from the services. "It seemed to me a barrier, preventing many needy people from joining us," explained Dr. Price. "We therefore discontinued this Sacrament at the healing services. They now consist of a sermon based strictly on the New Testament, and the laying-on-of-hands."

The rector devotes every Thursday wholly to the healing ministry, "in order," he says, "to do justice to the clear command of Our Lord to heal the sick."

He counsels by appointment throughout the day in preparation for the two healing services held at 12:30 and 5:30 in the afternoon. These are attended by approximately four hundred people of all faiths and none, of all races, rich and poor, united briefly as they kneel before the altar in their common need.

Some of these supplicants come from far away. A number have been sent to the healing services by their doctors, and a few physicians sit in the pews with their patients.

Scores of organic, functional, and mental diseases have been healed at St. Stephen's. "We have discovered," says Dr. Price, "that there is no disease that is incurable, and no problem which cannot be solved when God is allowed to take over."

Some of these healings have been instantaneous, as was the case with a woman whose hand was swollen to three times its normal size with arthritis. Immediately after she received the healing sacrament and prayer, her hand returned to its natural size, completely cured. The patient has dedicated this now useful hand to the service of the Lord.

Some healings, rather than "instantaneous," might be called "immediate," as in the case of a spastic baby carried to the high altar by Dr. Price, while her family knelt in prayer at the altar rail.

"The child felt like jelly in my arms," relates Dr. Price. "There was no coordination of arms or limbs. While I prayed, the baby suddenly started to cry with loud, piercing screams."

She continued to cry for two days. The family, frantic with anxiety, called the clergyman, who expressed his opinion that the healing was taking place. "So many experience this same distress," says Dr. Price, "while the battle for healing is going on."

When the infant finally stopped crying and slept, the miracle had taken place. She was completely cured. Today she is a healthy, robust child.

But many healings come more slowly, as did that of a three-year-old child, crippled with a club foot. His right foot was almost completely imbedded in the leg, but after six months of attendance at healing services, the child was completely healed.

The healing of a man with a medically diagnosed cancer of the bone didn't take quite so long. Scheduled for radical surgery, the patient received the sacraments of healing several times. The pain grew less each time he received the rites with prayer, until he was finally free of all discomfort. X-rays revealed what his doctor termed a "miraculous regeneration of the bone."

But however great the physical need, and however wonderful the healings, Dr. Price never lets us forget the necessity of placing disease in the perspective of man's total need, and healing in the context of God's total gift. "The Christian ideal is to have a God-filled personality not for health's sake, but for God's sake."

Nor does he pretend that it is simple to fulfil the essential conditions upon which healing usually depends. "Absolute relinquishment of self and personal ambition is never easy," he remarks. "Nor is it easy to lose one's resentment, and to make thankfulness a constant habit of our minds. But when people go all out to do these things, I have seen the healing power of God rush in with the force of a Niagara river and literally recreate every cell, every tissue, every organ; renew the whole personality—body, mind, and spirit."

The dignity and complete lack of sensationalism of the St. Stephen's services, the powerful support of those dedicated members of the healing Prayer Fellowship; the sound theological approach and deep spirituality of Dr. Price have proved to many ministers and laymen who had reservations that spiritual healing is indeed a revival of an honored and traditional ministry of the Church.

The Price ministry illumines for all to see what he believes to be the heart of the Gospel: "that the power of the Holy Spirit is within us to heal, to inspire, and to give life."

Before he lays on hands, Dr. Price faces the altar and, with out-stretched arms, prays this great prayer of consecration: "O Lord, take my mind and think through it.

Take my heart and set it on fire with love. Take these hands and through them bring to these thy suffering children, the fullness of thy healing power."

Again and again we see this prayer answered; for although Dr. Price makes clear that all are not physically healed, there are few indeed who leave the altar rail unaware of His Presence.

It is said that St. Stephen's Church was the first in Philadelphia to be electrically lit. The light that streams from her now cannot be measured in watts. Penetrating fifteen hundred centuries of darkness, its gleam has pointed the way to a knowledge of Him and of His truth that can transform the world.

The Reverend Richard E. Winkler

(EPISCOPAL)

RICHARD WINKLER, rector of Trinity Episcopal Church in the Chicago suburb of Wheaton, began his ministry of healing less than five years ago when a small group of interested persons began meeting to study prayer in all its phases, and to make intercession for the sick and needy.

"But as I look back now," comments the clergyman, "I think I have always believed in the principles of Christian healing."

Mr. Winkler and his wife, Dorothy, were married eleven years before he was ordained. During that time they saw several dramatic healings take place as a result of prayer. One which touched them closely concerned a member of the family who after a serious automobile accident was hospitalized with broken ribs, a broken vertebra, and a pelvis fractured in three places.

"Prayers were offered by our rector," Mr. Winkler relates, "and a rapid recovery resulted, her time schedule for the healing process being about half as long all the way through as that established by her doctors. One cannot be as close as this to such a healing without being deeply impressed by God's great love and healing power."

One case in Mr. Winkler's early ministry, involved a man whose doctors had given him six months to live following surgery for intestinal cancer. Prayers were offered daily for his recovery, and his condition steadily improved. Six months beyond his expected time to live, he returned to his physician for examination. The doctor was astounded to find him recovered. Today, four years later, he is alive and well, doing work which involves strenuous physical labor.

The faith of the prayer group grew as the members saw continual evidence of the power of the healing Christ, manifested not only in physical cures, or the rapid healings of emotional and mental problems, but in those healings of the spirit which led to conversion.

"It is true," reports Mr. Winkler, "That in the beginning my parish was wary of spiritual healing. I am sure that a large number suspected this, to them new, ministry of mysticism or even some spiritism. But through our prayer group there has been a steady educational process and a leavening growth among the parishioners; so that today in Trinity Church this ministry to the sick is accepted as a normal part of the parish life. Requests for prayers for healing now come from persons who would not have thought of making them a few years ago; and healing services are attended regularly by members of the parish who do not participate in the Prayer Group."

The Trinity Prayer Group is organized as a chapter of the Order of St. Luke. It includes Presbyterians, Congregationalists, Baptists, and others, as well as Episcopalians from nearby parishes, many of whom are members of similar groups in their own church. About one-third of the membership are men, and a number of young married couples are regular attendants at the meetings.

The regular Thursday night meeting of the group closes with a healing service in the Church, with prayers, hymns, and the laying-on-of-hands.

"We have found," states Mr. Winkler, "that the power of the Holy Spirit works in a marvelous way during these healing services held in conjunction with the Prayer Group meeting."

But the clergyman feels a need for the Holy Communion in Christ's healing work; so in addition to the Thursday night healing services he has instituted a weekly celebration of the Lord's Supper, followed by the healing rites. At this service sitters are available for young mothers who wish to attend, but a number of children prefer to take part in the worship and even come to the altar for the laying-on-of-hands.

Mr. Winkler has found that this is the service most frequently attended by visitors from other churches. It is followed by a coffee hour in the Parish Hall, "and it is here," says the minister, "that a great many visitors are introduced to the enthusiasm felt by those who have been active in the work of Christian healing." Through the healing ministry at Trinity, the Holy Spirit has touched and changed the lives of many.

It is a regular and now-expected occurrence that a physical change takes place at almost the same time as prayers for recovery are being offered, as in the case of a hospitalized patient suffering the excruciating pain of gall stones. Within the hour that prayers were said in her behalf, the pain ceased. The patient returned home the next morning, the scheduled surgery canceled.

Through prayers and the healing services, recoveries from all kinds of illnesses are invariably speeded far beyond the doctors' prognostications. Not a few are the spectacular healings which serve to build continually higher the faith of the Church.

A few weeks ago, for example, a woman in her sixties, suffering from a severe phlebitis, which prevented her from walking without the aid of a cane and made it impossible for her to bend her knees, attended the Tuesday morning healing service. Receiving Holy Communion, she suddenly found herself kneeling at the altar rail for the first time in twenty-two years. After the laying-on-of-hands, she walked a mile to her home, leaving her cane in the church.

Another thrilling healing was that of a patient who had suffered a coronary occlusion with severe damage to the heart muscle. The medical prognosis was poor, and an indefinite period of complete bedrest was recommended. Prayers were offered for her, and she received the laying-on-of-hands three times while in bed. After each time a decided improvement was noted. The improvement confirmed by electrocardiogram, the patient was permitted out of bed in just two weeks, and is now living a normal life with a grateful and healthy heart. She is, incidentally, seventy-seven years old!

But, as the Reverend Winkler emphasizes, it is the healing of the spirit, not of the body or mind, which is of primary importance. In this connection he cites the case of a man and wife who dramatically illustrate the totality of Christ's healing power.

This couple, not members of the Church, were referred to his prayer group for help. Their case was already in the divorce courts; the wife had been emotionally disturbed for some time, and the husband was the victim of serious ailments of both stomach and heart. Shortly after prayers were offered for this couple, a singular change came over their lives. The divorce suit was dropped; they were reconciled; and both were completely healed physically as well as spiritually. Members of no church until that time, they joined one in their community. The wife has organized an effective prayer group; the husband devotes much of his time to making hospital calls, and has encouraged a number of his associates to do the same.

"Just another of the many cases," comments Mr. Winkler, "where redeemed lives have gone on to witness God's healing power to others."

The clergyman also describes a personal situation which I have found characteristic of the results of participation in the healing ministry, whether as layman or minister. His three sons, aged thirteen, eleven, and two years, have never suffered a childhood sickness, regardless of exposure. This Mr. Winkler attributes to the protective power of God, to whom each day in perfect faith he commits his family. "Naturally we believe in medicine," he says, "but we also believe first in prayer at the slightest sign of illness."

Richard Winkler's experience with spiritual healing also typifies in another area the experience of the healing clergy everywhere. "As I look over my parish," he says, "and see the Holy Spirit at work in the lives of so many persons, I can say that most of the true conversions to Jesus Christ have come through the healing ministry."

This ministry at Trinity is impressive evidence of the power of the Holy Spirit to heal and to convert. This is the witness of the healing Church, providing the Christian world's best hope for triumph over the antichrist.

The Reverend Charles A. Sumners

(EPISCOPAL)

WHEN I discussed the beginnings of his fine healing ministry with Mr. Sumners of St. David's Episcopal Church in

Austin, Texas, the clergyman smiled rather ruefully and remarked: "I'm afraid this reflects the course of a number of ministers who, along with me, showed a very hesitant approach toward the acceptance of responsibility."

But hesitancy a few years ago was understandable. There was then little knowledge of the Church's healing ministry, and the whole movement might well have proved a wild flight of fancy on the part of a few fanatics. It is in great measure to painstaking theologians like Mr. Sumners that we owe the Church's increasingly widespread acceptance of spiritual healing today, for it was his concern with the theological validity of the healing ministry which dictated his caution. His prolonged study of the ministry eventually convinced him of its integrity and rightful place in the Church's entire ministry.

Mr. Sumners has been interested in healing longer than most clergymen to whom I have talked, for it was during his university days that he made a study of the "Emmanuel Movement," begun in 1906 by the Reverend Elwood Worcester at Emmanuel Church in Boston. This was the first rational and practical application of the psychological method of the problem of religion. Although it died out at the death of its founder, its influence is again evident in ministries such as that of Dr. Norman Vincent Peale, who uses much the same psychiatric-psychological-religious approach to spiritual healing.

Throughout his years at seminary Mr. Sumners maintained his interest. After his ordination he became increasingly convinced that the work of Christian healing was integral in the Church's life, and should be utilized as a regular part of the Church's ministry to her people.

"At the same time," the clergyman pointed out, "I felt the necessity of being on absolutely sound ground Scripturally and theologically before inaugurating this work."

Continuous New Testament study was to bring Mr.

Sumners added conviction, as were the accounts of other healing ministries which were by then available.

"But," he says, "I confess with shame that I was more concerned, first with being theologically sound, and then with the attitude of my fellow-clergy, than I was with the undertaking of a great venture of faith in the Name of Our Lord and Saviour, Jesus Christ. For even after I became convinced that this was the work of the Church and that the Church ought to undertake such a mission with courage and determination, it was still eight or nine years after I became rector of St. David's that I actually held a service of Divine healing."

The Reverend Sumners enumerated for me those four basic factors which finally made the institution of healing services seem imperative.

First, the unchangeableness of God. Either the New Testament is in error, or Jesus Christ performed mighty acts. If He did then, He can now.

Second, the unassailable fact of the practice of the healing ministry throughout the Church's long history. Healing services today are continuous with the tradition of the Church.

Third, all healing comes from God. Without question His healing mercy comes through medicine as well as the healing Sacraments; but no logical reason could suggest that the sacramental life of the Church should be excluded.

Fourth is the fact of modern man's need for healing of soul, mind, and body. The Church has a unique opportunity to bring to humankind a healing grace which at times may be supportive, at times primary, but at all times spiritual and sacramental for man's whole being.

When Charles Sumners made his decision to inaugurate a healing ministry, he had no precedent in his section of Texas. At just about the same time, however, and for the same basic reasons, another such ministry was to begin—that of Charles' twin brother, the Reverend Thomas Sumners of the Church of St. John the Divine in Houston. Both ministries have now been in operation nearly nine years.

The first of the weekly healing services at St. David's in Austin took place on July 1, 1948, and its format has not changed over the years. Following the service of Holy Communion, Mr. Sumners goes to the Prayer Desk in the Chancel for meditation on some fundamental aspect of the Christian faith. The subject of the meditation is often determined by questions which have been recently asked by members of the congregation. Following this period are the intercessions. Only Christian names are used, and the ailments for which prayers are desired are never mentioned. "If they are," says Mr. Sumners, "the ailment frequently becomes the center of thought, and not the mighty action of God, who, in full measure, knows the real difficulty."

After the list of names is read, with frequent pauses for thanksgiving to God for His healing action *now,* those who desire the laying-on-of-hands proceed to the Communion rail. The priest goes to the altar for a prayer of thanksgiving and consecration before he administers the healing Sacrament.

"Although we do not deny that God indeed endows certain individuals with special gifts of healing," states Mr. Sumners, "I think it extremely important that people realize that the efficacy of the healing service is not dependent upon any man, but upon the Sacraments. For this reason we make it a point to have my associate, the Reverend Albert Walling, sometimes assist with the laying-on-of-hands, and occasionally to take the entire service. By doing this, we affirm our conviction concerning the sacramental nature of God's healing action in and through His Church."

When I asked Mr. Sumners to tell me something of the

physical results of his healing ministry, he was inclined to dismiss the question as irrelevent. Nevertheless, the list is long of people whose spiritual lives have been affected by the healing ministry at St. David's, and who have received obvious and definable physical benefits.

A young man, for example, faced a radical operation for a cancerous colon condition. After receiving the laying-on-of-hands, he was not only physically healed by the power of God so that surgery was unnecessary, but, as a result of his experience, underwent a marked personality change. He is now happily married and a tireless worker in the Church. Such was the case, also, with a woman who faced an operation for breast cancer. The growth miraculously disappeared shortly before the scheduled radical mastectomy.

Then there was the dying child who received the laying-on-of-hands at midnight in his hospital crib and immediately took a dramatic turn for the better. He is today in perfect health. And the woman in her late forties who suffered a severe back and hip injury as the result of a fall. In continual pain, controllable only by sedatives, she attended a healing service, was immediately relieved of all pain and discomfort, and filled as well with the God-given vitality which is hers today.

"There are, of course, failures in healing which we cannot explain," comments Mr. Sumners. "All we can do is continue to try through diligent prayer and study to become a more effective instrument of his power and grace. However, I have never administered the Sacrament at any time or in any condition where a lack of physical improvement resulted in disappointment or despair."

During our interview Mr. Sumners suggested that his early conservatism in regard to spiritual healing may have placed him in the category of those condemned by Our Lord: "Neither will they believe though one rose from the dead." If this should be so, his present ministry of healing has surely redeemed him!

The healing ministry at St. David's reflects the humility, the love, and the faith of its administrant, filled now with the deep and abiding feeling that the mighty action of God revealed in Christ Jesus awaits only the mighty action of men who will respond; convinced that those who dare to believe in God's healing grace must act in His Name.

The Reverend Edgar N. Jackson

(METHODIST)

THE HEALING MINISTRY of the Reverend Jackson, of the Mamaroneck, New York, Methodist Church, is particularly interesting because of the pastor's own strongly scientific background and his unusually close association with the medical profession. By virtue of his extensive experience as a hospital chaplain, his membership on a committee studying psychosomatic medicine and spiritual healing, and his present position as administrative head of a clinic, his healing ministry forms a uniquely effective liaison between spiritual healing and medicine.

Pastor Jackson originally studied to be an engineer. When as a very young man he was first confronted with the healing power of prayer, he was torn two ways. The circumstantial evidence of healing was impressive, but his scientific training had, as he says, "instilled in me a good dose of healthy skepticism. I demanded a logical answer for everything." After he ultimately decided to eschew an engineering career and follow in his clergyman father's footsteps, he was to find that answer.

As a chaplain in a mental hospital he first observed the impact of thought and feeling on the functioning of the physical organism. Full realization of the enormous extent to which human emotions could influence the body, causing physical disease of all kinds, came to him during the war when he served as base chaplain at a replacement center. Here he sat in on the daily hospital staff meetings, where cases were discussed in detail. He learned first hand of the immeasurably destructive effects of fear and anxiety on strong bodies. Again and again he saw patients referred to the psychiatrist or chaplain for care, rather than to the surgeon or the doctor of internal medicine.

The impact of his early witness to the healing power of God had never wholly left him. By the end of the war, Mr. Jackson had organized several healing prayer groups for intercession, with exceedingly rewarding results. But he was eager to learn more of the science of human personality. Enrolling in a postgraduate center for psychotherapy, the clergyman pursued his studies, the only minister among a large number of physicians and psychiatrists.

This experience provided an unexcelled opportunity for him to check carefully his ideas on spiritual healing against the best medical judgments of the day. As he puts it: "Being exposed to other professional healing disciplines made me examine carefully the bases of procedure in any activity that had to do with the complicated structure of human personality. But while caution is desirable in any field dealing with the human soul, I concluded that caution should stem from that basic concern, and not from *fear in employing an adventurous faith.* I undertook my healing ministry fully convinced that there are resources available to the clergyman by tradition and practice, which are vitally necessary to complete health, but which obviously cannot be a part of the physician's practice."

Mr. Jackson emphasizes the substantial number of doctors who are in full agreement with this premise, and for this reason are now cooperating to the fullest extent with their colleagues among the clergy.

"Many of these," the minister comments, "accept the soul theory as defined in traditional religious terms, and not a few recognize the influence of spiritual healing. Though they can not understand all that is involved, they have verified what has taken place through medical examinations before and after."

One such case was a healing for an inflammatory skin disease, received by a woman who had been under a specialist's care for many months. Prayers were offered for her at the healing service, and a few days later Mr. Jackson received a telephone call from her physician.

"Mrs. X has just been in for her weekly treatment," said the doctor. "She appears completely cured. What on earth did you do for her at the church?" When told of the group prayer, he readily agreed that this must have been an important factor in her recovery.

The surgeon who operated on Mr. Y outspokenly refers to the patient's complete recovery as a "miracle."

Mr. Y was scheduled for a severe heart operation which involved the freezing of the body. A prayer vigil was arranged for the day of the operation. During surgery the heart stopped beating and did not function for eighteen minutes. When the heart action was restored, there was acute danger of loss of mental competence through lack of oxygen supply to the brain. Not only was the operation successful, but there was no sign of impaired function, and full recovery ensued.

In discussing these and many other similar healings, Mr. Jackson pointed out the variables which exist. Some patients, for example, knew they were being prayed for, and had the feeling of group support which in and of itself was clearly beneficial. Others, however, did not know they were the subject of prayer, and the group support factor did not enter in. One such instance concerned an alcoholic of long standing who, a year ago and unknown to him, was held in prayer at a healing service at the request of his wife. The following day he stopped drinking—without explanation—and has not had a drink since.

Pastor Jackson told me of other cases where the persons healed disavowed all faith in God, but either reluctantly agreed to attend a healing service or to permit the prayer group to pray for them. Such an instance was that of a woman who had had an operation for cancer. Faced with another, she was distraught, claimed no belief in God, and contemplated suicide. A member of no church, she rather unwillingly agreed to permit the Mamaroneck group to pray for her. When she reported for the pre-operative examination, shortly after prayers had been offered in her behalf, there was no evidence of the growth.

In reporting her physical situation before and after the healing, her doctor declared that the malignancy had not only been arrested, but had disappeared. Twenty-one months later, after repeated examinations, the patient showed no evidence of the growth. Her healing, as is almost invariably the case with unbelievers, resulted in her conversion. She has joined a church and organized a prayer group in the community in which she now lives.

Pastor Jackson comments that in some healings the illness was so clearly psychogenic in nature that a change in attitude was sufficient to explain any beneficial results.

"But we quickly move beyond the realm of easy explanation," says the clergyman, "when we see healings where an actual change of tissue is involved. It seems to me clear that the spiritual nature of man cannot be limited by explanation."

Believing that life is a spiritual fact, a point of view that has much support from modern science at this point, Mr. Jackson, through his healing ministry strives to be a channel for the healing and redeeming love of God. Through his ministry, he is seeking to live and practice the nature of God that was revealed in the life and teaching of Jesus.

"This," he says, "is not so much a philosophy as it is a way of life, rooted in a daring and adventurous faith. We do not so much seek to *have* a faith, as to *be* a faith. We do not so much seek to love in the abstract as to love in the concrete relations of life that engage us."

The healing services at Mamaroneck Church are simple and ritualistic, consisting of Scripture reading, a short meditation, the laying-on-of-hands, and prayer.

"Our praying," explains Mr. Jackson, "is not a medical exercise, not an assult on symptoms. Rather it is a determined effort to release life from the ideas that constrict and destroy it. In this way we do not interfere with any other form of healing that may be employed. We support it, supplement it, and move *beyond* it to the spiritual nature of man where true health is found. For we remember well the words of Jesus, 'Your faith has made you well.' "

When I asked the Reverend Jackson what he felt to be his primary purpose as a minister of Jesus Christ, he answered: "To help persons grow to an adventurous faith that helps to bring them wholeness of being."

This, I think, comes close to what Jesus meant when He promised a more abundant life.

The Reverend John H. Parke

(EPISCOPAL)

SPIRITUAL HEALING has never been a new concept to John Parke, the young rector of St. James Episcopal Church, Newport Beach, California; for his clergyman father was marvelously healed of tuberculosis when John was a small boy. Brought up in a home where, as he says, "the idea of healing through prayer and Sacraments was as natural as the air we breathed," it is scarcely surprising that Mr.

Parke should have considered healing a regular part of his total ministry. His belief was even further strengthened by a deep spiritual experience underwent while serving as Chaplain for the 261st Infantry in France.

Just after the Battle of the Bulge, the end of January, 1945, the regiment was encamped in the mud at Camp Lucky Strike, not far from Le Havre. Mr. Parke, along with many of his men, had succumbed to what was called "atypical" pneumonia; and after running a fever of 105 degrees for two days in a field tent, he was taken to a hospital in Dieppe.

Father Parke recalls that "after taking a great handful of sulpha pills in the afternoon," he fell into a sort of delirium around seven P.M., having a feeling he was hovering between heaven and hell, and very close to death. He remembers that around eight o'clock a nurse came in to take his pulse and temperature, and, as she left the room, she snapped out the light, leaving the door open just a crack.

"The next moment," relates the clergyman, "I had the most extraordinary experience of my life. A strange, ghostly light began pouring in from that crack, moved up toward the ceiling, then along the wall and directly toward me. I got up on one elbow and stared at this thing, terrified. Then with a feeling that this was some sort of angel of death approaching me, I began a rhythmic prayer, 'Jesus be with me' with every breath.

"As I prayed, the shapeless light retreated, but then, as fear returned, so did this apparition. I then decided to lie down, relax, and close my eyes, continuing the prayer. My heart was beating like a trip-hammer, and I was conscious that the light was now hovering right over me.

"Suddenly three ice-cold shocks wracked my body, followed by a flood of warmth, and I felt Our Lord's actual Presence with me more vividly than ever before or since in my life. The breathing came easier now. I could sense that the light was receding, and finally was gone, although I didn't open my eyes to look. My rhythmic prayer now became, 'Jesus, be with me forever.'

"A few minutes later the nurse returned, switched on the light, and, looking at me sharply, remarked; 'What's happened to you?' I simply smiled and said, 'I'll be all right now.'

"I slept soundly, and the next morning had a normal temperature. Ever since that time I have had more than an academic belief in the power of prayer. I have felt a deep certainty."

Mr. Parke's first healing experience was with sick children, for early in his ministry he discovered how responsive to prayer is the subconscious of a child, and how readily released in children is the healing power of God.

He mentions, for example, the times within the past year that he has received frantic calls from parents, saying that their new-born child had congestion of the lungs, and was given less than a fifty-fifty chance to live.

"Each time," reports Father Parke, "I felt I could meet the situation with confidence, first reassuring the mother, asking her to relax and just surround her baby with love, releasing it to God's loving care. Then donning a mask and gown, I went into the hospital nursery, looked down on the infant, set my breathing in harmony with the child's, visualized the lungs becoming clear, and thanked God for His healing power. In every case the child was out of danger within the hour."

Just a few weeks ago the clergyman received a call from another distraught mother. Her little girl, eighteen months old, was convalescing from pneumonia. Through vomiting and diarrhea, the child had become completely dehydrated and refused to eat or drink. She was receiving intravenous feeding in the hospital, but was making no progress. Her condition was precarious. "I laid on hands with the prayer of faith," says Mr. Parke. "Within half an hour the child took a bowl of Jello and, to the amazement of the nurses, began eating with normal appetite."

In every parish in which he has served since the war, Father Parke has instituted a healing ministry and organized a supporting prayer group, the members of which he personally selects. His weekly healing service on Thursday is invariably preceded by a prayer group meeting, after which he administers Holy Communion, followed by the laying-on-of-hands with anointing for those who desire it. Sometimes those who receive the sacramental rites are praying for themselves, but often they are seeking healing for someone else, for, Father Parke comments, "we find that the healing Sacraments received with special intention for the sick give added power to the intercessor."

An example of this is the healing of a woman suffering from cancer of the colon and an intestinal blockage. The clergyman was called to the hospital on a Thursday afternoon to see the sick woman. She appeared amazingly cheerful. "The doctor says I'm going to be fine," she announced jubilantly. "And the blockage passed this morning at about ten o'clock."

Father Parke made no comment, but noted that that was just the time the prayer group was praying for her. "I was reminded," he said to me, "of those passages in the Gospels: 'It was at the seventh hour the fever left him.' "

For a period of several weeks, there appeared among the other communicants at St. James's altar rail, an Eskimo from an Episcopal Mission in Alaska. The young man had been wounded by a polar bear several months before, and had suffered exposure for three days during a blizzard. As a consequence of this experience, he had developed a crippling arthritis. Sent to the warm climate of California in the hope that this would help him, he learned of the healing ministry at the Newport Beach Church. He traveled many miles by bus to attend services and received the Sacrament of Unction. He ascribes his healing progress to the power of God, channeled through this Sacrament, rather than to the change of climate.

Not long ago he stood on the steps of St. James's and read the notice of the Thursday healing service on the church's signboard. Smiling, he nodded his approval. "I wish I could see that sign everywhere," he said.

"Some day" remarked Father Parke, "I think he will."

The Reverend Crawford W. Brown

(EPISCOPAL)

DR. BROWN has established a notable healing ministry at the Church of Our Saviour, San Gabriel, California, where he assumed his present post as rector in 1953. Equally well known for his outstanding healing work in Washington, D.C., where he served as Canon of Washington Episcopal Cathedral for five years, it is fitting that he should be Chairman of the Healing Commission of the Diocese of Los Angeles.

Dr. Brown is an eloquent spokesman for the theological validity of the healing ministry.

"Healing," he emphasizes, "is not something that the Protestant Episcopal Church has suddenly become enamoured with. It is not something that has of this moment been given to the Church by an Act of both Houses of General Convention. It is an integral part of the corporate life and worship of the Church of Jesus Christ. It is sacramental, and, further, it was central in the life and teaching of Our Lord; and, as such, the Church has received the same."

This eminent Episcopal clergyman reminds us that in

Jesus Christ, God invaded history with power and with great glory. "This should be a glorious truth to all who profess Christianity and who call upon Jesus Christ as their Saviour and Lord.

"But when" he asks, "will this mighty truth grip and hold Christians everywhere, the clergy as well as the laity?"

Immediately after Dr. Brown came to the San Gabriel Church five years ago he organized the Prayer Fellowship which has so strongly supported his healing ministry there. Ever since then, this prayer chain has been operating eighteen hours a day, each member being responsible for fifteen minutes of prayer for the sick. Thousands of names are prayed for each year, requests being sent or called in from members of all churches.

The healing services are conducted without fanfare or publicity, except for a weekly notice that each Wednesday there is a Service of Holy Communion, with prayers and the laying-on-of-hands.

"The power of the Holy Spirit," says Dr. Brown, "has eloquently testified to the validity of all that is done and said here."

This would seem abundantly true, for God's power has reached down and touched many at these services.

Of the numerous healings which have occurred under Dr. Brown's ministry, one, the personal testimony of a well-known doctor, is offered here in full, as he gave it to me:

"Physicians have long recognized the close tie between spiritual and physical healing. Most of us appreciate the fact that when physical healing ends, it is possible for spiritual healing to complete the process.

"In my own case I was in a Naval hospital suffering with far advanced pulmonary tuberculosis. Specialists in this disease know that the patient goes through four stages before he may recover.

"The first stage is that of shock. He cannot quite realize what has happened to him, and the full import of his personal catastrophe has not yet impressed him.

"The second stage is a feeling of great depression. His whole world has collapsed around his feet, and the world looks very dark indeed.

"The third stage is that of resentment or belligerence. Why should this horrible disease afflict him? He knows his friends and associates are continuing their daily existence in good health, but he is confined to bed for a year or more.

"The fourth stage is that of hope. Perhaps there is a chance that he will get well—a chance that he may be able to resume his normal life if he spends the required time in bed, and if the medicines are effective in curing his disease.

"It is in this fourth and final stage that the spiritual healing plays such an important part in completing the cure of the body.

"My wife was invited by her mother to attend a healing service conducted by the Reverend Crawford Brown. She was so impressed by this service that she immediately telephoned me at the hospital and told me the hour at which these services were conducted weekly. I decided to take part in them, although from a great distance. By praying for help in regaining my health, perhaps our combined efforts would be of benefit to me. Amazingly enough, from that day on, my physical condition improved remarkably, and my spiritual health soared.

"One afternoon after I was permitted to be up, I was watching a telecast of a baseball game in the officer's lounge. I was joined by a Navy chaplain who was undergoing tests for tuberculosis. At the end of the inning he turned to me and said: 'Doctor, you take care of the bodies, and I take care of the souls. Let's get our bodies and souls together and go over to the sick ward and see if we can do some good.' How true his philosophy, and how effective could be our combined talents.

"When I returned home for convalescence, I was able to attend in person Dr. Brown's healing services. On each occasion I could feel health flowing into my body from his hands placed upon my head; and, hearing his prayers, I knew the power of spiritual help in healing my body."

This doctor, who has himself experienced the Presence and healing of the Holy Spirit, could understand the remarkable, instantaneous eye healing received by a high-school girl. Absent from school for a month because of a serious eye ailment, this girl heard of the healing services at Dr. Brown's church and decided to attend. So certain was she of healing that she took her school books with her to the church, planning to go straight on to school. After the laying-on-of-hands and prayer, she was indeed ready to proceed to school—for she found herself perfectly healed.

Dr. Brown stands convinced that the essential ministry of the Church is comprehended in Our Lord's command to teach, preach, baptize, and pray. He challenges all clergy everywhere when he says: "It is incumbent upon the clergy of the Church of the Living God to bring to the attention of all the people committed to their care the philosophies, the aims, the objectives, the faith, the Sacraments, and the True Word of the Living God, whose command of nearly two thousand years ago still rings in our ears. There is a terrific heart and soul hunger for spiritual nourishment; and only by feeding the whole man, body, mind, and spirit, with spiritual food that is available, will we be able to 'down' some of the rampant humanism and materialism, and quench some of the fears that sting men worse than the 'fiery darts of the devil.' "

The rector of Our Saviour makes clear that the reply of Jesus to the Sadducees is as relevant today as when it was first spoken.

"The same day came to him the Sadducees, which say that there is no resurrection. . . . Jesus answered and said unto them, Ye do err, not knowing the Scriptures, nor the power of God" (*Matthew 22:23–29*).

The Church is now charged with His Presence and with His power. Dr. Brown asks a cogent question of both clergy and laity: "Will we recognize the Presence—and will we use the power?"

The Reverend Richard Rettig

(UNITED CHURCH OF CHRIST)

WHEN ONE OF his seminary professors heard that Dr. Rettig of St. Peter's United Church of Christ,* Pittsburgh, had begun a healing ministry, he was astounded. "Not Rettig of all people!" he gasped. This was the general reaction of all who knew this clergyman, for Richard Rettig, outstanding intellectual, had made a name for himself throughout the Church as a modernist and liberalist of the first order.

"I attended a conservative seminary, which my father had attended before me," he relates, "but modernism was in the air, and I absorbed it like a sponge. I well remember the distress of my professors when I argued for a liberal interpretation of accepted doctrine. And curiously enough, I, of all my class, was the only one to depart from the 'faith once and for all delivered to the saints.' "

When Richard Rettig graduated from seminary he had, as he says now, "all the answers, intellectually, but I had nothing whatsoever to give to the hungry soul. My mind came between me and God, and although I never would

---

* This denomination is the result of a recently-effected union of the Evangelical Reformed and Congregational Christian Churches.

have admitted it then, the truth was that I was spiritually bankrupt."

For years Dr. Rettig preached a liberal Gospel, adeptly explaining away the miracles of Jesus. "Those I couldn't put aside so easily," he recalls, "I just never preached about."

It was four successive breakdowns of his back, culminating finally in a fusion operation, which were actually to lead this minister back to the simple, basic faith he had relinquished many years before.

"One of the firmest tenets of my faith is that God never sends sickness upon His children," comments Dr. Rettig, "but I do know that God uses all the experiences of life, and can make them work out for good to them that love Him. It was when I was lying flat on my back, unable to move, that I learned to know Him as I never could have otherwise."

This clergyman had never believed in spiritual healing, but within a few weeks after his return to his pulpit, the evangelistic ministry of Kathryn Kuhlman was brought to his attention. Extremely skeptical, but curious, he attended one of her services and was amazed at what he saw.

"I wondered," he says, "why these 'signs and wonders' should not take place within our churches, where I felt they really belonged."

At just about that time Dr. Alfred Price came to Pittsburgh to conduct a healing mission at Trinity Episcopal Cathedral. Dr. Rettig attended these services and was profoundly impressed. After a long conference with Dr. Price, followed by some intensive research on the healing ministry, he started in his own church to preach on prayer and faith, praying for the sick, by name, before each Sunday sermon.

Remarkable healings began to occur with increasing frequency, and names for prayer poured in until they became too numerous to read. Dr. Rettig then established a Wednesday night prayer group, where names were read until the list again grew too long to permit individual mention.

In 1953 the clergyman procured permission from his Church Board to hold weekly healing services with the laying-on-of-hands. These services, held every Saturday afternoon, last one and one-half hours and are conducted quietly and reverently.

"I pray as the Holy Spirit guides me," explains Dr. Rettig, "and I have been told that the prayers are so appropriate to the condition of the individual that it seems as though I had known the need of each."

Two-thirds of the persons who attend these services are not members of St. Peter's, but represent many diverse denominations. Many come from great distances. To this congregation, the pastor continually emphasizes the primary purpose of spiritual healing, which is not, as he makes clear, the curing of the body, but rather, the healing of the spirit. Also, lest there be any misunderstanding, he impresses upon his people the fact that the healing ministry acknowledges the reality of sin, sickness, and suffering, and encourages the use of medical science. To make this point doubly clear, he has printed on the prayer request forms, "This is not a substitute for medical aid."

A monthly prayer letter with a revised sick list goes to hundreds of people in some thirty-six states. The vast majority of these have agreed to pray for the sick and for the healing ministry at St. Peter's. Many are the healings which occur under this ministry, both through intercessory prayer and as the result of direct contact: healings of alcoholism, mental sickness, and physical disease of all kinds. In virtually every instance a deep spiritual regeneration has taken place in the individual concerned.

Some cures are instantaneous. A woman suffering from

blood poisoning, racked with chills and fever and in intense pain, attended a healing service en route to her doctor's. She was instantly and completely healed that afternoon at the church. A woman suffering acute pain from an internal hernia, went to St. Peter's a few days before her scheduled operation. During the prayer for the sick, she felt something like an electric current pour through her body. The pain increased almost beyond endurance (as is often the case in instantaneous healing) and then suddenly subsided. By the end of the service, she felt completely well. A visit to her doctor confirmed her expectation. "A perfect healing. No surgery required" was the verdict.

But Dr. Rettig points out that the majority of healings appear to be gradual. He cites, for example, the case of a man desperately ill with a grave heart condition. When the clergyman was called to the house, the patient's lungs had already filled with fluid (pulmonary edema). Diuretics had proved ineffective, and his condition was considered medically hopeless.

Before administering the healing rites, the Reverend Rettig talked at length to the man's wife, explaining to her the necessity, on her part, of what might perhaps be termed the ultimate in faith. "God has the last word," he explained. "There is nothing He cannot do. But He cannot accomplish His purpose until you learn to let go. You must be willing to commit your husband entirely to God, trusting Him implicitly."

This was far from easy for the apprehensive wife; but after much weeping and inner turmoil, she was able to say, and apparently mean: "God, he is Yours. Whatever You do is all right with me."

The clergyman then proceeded to the sickroom, and after praying with the patient, laid hands over his heart.

There was no immediately dramatic result, but within an amazingly short time thirteen quarts of fluid had drained from this man's body. He had lost thirty-one pounds in weight, and his blood pressure had dropped sixty-four points when he returned to his doctor. The physician shook his head, examined him again, then said: "I can't account for this thing, but you have a completely new machine inside you."

Richard Rettig frankly admits that he came close to intellectualizing himself out of faith. However, he discovered in time, and is now demonstrating for all to see, the dynamic power of practicing the full faith as opposed to the spiritual poverty which follows the equivocal belief of many modern intellectuals.

His former "erudite" and selective teaching, has been replaced by the preaching of an unadulterated Gospel, which points the way to holiness so simply that "wayfaring men, though fools, shall not err therein" (*Isaiah 35:8*).

This is a ministry of great spiritual power, founded on an arduously acquired child-like faith in the promises of Jesus Christ. It is an open channel for God's healing grace, as its leader bears eloquent witness to the eternal verity of Our Lord's Words: "If thou canst believe, all things are possible to him that believeth" (*Mark 9:23*).

The Reverend Robert A. Russell

(EPISCOPAL)

THE RECTOR of Denver's Epiphany Episcopal Church is a distinguished pioneer in the healing field.

It was more than twenty-five years ago, as a young minister just out of seminary, that Robert Russell took the healing ministry to the seven small mission churches in the mining camps of Colorado which he was then serving. Although spiritual healing was an entirely new concept to these mountain people, their response was overwhelming. The mountain chapels soon became too small to accommodate the crowds.

The young clergyman was then transferred to a small and moribund parish in Denver. This tiny church was destined to become, through its powerful ministry of healing, the second largest, the most dynamic and the most widely-publicized in Colorado.

In a matter of six months little Epiphany numbered among its congregation and membership many of the richest, most influential, and prominent citizens of Colorado. Loud-speakers were installed in the crypt of the old building, but the crowds kept pressing upon the little structure until it became necessary to move the congregation to the South Gate Masonic Temple. Here, after only a few months, the same situation was repeated, and it was finally decided to build the present beautiful church which is also known as The Shrine of the Healing Presence.

Dr. Russell's unusually long interest in spiritual healing is understandable, for, as he explains: "Being blessed with a mother of great faith and spiritual power, and having seen so many miraculous answers to her prayers, it is only natural that I should have grown up believing that faith can accomplish anything."

One of his early contacts with the healing power of God, and one which made an indelible impression upon him, occurred when he was a small boy. It involved the instant healing of his mother from a strangulated hernia, in answer to prayer.

"That incident occurred fifty years ago," recalls the clergyman, "but I shall never forget the story as she told it to us children the next day. She said that as she prayed for healing, the Presence of Christ was so real and so near that she actually placed her hand in His."

In the early years of his healing work, before his ministry at Epiphany had assumed its present time-consuming proportions, Dr. Russell held healing missions in Episcopal churches all over the United States. One of the first of these was at La Jolla, California.

Here a devout Presbyterian woman, who had traveled eighty miles to attend the mission, was instantly healed of double cataracts. When she returned to the oculist next morning, he was amazed to find no evidence of the cataracts for which surgery had already been scheduled. This dramatic healing of a woman well known and highly respected in her community was instrumental in Dr. Russell's meteoric rise in the field of spiritual healing.

From the beginning of his healing ministry Dr. Russell has combined a metaphysical approach with emphasis on the Sacraments. The thousands to whom the Healing Shrine has successfully ministered vouch for the efficacy of his method.

Epiphany Church conducts two public healing services each week in the Shrine, both well attended by people of all denominations. At the Thursday morning service, divine healing is invoked for all on the prayer list, each name being mentioned aloud.

The evening service of the same day includes instructions by the rector and the laying-on-of-hands.

The prayer group which supports this ministry is known as the Silent Ministry of Healing. It comprises men and women especially trained in prayer who are devoting their lives to God's work for humanity.

"They are proving daily," says Dr. Russell, "that physical, financial, mental, and spiritual difficulties can be overcome by scientific prayer."

The clergyman makes clear, however, that the primary purpose of spiritual therapy is not to make unhappy people happy; or poor people rich; or sick people well.

"These are only results," he emphasizes. "The primary

object is to help people realize the Presence of Christ."

He stresses the fact that healing lies in the total surrender of the individual to God.

"You must give Him your entire heart, mind, soul, and strength. In other words, you must 'put on the whole armour of God.' Only a part will not suffice."

To illustrate his meaning Dr. Russell cited the case of a devout woman who had asked him to pray for the healing of her broken hip which would not mend. In questioning the patient, the minister discovered that she was harboring a bitter resentment against the first doctor who had tended her injury; for he had set her hip incorrectly, with the result that it had to be re-set six months later by another physician.

In response to the woman's sincere assertion: "I believe that God can heal me," Dr. Russell replied: "Of course He can, but not until you give up this hatred which is generating poison in your mind."

"Well, there's nothing I can do about that," she answered, "for I shall hate that doctor as long as I live."

The clergyman left, unable to help her.

Several months later the woman again called him.

"I'm trying to love Dr. ———. Will you pray for me that I may be forgiven for the hatred I have been holding toward him?" she asked. She was subsequently quickly and completely healed, for she had "put on the *whole* armour of God," which in her case meant relinquishing her hatred and replacing it with love.

Dr. Russell is convinced that with absolute faith it is as easy to cure a cancer as a headache.

"Too often we open the mind through faith," he remarked, "and then slam it shut through doubt."

Not long ago, the clergyman was called to a hospital in the middle of the night. A seventy-year-old patient had fallen down a flight of stone steps, and for four days had lain in a coma with a fractured skull and other serious injuries.

Greeted at the hospital by a nurse and the patient's family, who had called him, Dr. Russell was told that three specialists had called the case hopeless. The woman was not expected to survive the night.

"Doubt and despair," says the minister, "are actually malignant forces operating against faith. They filled that hospital room. I asked the nurse to leave while I prayed, knowing that at a time like this, an unweakened and radical faith was needed; and that it was up to me to provide it."

Before the healing prayer was concluded, the patient had regained consciousness. The following day she went for a drive, and on the third day, went home from the hospital.

"Records of this sort are endless," commented Dr. Russell. "Undeviating faith invariably serves as the channel through which God moves."

The Reverend Robert Russell has dedicated his life to the restoration of the apostolic practice of healing in the Name of Jesus Christ by prayer, anointing, and the laying-on-of-hands. He has exerted a profound influence on the reestablishment of the identity of Christian healing with the whole Gospel of the Church Universal.

For many people in many churches, the name of this clergyman will be irrevocably linked with the twentieth-century revival of the great ministry of healing.

The Reverends John A. Collins and Williston M. Ford

(EPISCOPAL)

GRACE EPISCOPAL CATHEDRAL in San Francisco was one of the first churches in the United States to institute the ministry of healing as we know it today. Here in 1920, as the result of an American mission held by the gifted English lay healer, James Moore Hickson, healing services were started by the Very Reverend J. Wilmer Gresham, Dean of the Cathedral. His distinguished ministry was to continue for over twenty years.

Participating in the early development of the Cathedral's Mission of Healing were two young clergymen, John Collins and Williston Ford. They were to assist the Dean for some years until, transferred from the Cathedral to different parishes, they went their separate ways, each taking to whatever church he served the ministry of healing.

By strange coincidence these two ministers, whose experience in the healing field has run so curiously parallel (both are now chaplains of the Order of St. Luke), have found themselves reunited at St. Peter's-by-the-Golden Gate. Here the Reverend Collins, as rector of this church, is conducting an effective healing ministry, aided and supported by his colleague, Williston Ford, who, although retired from the active ministry, continues his healing work as chaplain of the St. Luke Mission.

History has seemed to repeat itself for these two clergymen at St. Peter's. For as their efforts were instrumental in bringing healing to the San Francisco area through the

Cathedral, so have they again restored this ministry to the community through their present church, which has replaced the healing services at the Cathedral, discontinued after Dean Gresham's retirement.

It was in 1949 that the Reverend Collins instituted his weekly healing services at St. Peter's after the congregation's interest had been sparked by visits from the Reverend John Gaynor Banks and Bishop Austin Pardue.

"From their inception," says Mr. Collins, "these services have attracted many people from faraway places." In fact, so widespread has been the interest and so urgent the demand, that it has been hoped that the healing ministry would soon be revived in Grace Cathedral. In view of the sentiments of Dean James A. Pike, newly elected Bishop Coadjutor of the Diocese of California, there is good reason to believe that this hope will be realized. Dean Pike made very clear to me his stand on spiritual healing when he recently said: "I am of course interested in and sympathetic to the revival and advance of the ministry of healing as any priest of our Church should be."

Meanwhile Mr. Collins has patterned his healing service after that used by Dean Gresham in the Cathedral.

The Tuesday evening gathering starts as a prayer group, remembering the names of those who ask help. Then follow the hymns and an address which immediately precedes the laying-on-of-hands. This rite is performed as though Christ were speaking through the ministrant, whose hands release His healing power.

The atmosphere of the service induces a very real sense of the Presence of Our Lord, "thought of as the Presence of Love," says Mr. Ford. "Christ being the eternal manifestation of love, His power presides and prevails in a very natural yet marvelous way."

Father Ford, in citing his own peace of soul and nervous rehabilitation which has resulted from his knowledge of the healing Christ, mentions the power of what he calls "spiritual relaxation" in a childbirth case of a few weeks ago.

The tense, frightened young mother went to the clergyman for help. After praying with her he gave her a simple meditation based on the words, "Be still and know that I am Love."

When the young woman arrived at the hospital, she appeared so tranquil that one of the nurses told her to return home until her labor had properly begun. The patient, however, insisted on examination; whereupon it was discovered that she was in the final stage of labor. Delivery was quick, and her recovery unusually rapid.

Through his healing ministry over the years, the Reverend Ford has continually emphasized that love heals; that God's infinite Love is the Healer; and that God above, dwelling within, is the focal or contact point of healing.

"Recognition of this truth," he says, "raises spiritual healing far above the level of magic or wishful thinking." This recognition, fostered by the healing ministry, results in many transformed lives, as was the case of a woman who had been under a doctor's care for several years, for a number of valid physical ailments. Physically sick, nervously exhausted, and mentally depressed over her long invalidism, the ministry of healing was finally brought to her attention by a solicitous friend. Skeptical, she nevertheless agreed to do some reading on that subject and attend a few healing services. Almost despite herself, she gradually became aware of the reality of the living Christ, who by His love heals all who turn to him. In a remarkably short time this woman was completely healed. Today, filled with gratitude and the love of God, she is radiant with a happiness which infects all those who come in contact with her.

"While we do not keep case records," says Mr. Collins, "there are continued witnessings given of healing."

In view of the number of cancer cases which have come to his attention, where resentment and hostility were invariably evident in the patient, Father Ford has become a firm advocate of the medical school of thought which is coming to believe that all disease may actually be psychosomatic or the result of stress.

He cites as a typical example the case of a forty-five-year old woman who was suffering from a large uterine growth. In talking to this patient, Mr. Ford discovered that she was harboring an overwhelming resentment against her husband because of his conjugal demands upon her. Through counseling and healing prayer, this patient was finally able to overcome her feelings of hostility and resentment. A short time after she had happily assumed her marital responsibility, she returned to the doctor for examination. There was no evidence whatsoever of the former growth.

Both Mr. Collins and Mr. Ford, as a result of their long experience in the healing field, are convinced that teaching and healing should go hand in hand. They recall the cessation of healing services at Grace Cathedral when Dean Gresham retired, and agree that "People had relied so much upon the loving personality of the Dean that his absence resulted in a gradual loss of expectancy. Unless teaching is made inseparable from healing, people tend to depend upon the power of a personality rather than on God."

They emphasize also that to "guarantee" healing or to anoint with consecrated oil without teaching the purpose of spiritual healing is dangerous and bound to end in disappointment, even though a temporary physical benefit may result.

"Without a prayer group," says Mr. Ford, "and without teaching, healing is able to rest only upon blind faith, self-persuasion, egocentric reliance upon one's own will, dependence upon some leader's personality, or passive credulity. None of these impart permanent cure or spiritual rebirth."

Participants in the healing ministry of St. Peter's-by-the-Golden Gate are conscious of the fact that, since Love is the Life of God, His Nature and His Being, each instant of Love heals. Touched by the Holy Spirit at work in this church, its members have come into a new awareness of a great truth: that Jesus Christ resides within each awakened soul.

Agnes Sanford

(LAY HEALER)

I VENTURE to say that there is no member of the laity in the United States who is wielding a greater or more widespread influence on the revival of healing within the churches than Agnes Sanford, daughter of a Presbyterian missionary and wife of an Episcopal priest.

Her first book, *The Healing Light,* published in 1947, has gone into nineteen editions and has been reprinted in seven languages. Not only has it guided innumerable laymen into a knowledge of the healing Christ, but it has served as both a revelation and a text book for hundreds of clergymen of all denominations.

Its author is a small woman of immense spiritual stature, vibrant with the love and vitality of God. A realist with a dash of mysticism, she is a curious combination of creative imagination and objective rationalism; of intellectuality and childish simplicity; of deep religiosity, yet with something of the scientist's dedication to the principle that the fundamental laws of the universe cannot be broken.

"The scientist," she writes "has faith in the laws of nature, combined with perfect humility towards these laws, and a patient determination to learn them at whatever cost. Through this humility, scientists have learned how to conform to the laws of nature, and by so doing have achieved results. Through the same meekness, those who seek God can produce results by learning to conform to His laws of faith and love."

Convinced that God does nothing except by law, Mrs. Sanford is equally convinced that He has provided enough power within His law to do anything that is in accordance with His will. Confident that His will is for health, and that within man's body are vital forces that make for health when God's love is channeled into him through faith, Mrs. Sanford's concern is that a patient's mind and body be open to the goodness and love of God. As she makes clear, "the infinite and eternal life of God cannot help us unless we are prepared to receive that life within ourselves."

It was twenty-five years ago that Agnes Sanford had her first experience with God's healing power. Her infant son had been ill for over six weeks with abscessed ears. As her prayers for his healing appeared unanswered, her bitterness and doubt grew. Then one afternoon a young minister stopped by the Sanford's home. Immediately on hearing of the baby's illness, he said: "I'll go up and have a prayer with him." Walking over to the crib, he placed his hands on the child's ears, and said a simple prayer, ending with a spontaneous word of faith: "Now shut your eyes and go to sleep, and when you wake up you will be all right." Instantly the baby fell asleep; he woke up the next morning completely well.

"This incident," says Mrs. Sanford, "turned on the light for me. It showed me that God is an active and powerful reality."

A year later, suffering from profound depression, she

sought out this same clergyman and asked his prayers. He laid his hands on her head, and prayed for the healing of her mind and nerves. "No problems were solved," recalls Mrs. Sanford, "because neither he nor I knew what they were. But I was marvelously healed. From that time forward, I began to learn. I followed this young minister's suggestions for prayer, and slowly the faith that I had said in words, unbelieving, came to me.

"I then asked him whether he thought a layman could learn to help people as he had helped me. He answered yes, and prayed for me to receive the gift of healing."

After a few experiments with prayer Agnes Sanford began to realize it was God's will that she enter the then virtually uncharted sea of spiritual healing. After a year of Bible study, "to see exactly what the Word taught about this matter," she began her work. "I knew," she says, "that I must go about this thing slowly; and I learned by doing."

It soon became evident that the young clergyman's prayer in her behalf had been answered, for she possessed an undeniable charismatic gift of healing, which has grown to an extraordinary degree over the years—a fact that causes her to believe that anyone with a sincere desire to heal can cultivate this gift by prayer and spiritual discipline.

By lecturing, writing, and conducting healing missions throughout the nation, many in conjunction with her clergyman husband, she has spread the word of the healing Christ. She works interdenominationally, but always within the framework of the organized Church. Clergymen of all denominations have come to accept the theological integrity of her teaching, as well as the evidence of the healing power of God which her work so thrillingly demonstrates.

Take, for example, the case of a small child dying of a brain tumor, who was brought to her for prayer and the

laying-on-of-hands. The medical prognosis was total blindness within a few weeks, followed rapidly by death. The
little girl was taken to Mrs. Sanford by her parents and
their Presbyterian minister, who knew virtually nothing of
spiritual healing. What he learned that afternoon was to
re-vitalize his ministry. The child received healing from
Mrs. Sanford and today appears well.

Or take the case of the man with a badly damaged
heart, who was instantly healed by God's power after he
received the laying-on-of-hands. Or the instant healing of
a pneumonia case. Or the healing within a week of a
woman whose physical health was shattered, and whom
psychiatrists had given up—a woman so seriously disturbed emotionally that she had made two suicide attempts.

The tremendously large number of remarkable healings
of this sort which have taken place under Mrs. Sanford's
lay ministry are well known. She is so constantly in demand to pray with and for the sick that it has been difficult
for her to concentrate on what, from the beginning, has
been her aim and purpose: to teach people to pray and
heal so that the ministry of healing may be restored to its
rightful place in the whole church.

Two years ago the way to do just this opened up for her.
A teaching center for spiritual healing was established in
Whitinsville, Massachusetts. She and her husband head
this School of Pastoral Care. Sponsored by eminent clergymen of many denominations and by a number of doctors
and psychiatrists, their school is, as Mrs. Sanford puts it,
"for the purpose of passing on to clergymen of all churches
what we have learned of faith and prayer. Our aim is to
help ministers to a better understanding of how they can
aid their people in illness, depression, alcoholism, emotional disturbances, and guilt complexes."

Mrs. Sanford explains that the sessions held at the

school are not retreats or conferences, but classes held to instruct the clergy in intercessions and the laying-on-of-hands; to lead them to a deeped realization of the spiritual power that is the heritage of all Christian ministers—the same power practiced by the apostles.

The response to the school has been extremely gratifying. At the request of many clergymen, its activities were recently expanded to include sessions for their wives as well as themselves; and, at the request of the Right Reverend William Lawrence, Episcopal Bishop of Western Massachusetts, at least one session each summer is to be held for lay people. But these lay sessions are strictly "extras." The emphasis and real purpose of the school is on and for clerical instruction.

Through this teaching center the healing ministry is being spread through the churches of America in a way not possible by any other means. Already the healing work of its "graduates" is becoming known. They come from as far south as Florida and Texas, as far north as the outposts of Canada and Alaska; they include Episcopalians, Methodists, Presbyterians, Lutherans, Congregationalists, Baptists, and others.

"Here we work together," says Mrs. Sanford, "in fellowship and unity in the world of prayer, where no compromise is necessary."

The contribution of Agnes Sanford to the healing ministry is two-fold: as a remarkable conductor of God's love, she fully demonstrates His healing power. As an outstanding teacher of His spiritual laws, she is handing on, so that it may perpetually flame within the Church, the torch lit by her conviction of the Kingdom which is within us all.

Louise W. Eggleston

(LAY HEALER)

SOME years ago Louise Eggleston, outstanding Methodist churchwoman, learned of the healing power of God released through prayer. Since that time, as founder and leader of the interdenominational World Literacy Prayer Group which meets at Ghent Methodist Church in Norfolk, Virginia, and as Spiritual Life Leader of the Virginia Conference of Methodist Women, Mrs. Eggleston has devoted her life to sharing her knowledge with others. Through her pamphlets on prayer, her work in churches all over the nation, and her activity and leadership in Christian Camp work, she has made, and continues to make, an outstanding contribution to the cause of spiritual healing.

In all her work, although it is interdenominational, she keeps the Church central; for she says: "All I have I've been given through the Church. I believe that it is the Body of Christ made visible on earth."

Mrs. Eggleston speaks with authority on spiritual healing, for she herself has twice been remarkably healed by God's power.

Her first healing occurred at the age of eight. When she was away from home on a visit to the country, she was seized with severe abdominal pain. When the home remedies of her hostess failed to alleviate the pain and fever, a country doctor was called in. He was unable to diagnose her case, but recognized her condition as critical, and urged her immediate return home while she was still living. Her parents were notified to meet the child with the best doctors in Norfolk. Two surgeons and the family phy-

311

sician made the diagnosis: ruptured appendix, peritonitis, with one chance in a thousand of surviving surgery.

The family doctor vouchsafed his opinion: "She will never come through surgery alive. My best advice is to commit her to the Great Physician for healing. He is the only One who can do it."

Her father, a Methodist clergyman, and her mother finally agreed. The parents and this Christian doctor met and prayed together for the small girl's life. She was marvelously healed.

From the time she became a teen-aged girl Louise Eggleston tried to follow the teachings of her parents, who constantly reminded her that God had saved her for a purpose.

"I considered myself a very good Christian" she recalls now, with a smile. "I never stayed away from Sunday school or church if it were possible for me to go. I even taught Sunday school. In fact, I did everything I was asked, except join a new prayer group. My excuse was that I was too busy to attend another meeting. The truth was that going to a prayer group meeting didn't sound nearly so alluring as the garden club or a bridge game."

Then at the age of forty Mrs. Eggleston became critically ill for the second time in her life. She had been in pain for some time before she sought medical advice. When she finally consulted her doctor, she was told that she had waited too long. Surgery, he said, would be useless, for the obviously malignant growth had metastasized. Finally at her family's insistence, the doctor reluctantly agreed to undertake what he considered a hopeless operation.

The little prayer group that Louise Eggleston had refused to join, prayed for her throughout the operation. When at the end the surgeon said she was still breathing but could not survive owing to the extensive damage of vital organs, the group continued to pray. Their faith was rewarded by the patient's complete recovery.

"So humbled was I by the Christ-like spirit of this little group," says Mrs. Eggleston, "that I promised my Saviour my life should belong to Him completely."

She has kept her promise, and has let God do with her as He wills. "Spiritual adventuring with the Lord," she says, "is the most thrilling experience one can ever know."

Mrs. Eggleston has done a great deal of research in prayer, and is by now wholly convinced that prayer has never caused God to change His will or break His spiritual laws. "Prayer," says Louise Eggleston, "changes *us* and makes us one with His will, His way, and His law. It is through our oneness with Him that we make contact with the Power that controls the universe."

She emphasizes continually that the primary aim in her life service is not physical healing, but the healing of the soul. Convinced that all disease begins in the soul, mind, and personality of men, and that no body can be permanently cured unless it is healed at the source of the disease, she refers to herself as a "soul surgeon."

"I know beyond the shadow of any doubt," she says, "that when we get the soul and mind in harmony with the will of God and His plan for our lives, the body will be made 'every whit whole,' regardless of its present condition."

Healing, in the opinion of Louise Eggleston, is like joy or goodness or success—a highway over which we travel to reach a higher goal, that of healing the soul.

She points out that Jesus met people at the place of their need, and used their awareness of some human need to reveal to them a deeper need. And so it is today that she ministers to human needs in order that the deeper need may be met.

When she prays with a person for healing, she always

lays hands on him in order "to be God's contact," as she expresses it. Unless she is asked, she does not tell patients why she does this; but she has found that this method of prayer brings a better response in the one seeking help.

She often gives the sick one a promise of Jesus to hold, saying: "You are holding onto a promise that Jesus gave us all. It is the Word of God upon which our entire universe is founded. It cannot fail, but you must notice that His promises always carry conditions. You must meet these conditions, for God is bound by His Own Laws."

Louise Eggleston can cite many wonderful manifestations of the healing power of God which have resulted from prayer.

A woman, for example, was dying of leukemia. A group of her friends met at the altar for prayer, meditation, and Holy Communion. An immediate improvement was noted in the patient's condition. She improved steadily, and her healing was a source of wonder and delight to both doctors and friends.

A woman suffered from tuberculosis of the spine; three inches in the middle of the spine had been destroyed, and three inches of the lower extremity. For a number of weeks devout friends prayed fervently for her recovery. One day she suddenly felt a warm glow pass up her spine. She cried, "I am well," and leaped to her feet. She could walk, and the healing was from that moment complete and permanent. Her doctor took her before a New York association, and said: "Before this happened I was an atheist. Now I am a Christian."

A child was operated on for a brain tumor. Throughout the ordeal of surgery, the child was surrounded and upheld by group prayer. She made a speedy and uneventful recovery. It was not until months later that Mrs. Eggleston learned from the operating surgeon that when the incision was made and the child's condition fully revealed, he knew she was wholly beyond medical help. As the child was obviously expiring on the operating table, the surgeons waited briefly before closing the wound, intending to perform a post mortem. They were incredulous as suddenly the child's pulse grew discernibly stronger, her breathing more regular. Conscious of a "strange sort of healing Presence" which seemed to envelop them all, the doctors closed the incision, having performed no surgery of any kind. The child's recovery was rapid and complete. Today, years later, she is in radiant health.

Mrs. Eggleston feels that the many healings of this sort which have occurred are the result of yielding to God, of allowing Him to do what He has been waiting for a chance to do.

"Let Him have you," she says, "so that He may heal you. For always remember that the price of spiritual power is unconditional surrender to God."

Louise Eggleston is herself a living testimony to the validity of her words.

Oral Roberts

(EVANGELIST)

MANY of us are by now familiar with the background of Oral Roberts, the thirty-nine-year-old revivalist—of how, three months before his birth, this son of a Pentecostal minister was dedicated to God by his mother; how, at the age of sixteen, a stutterer and long bed-ridden with tuberculosis, the frail boy saw a vision of Christ while he and his father prayed together, and so strong was the Presence that Oral rose from his bed, crying: "I am saved!"; how, five months later, the boy was taken to a revivalist healing service and heard the Voice of God say to him: "Son, I am going to heal you, and you are going to take my healing power to your generation"; how, completely healed that night of both his stammering and tuberculosis, young Oral began preaching some two months afterward; and how, twelve years later, while serving as the ordained minister of a Pentecostal Holiness Church, the Reverend Roberts received through fasting and prayer the revelation from God he had long been awaiting.

The evangelist will undoubtedly remain a controversial figure for as long as he continues to command such a tremendous audience; but I have observed with interest that as public knowledge of spiritual healing has grown, hostility toward the Roberts' ministry has diminished. Those who know most of the healing ministry, the healing clergy of the established Church, tend to be the most tolerant of the evangelist's work. They recognize the validity of his premises, even though they cannot accept his technique.

Episcopal Bishop Austin Pardue, for example, says: "While I couldn't possibly work as does Mr. Roberts, and temperamentally dislike his methods, I definitely *like* the fact that he is helping so many. There are great masses of people who seem to need such a ministry. Oral Roberts and others like him are reaching people their critics will never reach. I think it's presumptuous to blindly condemn and ridicule anyone working in Christ's Name. 'Judge not that ye be not judged' is something it behooves all of us to remember."

Several months ago the evangelist was invited to come to New York to participate in a seminar on spiritual healing with a number of eminent clergymen of conservative churches. Methodist minister Harry Robinson, Jr., voiced the opinion of most of those present, when he said: "Although I have some reservations about Mr. Roberts' manner, I nevertheless believe that he is a completely, sincerely dedicated man. There is no doubt of the many healings which occur under his ministry, and I am particularly impressed with his work among special groups, such as the American Indians, and his no-receipts missionary trips abroad each year. Furthermore his personal receipts seem so hedged about that they cannot become inordinately large, so he is not plagued with self-interest. He is serving sacrificially."

In his essential teaching Mr. Roberts actually hews closely to the line held by the traditional Church in its ministry of spiritual healing. His emphasis is continually on the soul's salvation, not the body's healing.

"I believe that physical health is the will of God," the evangelist states, "but I have no interest in healing apart from salvation. My concern is with the saving of souls, which is the greatest of all miracles."

This is the underlying theme of his ministry, evidenced by his preaching, and carried out in the format of his services, wherein he never prays for the sick until he has attempted to lead people to Christ. Convinced that "Faith cometh by hearing the Word of God," Mr. Roberts preaches his sermon first. He immediately follows it with a plea that those who accept Jesus renounce their sins and come forward. Only then does he offer prayers for the sick.

Healings of virtually every known ailment—congenital, organic, and functional—have been claimed under the Roberts ministry. The evangelist refuses to hazard a guess as to what percentage are healed; and no attempt has been made to estimate the number of genuine healings which occur, as opposed to the inevitable false claims.

A substantial number of healings brought to my attention are obviously of a psychotherapeutic nature. However, many claimed healings of both organic physical and mental disease appear entirely valid on the basis of the original medical diagnosis and the patient's apparently robust health several years later. That these dramatic physical healings appear to be accompanied by powerful spiritual regeneration would seem to remove the Roberts' ministry from any suspicion of charlatanism.

The case of Henry Holt, president of the New York textile firm which bears his name, is typical of many.

Supposedly dying of cancer four years ago, Holt was, as he puts it, "nagged into attending a Roberts campaign by my wife. A hard-headed business man and a skeptic, I was convinced the whole thing was a gigantic fraud. But I was just too weak to resist, so like a drowning man grasping at a straw, I had my handy man drive me down."

By the time Mr. Holt got in the healing line, after first being "saved," and then, in a smaller tent, praying for forgiveness for his sins, he was even more convinced than he had been in the beginning that the thing was a fake.

"And as soon as my turn came up to be 'healed,' " he said, "I intended to tell Mr. Roberts exactly what I thought of him in front of the audience.

"Preceding me in line was a club-footed boy who was seemingly healed. Then directly in front of me was a Methodist minister from Los Angeles whose wife, standing beside him, had a large goiter on her neck. I remember thinking, 'This I got to see.'

"At that moment Oral Roberts started calling on the Lord to heal that woman. All of a sudden she gulped, and to my amazement the goiter disappeared. I was absolutely stupefied—and in that instant my whole slant on life seemed to change. When it was my turn to face Mr. Roberts, I was still so stunned I couldn't answer him intelligently. My prepared speech excoriating him was forgotten. I vaguely remember him praying for me—and my surprise when I realized I was praying with him.

"After the prayers were over, I felt a tremor go through my system. A feeling of exultation seemed to wash over me, bringing with it a feeling of complete peace of mind and body which seemed to eliminate all my problems. I walked down the ramp, still dazed, but with a lightness in my soul it is impossible to describe."

Henry Holt claims that he was healed that night. Virtually bankrupt by the expenses of his illness, since regaining his health, he has worked hard to put his business back on its feet. "With the help of God, I am succeeding," he says.

As a consequence of his healing, he has regained all his long-lost religious beliefs. He and his wife have become faithful churchgoers, and powerful witnesses for the healing Christ.

"I'm not the emotional type," the business man assured me. "But I love my Saviour and will always testify to His almighty greatness. Mr. Roberts did not heal me, but he led me to the God who did. I shall always be grateful to him."

The Roberts' organization, manned by three hundred and fifty workers, receives, in addition to 150,000 letters a month, some 5,000 testimonies of claimed healings every week. These are carefully screened, and those which appear in his magazine, *Abundant Life,* are first investigated by a committee. If there is any doubt as to the authenticity of a healing, the account is not printed. "Of course we're not infallible," remarked the evangelist, "and we've made mistakes. But we do all in our power to reduce such mistakes to a minimum. We wait at least a year, and preferably two, before publicly acknowledging a healing."

Faced with the problem of all evangelists of becoming a "cult," Mr. Roberts takes every precaution to avert this. Although frequently asked to start a Bible school and send out missionaries, he adamantly refuses.

"As you well know," he said to me, "This is not a new 'movement.' I am simply preaching the Gospel of Jesus Christ—and I will work only through existing churches."

As a result of this policy many orthodox churchmen are

losing their antipathy toward the evangelist. They see and acknowledge the results of his revival in their own churches.

"I can't do a pastor's job," explains Mr. Roberts, "I simply haven't time. My task, my method, was given me by God, and I work as I have been directed. We are the shock troops to attract sinners, and bring them to God. It is up to the individual pastor to do the follow-up job."

The evangelist obviously has time during a meeting personally to lay hands on only a small percentage of those who seek healing. Healings, however, are by no means restricted to those he physically touches. Like the small, hunch-backed woman sitting in the last row during a recent crusade, whose back grew straight and strong as Mr. Roberts prayed for the sick, healings occur throughout the tent or auditorium.

"There is no healing power in my hands," Oral Roberts insists. "They are only points of contact."

Yet there is no gainsaying the clearly discernible current of power transmitted through these hands. Despite this fact, the evangelist vehemently denies the possession of a charismatic gift of healing. Only under some pressure will he acknowledge that he is a uniquely open channel for the healing power.

"If I had any choice in the matter," says Mr. Roberts, "I would choose the gift of wisdom. Whatever 'gift' I may seem to have now, it is not a twenty-four hour affair. It comes only with anointing, when the Holy Spirit is upon me. That happens most often when I am preaching. Even if I had time, I could not work privately with the sick. I just can't turn to healing at any moment of the day. As I preach I become more and more aware of the Presence of Christ, until finally the spirit of God takes possession of me —and using me, allows me to do things I could not normally do, of myself."

How many of the millions of souls saved under his guidance will remain "saved," no one knows. However, Oral Roberts' work is a dramatic demonstration that the healing ministry is the most powerful instrument of conversion the world has yet known. I suggest that an unprecedentedly large number of these conversions will last; for those who have visibly witnessed and tangibly felt the Holy Spirit do not easily forget the experience.

A man with a very great healing ministry within the Church, Dr. Alfred Price, says: "I feel that Oral Roberts is being used by God mightily."

Oral Roberts is what he claims to be: a simple man who loves Jesus; a man who is devoting his life to preaching the love and compassion of God, at the same time recognizing that the Presence of the Holy Spirit is a Presence of Judgment as well as of Grace.

Kathryn Kuhlman

(EVANGELIST)

FROM the beginning of her evangelistic career, the mission of Kathryn Kuhlman has been "to help those who are hungry for Christ to find Him"; and from the beginning, the theme of all her sermons has been faith.

It was twelve years ago, in Franklin, Pennsylvania, that members of her congregation suddenly began to claim spontaneous healings during her services. As the number of these healings increased, the Baptist-ordained minister began to preach on healing through faith. Thus began today's "miracle" services.

In 1948 she settled in Pittsburgh, and established the schedule to which she still adheres: two weekly services in Pittsburgh; one in Youngstown, Ohio; and every third week, a service in Cleveland.

Under this ministry I have seen tumors dissolve; the

blind see; the deaf hear; and the crippled walk. In none of these cases have I trusted my own vision, but have had scores of such healings medically verified.

To the frequent charge that such cures are hysterical and not permanent, Kathryn Kuhlman replies: "Those whom God heals stay healed." As many of the cases I have checked date from as long as twelve years ago, this statement would seem essentially true.

The answer to the charge that hypnotism or mass psychology is involved in these cures lies in the multitudinous healings which occur as the result of prayer requests and not personal attendance at the Kuhlman meetings.

One of many such cases is that of Mrs. Stella Turner, wife of an Internal Revenue worker in western Pennsylvania. She was operated on in 1952, supposedly for the removal of her gall bladder. When her abdomen was incised, the surgeon discovered that she had cancer of the gall bladder, liver, stomach, bowels, and pancreas. This diagnosis was confirmed by five attending physicians, who agreed that surgery was impossible and the patient's condition hopeless. Nine days later she was sent home from the hospital, in intense pain, to die.

A prayer request was sent in to Kathryn Kuhlman, written by the patient's sister and mailed by her husband at three A.M.

The following day the patient began what appeared to be pernicious vomiting. At the end of thirty-six hours she was without pain and confident that she had been healed. A subsequent check by her doctor confirmed the cure. "Five of us were not wrong," he said. "You have been healed by faith."

Mrs. Turner is today in perfect health. Both she and her husband are living dedicated lives in gratitude to God. Could this healing, and the numerous others like it, be attributed to either mass psychology or hypnosis?

But Kathryn Kuhlman's primary interest is in bringing souls to God; and, dramatic and awe-inspiring as are the cures of the body under this ministry, even more impressive are the healings of the spirit: the alcoholics, instantly healed, who have made Christ, not alcohol, the center of their lives; the drug addicts, miraculously cured, who live no longer for heroin, but for God; and the thousands of ordinary people like you and me, whose radiant faces and transformed lives reflect the God they have found under Miss Kuhlman's guidance.

The influence of this evangelist extends beyond the thousands of her personal followers and her two million radio listeners into many of the orthodox churches, for a substantial number of curious clergymen have attended her services and have been impressed. Her continual plea to "Start a healing ministry in *your* church; for every clergyman can and should have such a ministry," has not fallen on deaf ears. Some of the area's most effective church healing ministries have been instituted as a direct result of her inspiration. Furthermore, her insistence that her followers attend their own churches has resulted in a powerful spiritual revival in many community churches. As one clergyman confided to me: "Among my parishioners are many whose whole lives have been changed by the inspired faith of Kathryn Kuhlman. Now they never miss a Sunday, and have revitalized this church by their establishment of powerful prayer groups."

The fact that Miss Kuhlman has remained in one location for ten years and that her ministry has successfully survived the criticism which is the lot of all evangelists, is a tribute to her integrity. When asked why she does not extend the scope of her influence by traveling, her reply is: "My purpose is to save souls, and my particular calling is to offer proof of the power of God. I feel I can accomplish this more effectively by staying in one place where I am in a position to follow through on my people, and to insist that those who claim healings procure medical verification."

This emphasis on medical verification has done much to reduce the false claims of healing and the fanaticism which are inevitably associated with evangelistic healing. Insistence on scientific substantiation has not only contributed to the soundness of her personal ministry but to spiritual healing everywhere.

But if there are advantages to remaining in one location, there are also hazards; chief among them the overwhelming danger, in even so gifted a ministry as Kathryn Kuhlman's, that the instrument of His power, a blonde, slender evangelist, shall be mistaken by her devoted followers for the Source; that Kathryn Kuhlman may be worshiped rather than the Lord she represents. Of this peril the evangelist is well aware, and wages a constant battle to avert it. "I of myself am nothing," she repeats again and again. "It is the power of God, released by your faith, which heals you."

"My constant, overriding fear," she said to me, "is that I may grieve the Holy Spirit. No one knows better than I that without Him I am nothing, and have nothing."

I believe it is the genuineness of this fear which has thus far safeguarded her ministry from corruption or abuse.

The Reverend Gaius Slosser, D.D., eminent Presbyterian theologian, says: "Through the centuries there have occasionally appeared outstanding geniuses in the field of the spirit. Kathryn Kuhlman is one of these."

Many may, of course, continue to deplore Kathryn Kuhlman's evangelistic methods. For it is true that although, compared to many revivalist meetings, the Kuhlman services are decorous and well-controlled, compared to the traditional church, they are highly emotional. Yet dare we, who may prefer the orthodox church, disdain as "undignified" a method so abundantly endowed with the Presence of the Holy Spirit? Dare we who may believe in the sacramental approach disparage as "sensational" any service which is made so by the power of the living God?

The Reverend Owen Walton, Methodist minister and former executive secretary of the Council of Churches of Allegheny County, Pennsylvania, says: "Kathryn Kuhlman is undoubtedly bringing hope and faith to many thousands whom the established churches are not reaching at all."

The implication in this statement seems clear. When these established churches have universally revived the healing ministry within their own bodies, many of their people who are starving now for demonstrable evidence of the living God will no longer need to seek this evidence in tents and auditoriums. Meanwhile, for those thousands who have sought Him in vain at the altars of their own churches, Kathryn Kuhlman is pointing the way. She is providing the lamp that they may find His Kingdom in their hearts.

The Great Reconciler

THROUGH the healing ministry of the Christian churches, the Universal Church is meeting with the most conspicuous success, the greatest challenge in her long history. Through this ministry we see most clearly demonstrated the transforming power of the Christian faith. The healing Church offers us unimpeachable evidence that with the resurgence of the traditional faith there is a corresponding and unmistakable renewal of the Holy Spirit.

Events have proved that the layman wants, and has the capacity to receive, an anchoring, definitive faith. He no longer shuns religion because it is too difficult, or the wages of sin too high. He does not feel the miraculous truths of Christianity to be intellectually incompatible. He believes in the full use of his God-given mind and in the ceaseless pursuit of knowledge; but he has learned that a philosophy is a poor substitute for faith. In a perhaps instinctive recoil against the heresy of gnosticism, he has realized that the Kingdom of Heaven cannot be attained by the intellect alone; nor can knowledge, of itself, save souls.

"By their fruits ye shall know them." That there is power in the historic Church is not a matter of idle conjecture. We see its dramatic and incontestable demonstration in the healing Church. To the exact extent that the Church fulfils Our Lord's Commission, believing and acting upon His promises, so is the limitless power of the Holy Spirit being unmistakably manifested today.

As a result of his observation of the healing ministry at work, the modernist is beginning to re-define the word Christian. He is recognizing that it involves more than adherence to an ethical code; more than a vague, generalized belief in the "Fatherhood of God and brotherhood of man" precept. He is discovering that mental approbation of a Palestinian reformer's teaching cannot replace the heart's acceptance of the Man Himself. He sees operating in the healing church the unique power of the Risen Christ, the result of an unattenuated Christian faith. On the one hand is today's self-serving religion which conceives of God as a flunkey whose duty it is to serve us health and happiness on a silver platter; on the other, yesterday's concept of Him, who with unthinkable cruelty saw fit to afflict us with unbearable suffering and disease "for our own good." The seeking layman has come at last to rest between the two extremes in the healing Church. If the Church is rediscovering the boundless power of the Holy Spirit, so through exposure to this ministry, is the individual Christian becoming once again an unmistakable exponent of his faith. He has put on the "armour of light" of which St. Paul speaks. Regardless of whether or not he has been physically cured, he has been transfigured by the touch of the healing Christ.

The ministry of spiritual healing is proving itself to be one of the strongest of all religious ties which bind together churches everywhere. Doctrinal differences tend to be forgotten, and dogmatic dissimilarities overlooked. The only essential tenet becomes a universal awareness of the re-creating power of the living God, through His Son, Our Lord.

The Reverend Dixon Rollit, an Episcopal priest who is frequently called upon to minister to members of other denominations, cites a typical experience. "Just last week, for example," he reports, "I visited a four-bed ward in a large city hospital. In one bed lay the Methodist who had requested that I come to lay-on-hands. In the other three beds lay, respectively, a Lutheran, a Baptist, and a Roman Catholic. With bowed heads they all joined in the healing prayer. The following day all four patients showed what the doctors called a 'remarkable and unpredicted improvement.' "

While the healing ministry is only one of the many ministries of the Church, it is a fusion of them all. It is the catalyst which ignites the flame of faith that illuminates the whole Church and charges it with dynamic power. It is the ministry which is serving to unify the Christian world. For it is the unity of faith in the will and power of God to heal which is inspiring the sort of interdenominational teamwork manifested in one representative community during last Lenten season. Here the midweekly Lutheran Vespers service was conducted in a Methodist Church, attended by a large Presbyterian congregation, while an Episcopal minister preached and laid hands on those who desired healing. Side by side, not in stultifying uniformity, but in concord and unity in faith, we see here in action the Universal Church sharing the common prayer that it may be "delivered from all false doctrine, heresy, and schism"; jointly petitioning that it shall be "illuminated with true knowledge and understanding of His Word" (*Book of Common Prayer*).

It is in the Church Universal that the complete answer to spiritual healing must be found, as it is in the undivided Church that the full power and dazzling glory of Christianity will eventually be realized.

Healing is the ministry of great reconciliation, by which thousands have come closer to Jesus and are living redeemed lives in His Name. Through this ministry we glimpse a Christian Church, united by an unshakable faith in the totality of Our Lord's redemptive mission; an impregnable fortress, inviolable by reason of its foundation of immutable truth, against which the antichrist must hurl itself in vain.

Through Baptism and Holy Communion the Church offers us the means of spiritual regeneration. Through the preaching of God's Word it points the way to the Kingdom. Through the healing ministry, we enter in.

This is not to say that spiritual healing is the only way in which the Holy Spirit operates; or that it is the only road to belief in God. But for those of us who have for so long "looked through a glass darkly," seeing, no matter how we strained our eyes, only a blurred, distorted image, spiritual healing has proved the lens through which we have caught at last a clear, unclouded vision of the Christ. The irrevocable conviction, the certain knowledge that He lives is the miracle which transcends all others.